TO RESIST IS TO WIN!

with selected letters & speeches
Edited by Sarah Niner

Principal Translators
Jose Luis Perestrelo Botelheiro
Ana Noronha
Assisting Translators
Emmanuel Braz
Elizabete Lim Gomes
Balthazar Kehi
Cancio Noronha Jnr
Fabi Noronha
Palmira Pires
TAV Project Coordinator
Palmira Pires

AURORA BOOKS
DAVID LOVELL PUBLISHING

First published in 2000 by
Aurora Books
300 Victoria Street Richmond Victoria 3121 Australia
Tel +61 3 9427 7311 Fax +61 3 9428 4450

in association with
David Lovell Publishing
PO Box 822 Ringwood 3134
Tel +61 3 9879 1433 Fax +61 3 9879 1348

Cover photo by Armandina Gusmão
Cover design by David Constable
Design by David Lovell
Manuscript preparation by Geraldine Battersby
Page makeup by Ben Hider, Scott Howard
Print production by Sylvana Scannapiego
Typeset in 11 on 14 Bembo
Printed and bound in Australia

National Library of Australia
Cataloguing-in-Publication data
Gusmão, Xanana.

To Resist is to win!: The autobiography of Xanana Gusmão with selected letters and speeches.

Bibliography.
Includes Index.
ISBN 1 86355 071 2.

1. Gusmão, Xanana. 2. Political activists—Indonesia—Timor Timur—Biography. 3. Timor Timur (Indonesia)—History—Autonomy and independence movements. 4. Timor Timur (Indonesia)—Politics and government—20th century. I. Niner, Sarah. II. Botelheiro, Jose Luis Perestrelo. III. Norunha, Ana. IV. Title.

959.8603092

Australia Council for the Ar

This project has been assisted by the Commonwealth Government through the Australia Council, its arts funding and advisory body.

This project was supported and auspiced by the Timorese Association in Victoria

Contents

Foreword

There is an Indonesian saying — *Asam di gunung, garam di laut, bertemu dalan belange* (Tamarind from the mountain, salt of the sea, meet in a pot)—which explains the long journeys of Xanana Gusmão, leader of independent *Timor Loro S'ae,* and Jacob Rumbiak, a Melanesian independence leader from West Papua; both oppressed by the Indonesian regime and brought together in Cipinang, a first-class Javanese goal. We were determined to end the oppression and colonialism in our countries because we believe they debase the dignity of humankind and undermine the power of justice and the laws of God.

While we were in prison, Xanana and I overcame the boredom and the loneliness by organising activities—soccer, volleyball, badminton and basketball—by arranging prayer services and by caring for the small animals in our fruit and vegetable garden. These endeavours helped us change the goal's dry and suffocating atmosphere into a pleasant and peaceful environment. During our long internment we also sought to find peaceful ways to promote the march of our two countries towards independence.

The reality that exists now illustrates that the struggle and the sacrifice of the heroes of the Maubere People in *Timor Loro S'ae* have not been in vain, and this inspires my people to hope that the struggle and the sacrifice of our heroes will also not be in vain. We cannot repay these martyrs in earthly measure; we can only express our gratitude to them.

The dreams of the Maubere People are now a reality. Viva Maubere. Viva *Timor Loro S'ae.* Viva Xanana. The time has arrived for Xanana Gusmão to be recognised by the international community. The time has also arrived for Xanana Gusmão to present to the world the dignity and nobility of his people. Bravo to you, my friend. My prayers and best wishes are with you.

Your comrade

Jacob Rumbiak
Conveyor for the
West Papuan People

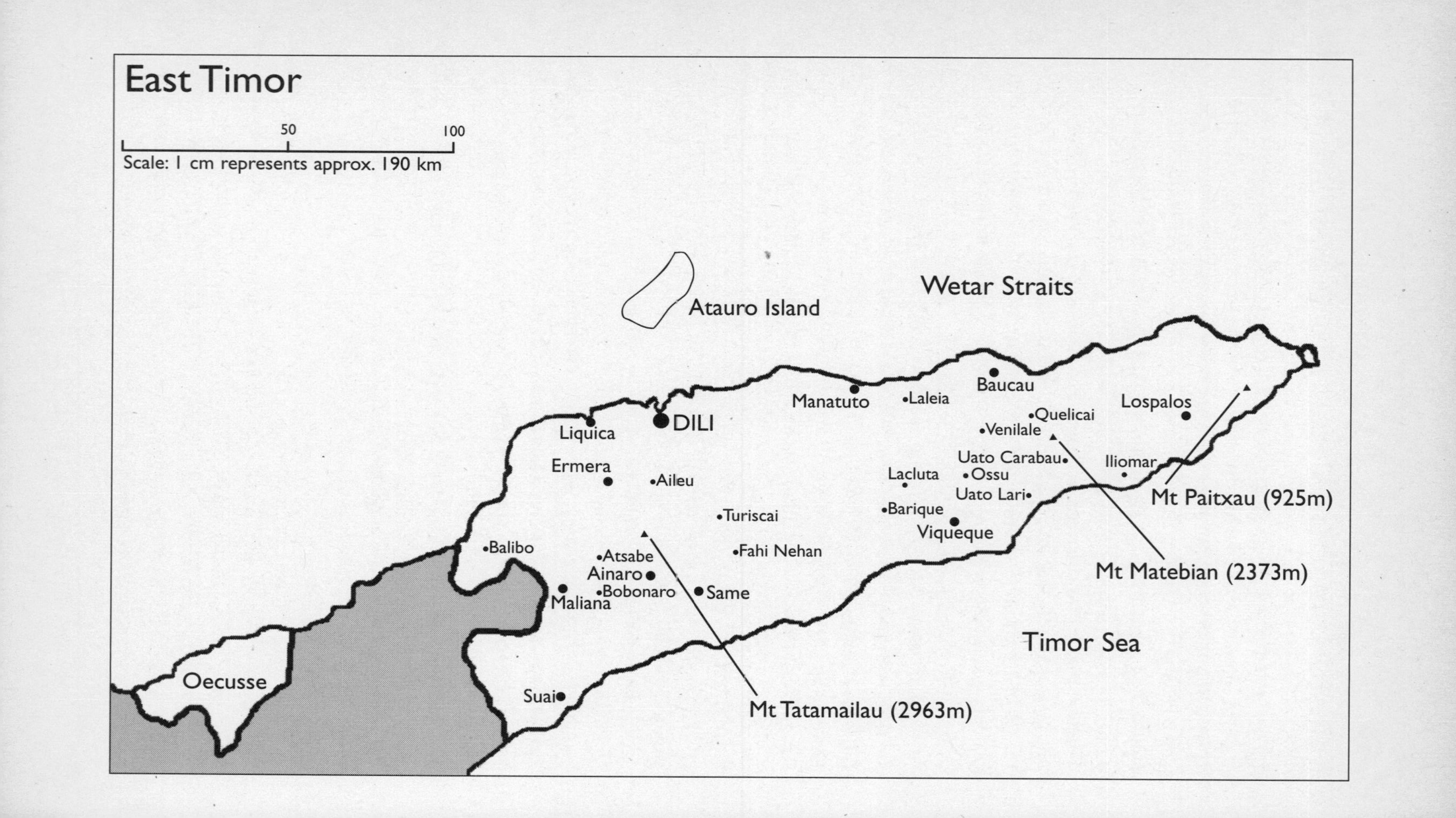
East Timor
50
100
Scale: 1 cm represents approx. 190 km
Atauro Island
Wetar Straits
Baucau
Manatuto
Laleia
Lospalos
Quelicai
Venilale
DILI
Liquica
Ermera
Aileu
Uato Carabau
Iliomar
Lacluta
Ossu
Uato Lari
Mt Paitxau (925m)
Barique
Turiscai
Viqueque
Balibo
Atsabe
Fahi Nehan
Mt Matebian (2373m)
Ainaro
Maliana
Bobonaro
Same
Timor Sea
Oecusse
Suai
Mt Tatamailau (2963m)

Editor's Preface

When I travelled to Dili in August 1991 I had never heard of Xanana Gusmão and had no idea of the horror that was a part of so many people's lives in East Timor. I found out the latter pretty quickly, especially when I arrived back in Australia to news of the Santa Cruz massacre in November. This event, shown repeatedly on television, drew another wave of Australians into the solidarity network that had been offering support to the East Timorese and their struggle since 1975. This time was a turning point and the Australian Government could no longer ignore what was happening just 600 kilometres north-west of Darwin. East Timor has grown to become Australia's most important foreign policy issue and made Xanana Gusmão a household name (even if many do not yet know how to pronounce it!).

By the time Xanana was captured in November 1992, I certainly knew who he was and joined the Timorese community and others outside the Indonesian consulate (and later at Foreign Minister Gareth Evans' house) to protest and appeal for his safety. But I still did not know very much about Xanana or that, as I was walking around Dili the year before, he had been living in an underground bunker planning the next move of the resistance (a meeting with the Portuguese Parliamentary Delegation). And of course I did not know that nearly ten years later, because so little was known about him, I would be working on his biography. At some point while researching Xanana's life I realised that I had files full of his writings, sourced from friends' and many solidarity groups' filing cabinets, and that they would fill a book.

I have come to realise that these words show Xanana's unfolding as a leader: from traumatised and passionate writings full of bloody torture and pleas that outsiders might simply acknowledge what was happening; to sophisticated, subtle and often beautiful letters and poems, written to all manner of people around the world; alongside his continual pleadings to his people to keep resisting, to stick together and to remember who they are. These words also show Xanana to be a unique political leader, one who had never sought political power and still does not, asserting that he just wants to be a farmer in free Timor *Loro Sa'e*.

There would have been no book were it not for all the hard work of the translators, especially Jose Botelheiro and Beti Gomez who gave up more that a year of Sundays to work with me on the autobiography and other pieces. Also, thanks to the Timor Association of Victoria's Palmira Pires and Ana Noronya for their labor in translating so many pieces. Justino Gutteres helped me many times with background. I would like to thank the Australian Society of Authors, the Australia Council and Latrobe University for assistance with translation grants. Much appreciation to the Xanana Gusmão Support Office in Jakarta and to José Ramos-Horta, to Kirsty Sword, Louise Byrne, Patsy Thatcher (for the original spark) and Kevin Sherlock. Thanks to the Portuguese newspapers, *O Publico* and *Diario de Noticias*, for their kind permission to reproduce interviews, as noted, as well as to Edicoes Colibri, publishers of a similar collection of Xanana's writings in Portuguese. To the staff of *East Timor News*, *Matebian News*, the East Timor Talks Campaign, ACFOA and the CNRM office and also to Robert Domm who provided one or other of the pieces here. To Michael McGirr and David Lovell for their patience with the manuscript, to Mary Aitken for adding style and polish to selected pieces and to the Sangsters for their hot tips.

And of course thanks and peace to Xanana Gusmão who kept up the fight and wrote most of these pieces in unimaginable conditions. May he get to sit and rest one day on Mt Paitxau, that kept him safe, and write much more.

Sarah Niner

Resistir è Vencer!
To Resist is to Win!

This collection reveals many things. It traces the development of the Timorese resistance over the last 24 years. The documents explain how the Timorese resistance transformed itself, with little contact or help from the outside world, from a ravaged group of guerrilla fighters scattered over the land in the late 1970s into a cohesive, inclusive structure, recognised, and aided internationally, as a legitimate cry for self-determination.

The collection also displays, at times, my frustration at our plight and at those who have been a party to it or those who have looked the other way. But it also documents my heartfelt thanks to those friends of Timor who have supported us.

It shows how many Timorese, fearful, intimidated and confused, who had abandoned the struggle, have returned. The waves of wounds to the Timorese people are the consequences of both internal and external conflicts. They come from our thorny civil war, and from the problems of our early years in the mountains and the related acts of revenge, as well as those inflicted by the Indonesian military and those Timorese serving the integration process. Our internal wounds were mended under the continued and increasing pressures from without. Many of these wounds and those relationships destroyed by the effects of this seemingly endless war have been healed.

The letters, statements and messages published here record intimately the tortuous route by which all these things have occurred over the last 25 years and they reaffirm over and over how the will of the East Timorese people to choose their own future has remained alive against tremendous pressure. It is this will of the Timorese people that inspired me to keep fighting and take up the responsibility of leadership. It was the people who requested that the heroic Falintil guerrillas keep fighting and never surrender. It was the people who supported us, fed us and revived us and sent us back into the mountains.

I have learnt, as they say, 'on the job'. My writings show that I have often struggled in my leadership to find new ways and forms to assert the rights of my people in a journey that has demanded of all of us so much patience, empathy, flexibility and innovation. It was never my ambition to lead my country but the crisis in my Homeland led me to this fate.

Falintil's duty is nearly at an end; we have secured the right of the Timorese people to choose their future. This was the dream that kept us alive in the mountains of East Timor. Today we feel we are on the last leg of our long journey to self-determination.

It was always necessary for us to resist because by simply resisting we knew that we were on the road to victory. The essence of the spirit inherent in our struggle was *Resist in order to win* and the act of resistance meant to win!
Xanana Gusmão, Salemba, July 1999

Xanana Gusmão — Timeline

Childhood 1946-62

1945 World War II Japanese occupation of Timor ends after three years and the Portuguese administration recommences. Forty thousand Timorese died as a result of the war.

20 June 1946 José Alexandre Gusmão born in Manatuto, second of eight children and eldest son.

1947 Xanana's father is transferred to Lacluta then on to Ossu to teach at local schools.

1954–1958 Xanana attends St Theresa's primary school in Ossu, Vikeke, a remote and underdeveloped area of East Timor. He witnesses prisoners whipped at administration posts and forced into labour by the Portuguese government.

1 May 1959 Armed uprising against the Portuguese administration based in Wato Lari and Wato Karbau, near Vikeke. A series of riots and attacks on Portuguese posts occurred and the Portuguese were forced to raise a militia in the neighbouring area of Lospalos to put down the rebels.

1959–1962 Xanana attends *Nossa Senhora de Fatima* seminary, a highly-disciplined environment run by the Jesuits, in Dare in the hills overlooking Dili. Fellow students include many future political leaders of East Timor such as Nicolau Lobato, Francisco Lopes da Cruz, Xavier do Amaral. Although absorbed by the arts and humanities and excelling at sport, Xanana was unable to finish his studies in this environment.

Young Adult

1962–1964 Xanana leaves seminary and begins working in various jobs in Dili: as a typist, draftsman, wharf-side worker and fisherman. His studies at the *Liceu Dr Francisco Veira Machado* are continually interrupted due to lack of resources. He plays sport—basketball, soccer, gymnastics, volleyball—and this proves to be his entrée into Dili society.

1965 When Xanana is 19 years old he meets his future wife Emilia Batista.

1966 He begins work in a permanent public service position and is able to continue with his education.

Adult Life

In the late 1960s modern fashion, music and political ideas find their way through the censors to a neglected Portuguese Timor. Xanana becomes a member of the indigenous sporting club *Uniao* and learns a Timorese version of history from its older members.

1968 Xanana is recruited into the Portuguese Army to serve three years of national service. He rises to the rank of Corporal.

1969 Xanana marries Emilia Batista.

1971 A son is born and Xanana returns to the public service and to study.

Xanana associates on the fringes of an incipient anti-colonial, nationalist organisation founded by José Ramos-Horta, Mari Alkatiri and Abilio Arujo. He edits political articles by Borja da Costa but mostly they are censored. He becomes more critical and dissatisfied with the public service and the unjust colonial system.

Revolution and Decolonisation

25 April 1974 The left wing coup, the *Revoluçao do Cravos*, in Portugal, results in decolonisation for Timor. Xanana is fearful the Timorese will be unable to run their affairs as an independent nation. Unable to obtain a government loan to start a farm he becomes angry and disillusioned and leaves his government job. He moves to Darwin, decides to emigrate to Australia and returns to Timor to collect his family. Because of his growing political involvement they do not emigrate.

May 1974 Decolonisation of the country begins with the Governor announcing general elections and calling for establishment of political parties.

October 1974 Indonesia begins a covert destabilisation operation, including subversive radio broadcasts from across the border in West Timor.

1975 Xanana begins working as an apprentice electrical mechanic. There are reports of 20,000 strong political demonstrations.
March 1975 General elections begin.
May 1975 Xanana is swept up by the changing political climate and joins pro-independence party Fretilin.
26 May 1975 Following internal disagreements UDT withdraws from coalition with Fretilin.
July 1975 In local elections held under the auspices of the decolonisation committee 90 per cent of newly elected *Luirais* are Fretilin members or supporters.

Coup and Civil War

11 August 1975 UDT stages a coup and takes over strategic parts of Dili.
15 August 1975 Fretilin calls for armed struggle to oppose UDT coup.
17 August 1975 Xanana is arrested at Fretilin HQ and imprisoned in Palapaco.
20 August 1975 Foundation of Falintil. Fighting has broken out in rural Timor.
27 August 1975 Governor Pires withdraws to Atauro; 2000 refugees flee to Atambua and are kept in refugee camps by Indonesians.
September 1975 Fretilin finally regains control of the country and UDT prisoners, including Xanana, are liberated. Xanana begins producing the paper *Timor Leste: Journal do Povo Maubere* and becomes Vice-Secretary of Fretilin's Department of Information with Borja da Costa. They are responsible for media and press affairs.
October 1975 Indonesia begins attacks across the border from West Timor. On the 16th five foreign journalists are killed in Balibo. Xanana volunteers for service at the border.
28 November 1975 In a formal ceremony: Fretilin declares 'The Democratic Republic of East Timor' with 2000 people present. Xanana films the event.
30 November 1975 Xanana travels to the border area to help gather information about the movement of the Indonesian troops.
The Balibo Declaration inviting Indonesians to liberate East Timor is signed by compromised UDT and APODETI leaders. Indonesian Foreign Minister Adam Malik formally declares that East Timor has been integrated into Indonesia.
7 December 1975 While returning to Dili, Xanana witnesses Indonesia's full-scale air and sea invasion from the hills above the town. In the following days he goes to Balibo to HQ with Nicolau Lobato and then to the outskirts of Dili to search for his family.
11 December 1975 Ramos-Horta arrives at the UN in New York.
12 December 1975 UN calls on Indonesia to withdraw.
17 December 1975 Pro-Indonesia Provisional East Timor Government set up on warship.
22 December 1975 UN Security Council condemns invasion.
25 December 1975 15-20,000 additional Indonesian troops land in East Timor.

Initial Occupation

Xanana hides in the mountains of Timor with many other East Timorese, fighting Indonesian troops and living off the land. He travels from Mota Ulun across the mountains by foot to Manatuto.
February 1976 Lopes da Cruz, President of the Provisional Government of East Timor and former UDT leader, claims 60,000 East Timorese have been killed since the invasion.
May 1976 Xanana attends historic meeting of resistance in Soibada and is redeployed to the Eastern regions.
31 May 1976 An East Timorese 'Popular Assembly' is convened by the Indonesian military. It approves a petition, addressed to President Suharto, calling for full integration with Indonesia.
November 1976 As result of occupation, 100,000 East Timorese have died.
December 1976 Xanana attends political meeting and school at CASCOL and begins to read Mao's 'Little Red Book'.
7 May 1977 Fretilin forces report that they control just over 80 per cent of the territory.
September 1977 First stage of Indonesian Campaign of Annihilation.
28 November 1977 UN General Assembly rejects integration and calls for act of self-determination.

December 1977 Xanana becomes Deputy Political Commissar in Ponta Leste, with Manecas Ma'Huno as military commander.
6 April 1978 Lt-General Yusuf is appointed Commander in Chief of Indonesian armed forces. He states resolution of East Timor is one of his priorities.
May 1978 Second stage of Indonesian Campaign of Annihilation.
September 1978 Xanana supervises march of population fleeing the east to Mt Matebian.
20 November 1978 UN General Assembly calls for withdrawal of Indonesian troops and an act of self-determination.
22 November 1978 Encirclement and fall of Mt Matebian, the last resistance base in mountains.
12 December 1978 Radio Maubere stops transmitting.
December 1978 Deaths of President Nicolau Lobato, leader of Eastern region, Vincente Sahe and others signify the end of initial resistance and leadership. Xanana escapes from Matebian back to East and adopts guerrilla formations.

Establishment of Leadership

13 December 1979 UN General Assembly passes resolution condemning the Indonesian occupation and calling for act of self-determination.
1979–1980 Reorganisation of resistance structures begins. Xanana walks from village to village to consult with the people about the continuation or conclusion of war and to contact any remaining resistance. Receives overwhelming response to continue. Sets up small clandestine independent guerrilla units and bases.
June 10–11 1980 An attack on Dili is mounted by resistance forces.
1981 To facilitate the reorganisation of movement and define ideology of new struggle Xanana writes two reports: 'Homeland and Revolution' and 'Themes of War'.
March 1981 First National Conference on the Reorganisation of Country. CRRN formed and Xanana appointed leader.
Mid 1981 The 'Fence of Legs' or 'Final' Operation is launched by Indonesian military.
October 24 1981 UN General Assembly repeats its call for act of self-determination.
September 1981 Surrounding of Mt Aitana and Lacluta massacre. Food shortages and famine are reported internationally.
1982 Xanana recommences communications with the resistance outside the country, the United Nations, human rights groups and diplomatic channels.
4 May 1982 Elections held in East Timor in which official Indonesian party Golkar wins 98.8 per cent of vote.
3 November 1982 UN General Assembly again condemns annexation and calls for act of self-determination. Secretary General instructed to initiate discussions with 'all concerned parties'.

Cease-fire and Kraras massacre

1983 During the 1980s Xanana makes a number of attempts come to a peaceful settlement with the Indonesian invaders. Along with war-weary Indonesian troops localised cease-fires negotiated and in March a regional cease-fire is agreed upon by Xanana and Indonesian military representatives. But in August the Kraras massacre signals end of cease-fire. And in September a state of emergency declared and a new Indonesian offensive, Operation Unity, is launched.
1984 Operation Unity ongoing and its consequences convince Xanana to cease operations that may lead to civilian reprisals like Kraras.
25 July 1984 UN Secretary General states that little progress has been made on negotiations between Indonesian and Portugal. Discussion deferred.
1985 Xanana liaising with emerging clandestine movement of civilian and student resistance in East Timor (mainly in Dili but also in Indonesia). The generation of Timorese who have grown up under Indonesian occupation see Xanana Gusmão as a charismatic leader of the national resistance.
18 August 1985 Australian Prime Minister Bob Hawke recognises Indonesian sovereignty over East Timor on behalf of his Labour Government.

24 September After again deferring action on East Timor the UN oversees first formal contacts between Portugal and Indonesian since the invasion.

9 December 1985 Australian and Indonesian governments announce they will jointly develop the petroleum reserves in the Timor Gap.

Restructure of the resistance

31 March 1986 Fretilin and UDT announce formation of a coalition.

4 September 1986 Newly-elected Social Democrat Government in Lisbon states they have dropped the demand for East Timor's self-determination.

1987–88 In a reorganisation of the resistance structure, Xanana declares Falintil a non-partisan 'national' army. In 1988 he relinquishes membership of the political party Fretilin, believing the fight for a free East Timor transcends political loyalties. He establishes the National Council of Maubere Resistance (CNRM) and is declared leader.

Feb 1988 Indonesian Government invites Portugal to send an observer mission to East Timor.

November 1988 Suharto visits East Timor and announces that, from January, eight of East Timor's 13 districts will open up to entry to Indonesians and foreigners.

15 July 1989 A short Indonesian military offensive is carried out in advance of Pope's visit. Its primary aim is to capture Xanana.

October 1989 Pope John Paul II visits East Timor and a huge demonstration in Dili signals the beginning of a phase of urban political demonstrations organised by the emerging youth resistance.

11 December 1989 Australian and Indonesian governments sign a joint treaty to explore the Timor Gap area.

17 January 1990 US Ambassador meets with group of demonstrators in Dili. They are dispersed violently after his departure and least two are killed.

September 1990 Robert Domm interviews Xanana in mountains camp in Ainaro. Reports published internationally and Xanana becomes known to the outside world for the first time. Leads to reprisals.

February 1991 Xanana travels to Dili from Ainaro area after near capture. He lives in secret underground bunker and is able to travel the territory.

Late 1991 Resistance begins to prepare for the visit of the Portuguese Parliamentary Delegation, planning a formal ceremony.

Late October 1991 Two young demonstrators are killed protesting the cancellation of the Portuguese Parliamentary Delegation.

12 November 1991 A massacre of hundreds of East Timorese occurs at Santa Cruz cemetery at funeral procession of those killed at demonstration. Events are shown on television screens world-wide.

February 1992 Xanana voices despair at the international community over lack of actions concerning the Santa Cruz massacre.

September 1992 Abilio Soares becomes the last Indonesian appointed governor of East Timor; takes over from Mario Carrascalao.

Xanana's capture and imprisonment

November 1992 Xanana captured in Dili and many others are arrested also, including those who hid him and members of his family. He is taken to Bali and Jakarta amidst international protests.

December 1992 Xanana appears on Indonesian TV stating that the struggle is over.

February–May 1993 Trial in Dili. He is sentenced to life imprisonment and refused permission to make defence statement. He is transferred to Salemba prison then to Cipinang in Jakarta. Ma'Huno becomes leader of the resistance in Timor but is soon captured and Konis Santana fills his place. In Cipinang, Xanana meets and mixes with other Timorese and Indonesian political prisoners, while maintaining contacts and control of the independence struggle from behind bars.

July 20 1993 Indonesian Government gives go ahead for talks between pro and anti integrationists. Pro faction is headed by former UDT leader, Lopes da Cruz.

December 1993 Pro and anti integrationists talks go ahead.
1994 Youth resistance begins campaign of entering foreign embassies in Jakarta.
January 1994 UN special rapporteur on East Timor, Tamrat Samuel, visits Xanana in Cipinang to formulate new initiatives for the next round of talks between Indonesia and Portugal. Xanana is denied visitors after writing protest letter.
February 1994 Both Xanana and Bishop Belo respond negatively to the 'reconciliation talks'.
July–September 1994 Xanana permitted to meet with legal aid and with Indonesian military.
September 1994 Melbourne auction of Xanana's paintings composed in Cipinang to raise money for the resistance.
November 1994 Xanana's Autobiography and other writings published in Portugal.
12 November 1994 29 East Timorese students enter the US Embassy during APEC meeting.
14 November 1994 Speaking to Suharto, President Clinton is 'firm and forceful' on the issue of human rights in East Timor.
January 1995 Indonesia and Portugal allow UN talks among Timorese.
May 1995 Xanana hospitalised with kidney problems.
June 1995 First Intra-Timorese Dialogue (AIETD).
July 1995 UN-sponsored Indonesia-Portugal Talks agreement to preserve East Timorese culture and Intra-Timorese dialogue.
July 1995 Half of East Timorese signatories to the 'Balibo Declaration' retract.
August 1995 Xanana is put in solitary for writing letter to Beijing World Women's Conference.
December 1995 Interview with John Pilger published internationally. The Indonesian Government denies its authenticity.
29 February 1996 During the formal meeting with President Suharto, Portuguese Prime Minister Antonio Gutteres announces willingness to open 'Interest Section' in return for release of prisoners including Xanana.
February 1996 UK Ploughshare women disarm BAe Hawk plane bound for Indonesia.
19–22 March 1996 Second Intra-Timorese Meeting Final Statement does not include demands of external resistance including release of Xanana Gusmao.
June 1996 Xanana turns 50.
27 June 1996 Eighth round of talks between Indonesia and Portugal; only resolution is to build Timorese cultural center in Dili.
October 1996 Australian Senate passes unanimous motion supporting East Timorese self-determination.
November 1996 Nobel Peace prizes awarded to José Ramos-Horta and Bishop Belo. Bishop Belo arrives in Dili; tens of thousands of Timorese welcome him.
27 Mar 1997 Xanana meets again with UN Envoy Jamsheed Marker.
April 1997 Xanana calls for referendum.
July 1997 Secret meeting between President Mandela and Xanana at Indonesian palace guesthouse.
August 1997 Mandela recommends Xanana's release.
October 1997 Third UN-sponsored Intra-Timorese Dialogue

Leader of CNRT

April 1998 National Timorese Convention held in Portugal establishes the National Council of Timorese Resistance (CNRT) to replace CNRM. This non-partisan national organisation is the new umbrella for Timorese resistance. It brings together different political nationalist organisations and unanimously elects Xanana Gusmão as President.
May 1998 Suharto resigns following student pro-democracy pressure from Indonesian public. The new Indonesian government allows unprecedented access to Xanana. Western press allowed into Cipinang Prison to interview political prisoners for the first time. Xanana in interview states that he does not have great faith in the Habibie administration, but that it is a step toward freedom for East Timor. José Ramos-Horta leads East Timorese and international calls for Xanana's immediate release.
August 1998 Secret meeting between BHP representative and Xanana. Xanana reassures BHP that an independent Timor would respect mining company rights.

5 August 1998 Agreement between Indonesia and Portugal to undertake, under the auspices of the Secretary General, negotiations on a special status based on a wide-ranging autonomy for East Timor

Nov 20 1998 Portugal suspends talks with Jakarta on East Timor after reports of a massacre.

January 1999 Australia suddenly changes foreign policy on East Timor to one of 'self-determination'.

February 1999 Xanana is moved to house arrest in Salemba, Jakarta. He further warns about possible violence and calls for armed international peacekeepers, but nevertheless agrees to proceed with the referendum.

16 Feb 1999 Tens of thousands of people in Dili attended the burial of a 25-year-old man shot dead during an incident between pro-independence and pro-Indonesian youths.

3 March 1999 Indonesian President B. J. Habibie announces that if, in a 'process of consultation', the majority of East Timorese rejected autonomy in favor of independence, Indonesia would grant independence. Xanana begins calling for a cease-fire, disarmament and real Indonesian troop reductions.

5 May 1999 Agreement between Indonesia, Portugal and the UN to put a special autonomy framework to the East Timorese people through a 'popular consultation' and for the UN to establish a United Nations mission, UNAMET, to do so. The Government of Indonesia made responsible for maintaining peace and security in order that the popular consultation could be 'carried out in a fair and peaceful way in an atmosphere free of intimidation, violence or interference from any side'.

30 August 1999 Ballot is carried out.

4 September 1999 Results of ballot announced: 78.5 per cent of East Timorese vote for independence by indicating the CNRT flag on the ballot paper.

September 1999 The pro-integration militias, with substantial Indonesian military backing, engage in a period of uncontrolled terrorism. An unknown number of East Timorese were killed and over 200,000 forcibly displaced into West Timor and other parts of Indonesia. Xanana is released amidst military slayings in East Timor. He takes refuge in the British Embassy and then flees to Darwin after receiving death threats.

15 September 1999 The terrifying violence in East Timor finally spurs USA to pressure Indonesia into accepting a peacekeeping force. The UN Security Council authorises an Australian-led multinational force to restore peace and security in East Timor.

Xanana returns to a devastated East Timor and makes emotional pleas for all Timorese to return home, to forgive and to rebuild.

AUTOBIOGRAPHY

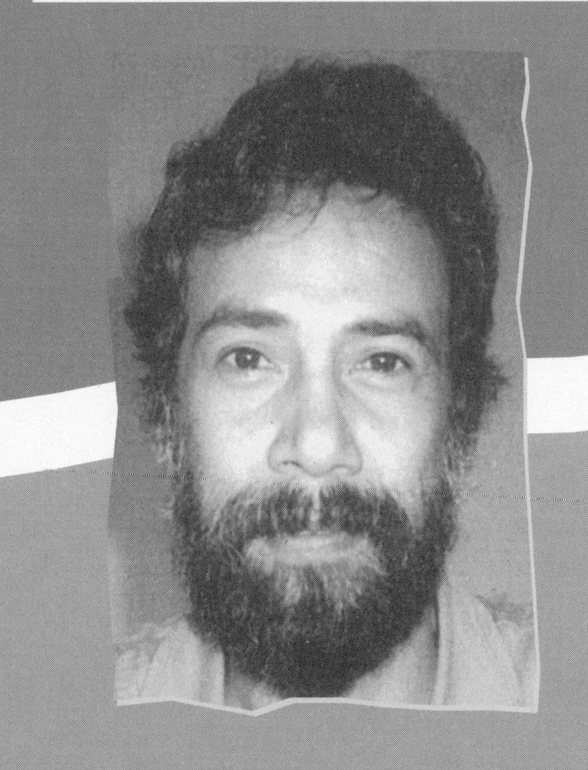

Autobiography

Xanana Gusmão wrote this part-autobiography in Cipinang Prison in Jakarta in 1994 at the request of a friend from the Portuguese solidarity group, CDPM, Commission for the Rights of the Maubere People.[1] *He wrote it in clandestine moments with no other reference but memory. A fellow East Timorese prisoner, Joao Camara, jailed for organising a demonstration in Jakarta protesting the Santa Cruz massacre, typed up the 45-page manuscript on a clunky old Remington typewriter in his cell. The loud thudding of the keys often made him fear detection. The manuscript is dated 30 September 1994 and its pages were smuggled out to Portugal where it was published as the centrepiece in a collection of Gusmão's writings entitled 'East Timor: One People, One Homeland'. Headings and notes have been added.*

1. Growing up (1946–1974)

Childhood 1946–62

Immediately after the Second World War, the pride of Manatuto was the ruins of Saint Isabel College, once a Catholic boarding college for girls. These ruins acted as a symbol of the break between the two historical periods of Portuguese presence. As the obligatory stopping point on the way to the college and to Soibada Catholic mission, Manatuto—a town on the north coast of East Timor—was heavily influenced by religious teachings, captivating for some but slavery for the majority. At the college, the nuns kept the hands of the young local girls busy, teaching them embroidery, crochet and weaving. The girls knew the stories of the Old Testament word for word and would never have mistaken any of the faces of the apostles and saints. Yet maybe those busy hands also had time to sign love letters, in between cooking lessons, providing a powerful attraction to the young students at Soibada.

Nearby, in my village of Laleia, on a small hill scorched by the sun, rested sacred stones that were a special home for the *Luliks*, indigenous sacred objects that were called demonic by the church but to which the people would run with

[1] José Ramos-Horta explains the political origins of the use of the indigenous word 'Maubere' in his description of the beginnings of the political party Fretilin. 'I began therefore to concoct our own version of social democracy by coining the word Mauberism—from Maubere, a common name among the Mambai people that had become a derogatory expression meaning poor, ignorant. Though vaguely defined without any serious theoretical basis, Maubere and Mauberism proved to be the single most successful political symbol of our campaign. Within weeks, Maubere became the symbol of a cultural identity, of pride, of belonging' (Ramos-Horta, 1987, p.37).

prayers, as if to their guardian angel. My father, the only son of a poor peasant family, was native to Laleia. He was sent to Manatuto after his teacher training and he married my mother who was also from a poor family of peasants. The only thing these peasants had to sell to the landowners was their labour.

I was born in Manatuto. My mother said it was either on the night of the 20th of June or in the early hours of the 21st, 1946, in the scorching heat that ripens the rice. By then, my sister Felismina, born two years earlier, was probably enjoying childhood delights in the balmy afternoons of a coastal village: an earthen bowl of steaming chicken soup, with locusts from the plains at harvest time, or with *balichao*: seafood preserves whose aroma of algae would waft even into a child's dreams, interrupted by shrieks of fright at the sticky touch of dead octopus and amid stories of crocodiles. Only the Bible and the civilisation of colonialism were able to destroy the bonds that tied the Timorese to their pair of goats, their vegetable plot and their belief in sacred sites.

I was one or two years old when my father was transferred from Manatuto to Lacluta. In the steep and foggy mountain ranges called Bibileo-Aitana, another sister, Lucia, was born. Not long afterwards, my father was transferred further east to Saint Theresa's mission in Ossu. I still remember vividly the journey on horseback, possibly with my father, along a sandy riverbed, beneath the sad moan of the *kakeus*, casuarina trees, which seemed to be responding to the inconsolable cooing of the small turtle doves, a sound which always managed to imbue the solitude of the wilderness with a penetrating bucolic melancholy.

Ossu was a temperate hamlet with a castle. It reminded us of the tale of Guimaraes Castle, the home of the first king of Portugal, King Afonso Henriques. Guimaraes acted as the cradle for a nation of whites. The only whites we knew were the priests, irate in their sermons and violent in the schools, and the *chefe de postos* who, it was said, were the senior administrators of a country we could not conceive of.

A childhood of lofty dreams! Dreams of being a schoolteacher like my father. It was a magnificent title enjoying the respect of everyone, deeply regarded by the *Lurais*, the traditional chiefs, and having the confidence of the Chinese merchants. Once every few months an old Chevrolet would pass through, making a din, frightening sleepy buffaloes, upsetting the dogs and scattering the noisy hens. The children would come running out from the few houses of the hamlet to the shop to smell civilisation in the petrol fumes and in the awful smell of copra. Although the smells made us sick they fixated us. We returned home at night to a few smacks from a welcoming father; and to quieten our cries our mother would tell us stories of bandits and of a monster, like a machine, which ate naughty children.

My father's monthly salary was 60 *patacas,* silver coins. I heard him say this many times, sometimes full of tenderness and other times tainted with bitterness due to our poverty. Nevertheless my childhood was a happy one; I was free to run on the grassy slopes in muddy rains and in a temperate and healthy climate. Ossu valley was like an open shell squeezed between the mountains of Mundo Perdido, Mau Laritame and Builo. Once a year, as students, we would go to work on the corn harvest at the mission vegetable gardens. The leeches rising from the fertile smell of the rotting leaves and branches would frighten us. They seemed to be waiting for us, nature's blessing!

My two oldest sisters became boarders at the college run by the Canossian nuns, so I was left as leader of a line of little girls. As a son, I was the blessing from God for my father, the answer to his prayers. I had many duties at home and was envious of the boys I went to school with who lived in at the boarding school and did not have to look after their little sisters. I would run away to play with other boys from the school where my father taught. The priests at school scared me but the sisters, mostly Italian, made me believe in angels. They were really saintly and became good friends of my family.

My father loved reading and subscribed to the Catholic magazines, *Flama*, *Noticias de Portugal* and others. He used to read to me and I began to read with him—little tales. My mother told us stories about the Japanese occupation, about my grandparents, and my uncle, a brother of hers, a telephonist who had managed to land himself a job in Dili. He was to be our chance to break away from our small world, move to Dili where I could get an education and, according to my father, become a good Portuguese. My father had accumulated 'the benefits of civilisation' which, although not many, had nonetheless allowed him to clothe and educate all his children, something most Timorese would never be able to do. He also had a part-time job as inspector in *Senhor* Ricardo's cheese and butter factory.

By nature I was already a rebel, but the regular beatings I received at school were just passing pain. It was a happy childhood, full of presents, godparents and godchildren because of the position of my schoolmaster father. He discussed the latest Portuguese 'Development Plan' with his own small circle of friends from the town who were 'assimilated' like him.[2] He spoke of Salazar, the statesman who ruled Portugal as a dictator, as if he had actually met him in Soibada. I admired my father in those days. He bought a horse and off he went

2 An *assimilado* was an indigenous Timorese who had mastered Portuguese, paid tax, been baptised and taken a Portuguese name. The *assimilados* were given voting and Portuguese citizenship rights and were eligible to receive an education. These policies were a result of Salazar's 1930 Colonial Act.

to some election or other in the town of Vikeke.[3] He was not political but had become an 'assimilated' Timorese, who tried to cut the ties between his children and the barefoot Timorese culture. My father was not a proud man. He was simple, reserved and principled. I liked his profile; he was erect, sure of himself, and I could always recognise him from afar by his ever-present hat. My father belonged to a specific link in the chain of East Timor's colonial history. After the Second World War, a handful of schoolmasters, earning a pittance, assisted the colonial power to try to recultivate a nation and, imperceptibly, reinforced the domination by cross and sword, alongside a feudal authority.

I saw prisoners at the administration post being whipped; they groaned as they were forced to stand on the burning rocky ground in the scorching sun with feet shackled. Sometimes, in my boyhood escapades with school friends, the sons of *Lurais*, I also saw agents or local people setting off in search parties, or returning with a crew of bloodied offenders who had not shown up for forced labour on the roads, or the obligatory service as *asu-lear*, manual labourer, in the homes of the colonialists, Chinese and assimilated Timorese.

One day I got home from school to find my mother weeping inconsolably. Her brother, my uncle, the telephonist—and possibly my only hope of a future education—had died. After I took my end of primary school exams, the problem of my education became worse for my worried father, who wanted his only son out of his seven children to be somebody. 'You are going to the seminary!' he said. There was no alternative. But I did not want to be a priest. I had never seen a Timorese priest and the white priests frightened me. I hated them for beating us so much at school. But I had to go along with it.[4]

We went to Dili, which we knew at the time as the *praca*, the market-square. It was a very dusty market; you could smell the pig excrement. The pigs were on the loose, fossicking through the smelly sewer that was the habitat of noisy ducks and hungry dogs. I remember a rotting hut made of half-eaten away straw, with a dirty counter made from packing crates. This was the shop. The Chinese proprietor sold petrol and fried rice cakes made from the family leftovers and children's clothing made of his fat wife's dirty petticoats. She used to wear wide Chinese pants made of a nondescript blue and so stained that

---

[3] 'Viqueque' is the Portuguese spelling and 'Vikeke' the indigenous spelling. Both usages appear through this text.

[4] The seminary was the *Nossa Senhora de Fatima* minor seminary in Dare, in the southern hills behind Dili. The Dare seminary became famous for producing nearly all of East Timor's indigenous political leaders of the 1970s of all shades of the political spectrum. It was a highly disciplined environment run by the Jesuits. The education was free to those bright enough to be selected by the priests. It was the only option for Timorese from poor families to get a secondary education, especially those with nowhere to stay in Dili, preventing them from attending the local high school there.

even the best soap, manufactured from copra oil in Baucau, could not get them clean. The kind shopkeeper allowed us to leave our mat, suitcase and tin of sweets behind the counter and he also gave us water from a well behind the house. That night my father and I slept on the dusty veranda, sharing a mattress and a common anguish, eating our bread and tin of sardines. At least we were more civilised and assimilated than the Chinese was the sentiment I felt in my father's sighs! We went from house to house, from friend to friend and possible relatives. We even went to the ecclesiastical centre. We found the sun was absolutely unbearable that July 1958. No one would accept me.

'There's no other choice; you are going to the seminary to continue your studies', my father said.

I never even thought of asking the question later: Where did we sleep on those nights before being able to find a car to return to Ossu? Certainly there was the veranda of that welcoming shop.

Just as in primary school, I was not a diligent secondary school student. At the seminary the nightly saying of the rosary and constant novenas and prayers used to send me to sleep! I remember that I never got more than 13 out of 20 marks and even less for behaviour. Even if I had wanted to I was never allowed to join the Sons of Mary Apostolado. I took my revenge when I left the seminary by stealing one of the big sashes reserved for the heavenly-minded, usually earned one or two years before going on to the senior seminary in Macao.

One homosexual priest enraged me so much I helped to expel him. He went on to become a prison chaplain in Mexico.

My predecessors at the seminary learned English and French and arrived at the senior seminary knowing more of those languages than the language of the church. Then suddenly they stopped teaching French and English and instead there was an increase in the hours of Latin and religion.[5]

There was a Timorese priest, Jacob Ximenes, who encouraged discussions about religion and I always enjoyed taking the part of the Protestant, the incredulous, the atheist. The priests taught me to draw and my friend Domingos helped me to improve my paintings. I tried to compete with the beauty of the *scenarios,* stage sets, of my classmate Ricardo.

From my first year, Father Leoneto knew my total inability with music. Father Isac was a great friend: if I owe my father my love of reading then I owe Father Isac my love of the Portuguese language. I stole *Flamas* and *Noticias de Portugal*; I used to spend hours kneeling down reading in the quarters of Father Zuloaga, the Spanish Rector, who insisted on trying to make a priest of me.

[5] The suppression of secular languages such as French and English came as a kind of warning to the seminarians not to look beyond the priesthood.

The seminary was like a prison for minors that offered all the sexual inconveniences of puberty without the presence of women. In 1962 I had my first long holiday break.[6] We were divided into groups according to the missions to which our families belonged and we stayed with relatives. My father had been transferred to Bacau so I went there. I made pastoral visits with Father Brito and had some days at home and some at the swimming pool. I loved swimming and we boys hurried anxiously back to the pool because many of the girls from Dili swam there. What stupidity, I used to think of the pastoral work. I pretended to be sick so I could stay at home, then I would go to the swimming pool while others proceeded with the pastoral visits.

'My Holidays' was the first essay we had to write in the following school year. After reading it, Father Isac called me to his room and said, 'I don't give you too many more months here'. I protested, 'But this is only an essay, Father!'

Father Rabago gave me two months to meditate. He was my sex educator and I have much to thank him for: his friendship and being my confidant. Even after I left the seminary he continued to be my counsellor.

By the time I ran away from the seminary, my father had been transferred to Manatuto and I cannot remember if it was a surprise for him when I returned home. I had already done something similar in Ossu when I had run away to Viqueque just as the exams were starting. I had run away with a delegation to organise the festivities for the arrival of some governmental department head, but on the third night I was awoken and forced to return with one of the priests, a superior of the mission.

The punishments on my return to the seminary did not correct me and maybe, in truth, even my father was never convinced that I would spend much more time there. During the first few weeks back at the seminary the harsh environment was frightening. We were taken on a retreat to a remote place near Dare. On the second and third days we planned to escape. Afonso would be our guide. On the fourth day, the day chosen for our escape, after lunch we were allowed to speak and play again so we forgot about the plan.[7] In the end I simply told Father Rabago that I wanted to leave the seminary and go to the *Liceu*.

'You'll have to apply for the equivalent of the regular Portuguese education system and you can only enrol for next year', he said. 'I'll try to help you', he promised.

---

6 This break was part of the priesthood training in pastoral care and was spent in the student's home diocese.

7 Afonso Redentor Araujo, brother of Abilio Araujo, former Fretilin leader, was a friend of Xanana's and his senior in Fretilin. He was a good musician. He was killed in the mountains during the Indonesian occupation.

Young adult 1963–67

What I did not know was that outside my prison—that antechamber for saints—life had changed for the worse. I admired my father's spirit of sacrifice and my mother's ministrations. I was an extra mouth to feed and it wasn't a small one. My sister Felismina was a pre-school teacher and already was helping the family with her monthly salary of 300 escudos. My father earned his 700 a month plus some miserable family allowances for each child of school age. He was responsible for all of us, two boys and six girls.

An uncle wrote to my father, offering to take me into his house in Dili. I started learning French but there were problems that forced me to return to Manatuto. I got work in the morning as a draftsman at MEAU, the *Missao de Estudos Agronomicos do Ultramar,* and in the afternoons I taught Portuguese in the Chinese school.

My mother saved up some money so I could return to Dili the following year to try night classes at the high school, the *Liceu Dr Francisco Veira Machado*, and to look for work. However, my three years at the seminary were not recognised by the Portuguese system since there were considerable differences in the curriculum. I would have to start again in the first year. But there were other needs to consider, so in the mornings I got a job typing in the Health Service. In 1964, after a year's practice, six months of which was without pay, there were vacancies announced for 15 office workers. I was confident and managed to get twelfth place, but then they only took on four people. This was the first of life's disappointments! The first feelings of rebellion! Women, *mesticos*, and sons of important people always seemed to get preferential treatment. Why should they?

Many of my colleagues, after studying for a year at the seminary, joined the *Milician* sergeant's course. Not for me; I did not want to be a soldier, so I went back to Manatuto. My father spent his life travelling that narrow colonial world and did not even have a plot of land on which to grow one ear of corn. When I was looking for firewood in the meadows with Lucia and Celina I dreamed of having horses and thousands of cattle just like the cowboys in the movies we watched through a hole in the wall at the 'Sporting' club.

Months later I received a telephone call from Pedro Melo, my best and inseparable friend, asking me to come back to Dili. He used to buy magazines, have books and subscribe to a royalist paper, the name of which I don't remember. Pedro was the 'single guy' because another friend, Azorio, had stolen his girlfriend. Pedro was very methodical and never got angry. His door was always open to me when I was tired of *kore-metan* parties,[8] or arguing with friends or when I was searching for debates, 'relaxation' and reading.

Two of my colleagues had accepted public service jobs, receiving 30 escudos a day for the first three months.[9] All eleven of the others offered this deal had refused, so I was called in. I refused the probationary period because I had already worked without remuneration for six months but I was forced to accept it anyway. Three months later—no raise. I protested but was forced to wait another two months. A Portuguese woman, a wife of a low-ranking officer was accepted straight into a base-grade position. She was expecting a baby and would spend all her time knitting. Three months later Elvira, one of my female colleagues who had accepted the job at the same time as I had, got a raise.

I knew what the Head of the Department, Inspector Matias, was like, so I knew my protests were to no avail. There were only three of us in that section in the Department of Health: the Administrative Officer, the Accounts Manager and me in the Statistics Section. Since I had already worked with no remuneration for more than half the year, I started coming in late and leaving early to try to make the time I worked correspond to the salary. The Inspector screamed at me and I yelled back. Three months later Elvira was given the full salary. I suggested to a colleague that we should write in protest about it but he did not want to. I went direct to the boss's office. I insulted him and wanted to punch him and I was sacked. I also left the *Liceu* because I could no longer pay the school fees.

I lived with an old fisherman. At night his nephew and I used to steal a *beiros*, a small boat, and go out on the high seas to cast our hooks. We would return at dawn to sell the fresh fish, usually to the Chinese. We had lucky days but there were also nights when we fought the currents and winds, arriving back at the beach without any fish, famished and exhausted.

I was running from department to department looking for a job and finally I was recommended to the Governor's Department. Captain Carneiro, if I am not mistaken, was the head.

'Qualifications? What do you know? Have you ever worked? What is your name?'

'Gusmão, in Health', I said.

'Ah! Gusmão, what does Health say of you? Receptionist, bring me the note from Health on Gusmão.'

I understood, apologised and went back to working on the sea.

---

[8] *Kore-metan* is the traditional Timorese commemorative celebration that signals the end of the one-year mourning period after a death. It is open to everyone who attended the funeral and usually the whole community goes.

[9] The average wage for a person of Xanana's age at the time was equal to three Australian dollars, about 17 escudos, per day for a Dili worker over 18.

I counted the many times I bowed, swallowing the words the whites flung at me. Colleagues were admitted to the public service with such ease, they were the children of staff, big shots who had the right blood that permitted them to speak Portuguese with the right accent. We swelled the number of thinkers amongst the *tintanas,* those who spent their nights drinking red wine, and the frustrated. We were not hooligans or violent. Among us were the virgins straight out of the seminary who went off as dusk came, *mestiços,* who were just all talk, and troubadours, who defied the dogs with their singing and wooing of the hearts of girls whose parents reacted with insults and threats. In those youthful days I knew that tomorrow would have to be something different, something that could be counted in escudos. Many times I apologised, looking for work, yelling my thank yous at people.

In 1965 the sea became stingy so I went to work on the wharf as a stock-taker for the *Sociedade*[10] unloading ships. Eventually I left, physically exhausted, and sought refuge and rest in Manatuto.

'You only remember home when you're sick', said my father.

'I won't stay long!' I answered.

Fully recovered, I returned to selling fish at dawn in Dili at Lecidere and Bidau whose beaches had become a salty path full of the whispers of the sea in my life. In 1966 I finally got a job at the *Sociedade* as a civil engineering drafts-man. I returned to the *Liceu* at night to complete the final year of junior high.

My life was not all sadness, my difficult youth not all without its brighter side. Sport was my passion and it provided me with a passport to all the social events and parties. The indigenous sporting club *Uniao* [11] was known as the 'indigenous home' for stray players, drunks and *kore-metan* parties, and membership meant a free ticket into any wedding party or birthday dance in any neighbourhood. We were smiled upon. These parties danced to the strains of Abril Metan's eloquent violin which delighted in seeing old couples return to the time of their youth amidst a difficult and restless group of young men who stole away their daughters and threw vengeful punches afterwards.

Several clerical vacancies were announced in Civil Administration and I applied. I got my first decent job. I said goodbye to the old fisherman who only knew how to smile. He smiled even if the sea deprived him of sardines when he fished way out where the waves started to flower.

---

[10] *Sociedade Agricola Patria e Trabalho* (SAPT) was the largest Portuguese import/export company, established in 1897.

[11] The *Associacao Desportiva e Recreativa Uniao* was a sporting and recreational club founded by 12 native Timorese with the assistance of Portuguese Catholic missionary priest, Ezequiel Enes Pasqual. The club was exclusively native Timorese.

Army and marriage 1968–74

One of my colleagues, Justino Mota, was one of those people who saw the injustices and difficulties of a future condemned to working in the miserable public service. Our limited options, the great Portuguese economic development plans and the incentives given to the Chinese, were the natural themes of our conversations. Still, I went about tidying up my life: I bought books and read. My mother and four sisters were living with me. Lucia was teaching. On Easter Sunday night, 1968, I returned home drunk and found my *palapa* palm hut on fire. That part of my life that had come from the dust had turned to ashes! Months later the local Council Administration sent me a recruitment notice and in August I joined the Portuguese army. I could no longer avoid national service and went out to salute many of my old seminary and *Liceu* colleagues.[12]

In 1969, I married my fiancée, Emilia, in a registry office, having insulted the priests. Ever since September 1968, Emilia had been forbidden by her father to continue our courtship. In 1969, he made her leave her home. Inexplicable? Because I was just a soldier? Because I was poor? Because I was native? Only he knows.

At the beginning of 1971 I managed to obtain a *passa a peluda*, an army discharge, early. I had joined the army, and left it, with a spirit of defiance and disobedience, but I also learned how to do what I did not want to and what I did not like. Positions for Timorese at the rank of sergeant were increased and paid well and continued to be a lure for me.

The public service, my only other option, was a necessity for survival. It gave the feeling of belonging to a higher social class. It was entry into an elite group that was growing in Timorese society. In the previous generation this elite was restricted to just a few *Chefe do Posto*s, nurses and aristocrats. A job in the public service that had been so hard to obtain in the previous decade had now become a real lottery. Previously knowledge (even if very circumscribed) guaranteed entry and, while this continued to be so, in the 70s it was applied a lot more efficiently. The Timorese elite was growing and climbing the rungs of that bureaucratic ladder of state. Was all this a sign of the times? Was development all there was? The growing public service was the only living symbol of civilisation![13]

[12] National Service was for three years. There were about 3000 soldiers and 7000 reserve soldiers stationed in Portuguese Timor. By 1974 most ordinary ranks and non-commissioned officers were Timorese.

[13] A marked increase in educational facilities and an expansion of jobs in the public service and army for native Timorese offered by the Portuguese administration occurred in the 1960s and 70s. Some commentators argue this increase was a direct result of the 1959 Viqueque uprising when the Portuguese were 'forced to refine their methods of repression'.

Smoking on the Esplanade

This newspaper piece, by J. A. Gusmão, published in A Voz de Timor *on 24 April 1975, was part of a series of fictional dialogues between two characters, both public servants in the Portuguese Colonial administration. Their conversation highlights the growth in size of the Public Service and the resulting change in work ethic, also affected by new political and anti-colonial sentiments circulating in Dili. The first democratic elections, the result of which preceded a civil war in August, were only two months away. Xanana carefully illustrates the generation gap in a society in such changing times. Portuguese spending in the early 1970s had increased from US$1,251,622 in 1972 to $5,075,189 in 1973 (Jannisa, 1977, p. 156) and much of this went into education, infrastructure and the public service.*

Enjoying the pleasant afternoon at the Hotel Resende, Rodrigues, a dignified old man carrying the heavy burden of having to provide for his many children and having achieved little in his life-long work as a typist, is consoling himself with a cigarette.

Along comes Sousa, a well-known youth, well paid and unaffected by his everyday problems. He disturbs Rodrigues' thoughtful state of mind.

Sousa: Hi, Rodrigues, what's new?

Rodrigues: Nothing new my friend, and you?

Sousa: As usual. You should stop thinking so much. Do what I do, my old friend: live life without a care.

Rodrigues: Obviously you don't have the problems that I do.

Sousa: Problems? What problems do you have?

Rodrigues: Problems at the office. It's all in a mess and it's upset me, you know?

Sousa: Upset you? Well you don't say … sensitive, hey? What order of problems are they?

Rodrigues: What order? You mean disorder! Imagine, in that office where I have earned my daily bread as a typist for 29 years, I have never seen it so out of control, so full of empty heads!

Sousa: Oh, Rodrigues! These are new times. Your time has passed. You've worked too hard, right? See the state you are in? Physically worn out, to say nothing about your inner spirit.

Rodrigues: I behave like a good Christian who does his duty. I am not like you young playboys—bad-mannered—I am sorry to say, but it is my conscience that guides me. All you lot know how to do is waste all your money on wine. So now, I'm a nervous wreck, to see you all earning all this money and working so little for it.

Sousa: There you go again, mad with jealousy. It's just not on and even more so at your age, my old man! Let it be, because you were just the same in your time.

Rodrigues: No, Sousa. You can believe that what little I have earned is due to my own efforts and I don't envy the position of those hangers-on. What makes it so pitiful is to see them being so unproductive.

Sousa: Producing what, Rodrigues? Can't you see that the population has increased, that the problems are greater now, and that … well, to facilitate the task, we need to put on more people, to evenly distribute the work? Don't think about it—the days of slavery are over—that was your day.

Rodrigues: Yes, and the truth is that people nowadays are only interested in how much they earn. They think all the rest is rubbish!

Sousa: I can see that you are becoming conscious and coming to terms with the changing times, the turn of the tide. Are there more people asking for jobs? They have to be paid the basic wage to keep up with the cost of living, etc, etc … Well, here goes another 'Laura' [a brand of beer].

Rodrigues: No. No, no more for me.

Sousa: One more, go on. Hey, Manuel, bring me another tall one and two glasses. We can clear up our misunderstanding over another beer, Rodrigues.

Rodrigues: No, Sousa, you don't understand me.

Sousa: What you need to do is to go with the flow.

Rodrigues: I can't stop being myself, don't you understand?

Sousa: Forget about these stories, Rodrigues, while the bottle is still not empty. Even I am a supporter of … er, I say, er, of, well, I don't have one yet. [He is talking about supporting one of the newly created political parties; the two main ones are UDT and Fretilin.] Understand, because of the way I feel, of living in the present. Then, er, as I was saying, to continue this kind of life—I'm not sure if you understand me—in which we live happily, in peace, calmly and harmoniously, not anxiously, not putting our moral integrity and professionalism in danger and, er, all our work, our efforts justify that, er, we have our ambitions, rather just ambitions as it happens, that motivate us to get though those six hours of work!

Rodrigues: Six – long – hours!
Sousa: I'll give you a lift.
Rodrigues: No, thanks, the walk will do me good. I'll see you tomorrow.
Sousa: *Tchau!* Tomorrow we will continue our conversation.
Rodrigues, even more subdued, walks away with his own thoughts.
Sousa: For goodness' sake, some people!

I met Borja da Costa in the army.[14] Lots of colleagues from high school and from earlier social gatherings were starting their own families. It was usual for people starting a family to gradually leave the chat out on the street, and spend more time at home. However, Justino Mota, along with a few others, always had time for chatting and grumbling and another new group of young people soon was formed. It was customary to find them on the Esplanade, deeply engrossed in society gossip. The Chinese and their smiling diplomacy and red envelopes;[15] bosses, their integrity and professional abilities or otherwise, governors and their policies, taxes and prices; the 'terrorism' in the African provinces[16]; day-to-day life in the civil service—these were all topics that reflected a dissatisfied character. We all simply wished that the whites would go away without the slightest thought to anything beyond that.

I convinced my father to make a request for consideration of service rendered to Bishop Joaquim Ribero. The Bishop answered in a pastoral letter that anyone who was not happy in their job should leave, but the mission did not have any extra money. I had got my father into trouble and felt guilty.

The public service was a routine of paper shuffling, unproductive and false—that was our perception of it—but it was a necessity because we had no other choice. Borja da Costa was starting to write a few articles which he gave me to read. We exchanged points of view and he convinced me of his. They

[14] Francisco Borja da Costa was the son of a Liurai from the south coast of East Timor and attended Soibada College and Dare seminary. He joined the public service in 1964 and did his national service 1968-71 at Laclubar (at the same time as Xanana but in a different place). A poet who wrote nationalist verse in Tetum Terick, he went to Lisbon in September 1973 and was 'politically oriented' by more radical Timorese there. Borja returned to Timor and worked with Fretilin. He was shot dead on Dili wharf by Indonesian soldiers on the day of the invasion.

[15] It is Chinese custom to pass bribes or gifts, indeed all money, in red envelopes.

[16] 'Terrorism' was how the Portuguese government described the armed movements for independence in the African colonies. Timorese students returning from Lisbon and some more liberal army personnel were aware of the true nature of the conflict. After being cut off for so long, Portuguese Timor was beginning to receive uncensored news of the rest of the world and anti-colonial and incipient nationalist sentiments were beginning to be expressed.

were not incisive articles; more metaphors of the situation outlining a society of three worlds—the colonists, the assimilated and the people. Only two of his articles were published and they were so heavily censored that only imaginary descriptions with no real meaning remained. We quit. I was sick of the public service. I wanted to free myself from the need to put up with the whims of the bosses and from the anchor that forced me to serve that regime which continually shut our mouths with our monthly bread.

There was a story of an old *Tinoco,* a Timorese man, who said to a governor, 'Aren't we glad Timor is like a boat that leaks but does not sink?' and this became like a catch-phrase! We felt distress and impotence because of many things: a Legislative Assembly that only signed documents; an army major who was forced to return to Portugal because he had been committed to a mental institution; inspectors sent to Timor who did not report on all the bridges that were falling down; the oil we were never sure existed or not;[17] a poll in which we were told to place a cross in front of the absentees so that we could reach 60 per cent attendance because our list of voters had reached little more than 20 per cent; the African wars that were costing the lives of so many Portuguese soldiers. A feeling that we were simply being tamed, that we were unable to cut those colonial chains, distressed us. We felt impotent because we could do little more than comprehend our situation for what it was.

The return from Angola of those exiled in 1959 was a new way to understand what had happened 15 years before.[18] At the time, in the seminary, I only knew that there was almost a war, and the word PIDE, the Portuguese Secret Police, became well-known from then on. The increase in the military, compulsory national service and the creation of the second-line army reserves were all understood as tactics necessary to contain the eventual rebellion of the Timorese. The returnees from Angola were 'heroes'. I had always enjoyed stories, told in whispers by the older residents of Dili—the old elite made up of nurses, employees of the printing industry and a few old retirees—about the 1959 case in Dili when the clubhouse of *Uniao* was burnt down and why that

17 Oil explorations were run by Australian and British companies, sometimes aided by American experts. Although promising, the two world wars and Portuguese red tape hindered the explorations.

18 On 1 May 1959, an armed uprising against the Portuguese administration arose in Uato Lari and Uato Karbau, near Vikeke. A series of riots and attacks on Portuguese posts occurred and the Portuguese were forced to raise a militia in the neighbouring area of Lospalos to put down the rebels. The rebellion was instigated by a group of Indonesian army officers who encouraged this anti-colonial rebellion against the Portuguese in a spirit of solidarity, just as they had done against the Dutch. Around 160 lives were lost and 60 Timorese were exiled for their part in the rebellion. Both UDT and Fretilin claim this event as a formative influence.

club had become a symbol of anti-colonial and sometimes racist sentiments against the Portuguese and Chinese.

Now I wanted to be free of saluting the whites, free of bowing my head like the old public servants, just so you could eat and educate your children. I tried to ask for a loan to start life as a farmer. Alves-Aldeias, my army Sector-Commander, without trying to persuade me to give up on this idea, told me, 'You know me. I am an officer. If the agricultural services agree with your plan I will only have to approve it'.

Mario Carrascalao, the Head of Agriculture, had gone to Tomar to participate in a meeting of the ANP [*Associao Nacional Popular*, the official right-wing Portuguese government party], which was the only official political party of the time. Two technical engineers, who were temporarily replacing Mario, welcomed me with great enthusiasm and confessed, 'Here we receive a house, car, money and we vegetate. What we learnt is dead. Count on us for your project. We will not ask for payment because it will be an opportunity for us to apply what we have learnt'.

The pair even told me, 'Go to the Loes region; we have analysed the soil there and it is fertile. The problem is that you will have to wait for the Chief, we cannot decide anything.' But Mario Carrascalao did not agree and demanded that I ask for a bigger loan. I tried to make him understand that I was not prepared to pay debts on a loan larger than I needed. And so died my dream of not depending directly on the power of whites. No, I was not a racist and nor am I now; I just wanted to be free of that system.

2. The last days of Portuguese Timor (1974 – 1975)

The Portuguese Revolution and decolonisation 25 April 1974

Paradoxically, I was frightened when the 25th of April 1974 came along, with the 'Carnation Revolution', a left-wing coup ousting the fascist government in Lisbon.[19] Could this mean independence? How? Our old Timorese elite was no elite, just a bunch of civil servants who, in their everyday conversation, sinned

---

[19] The coup meant eventual decolonisation for East Timor. This process included the call for the establishment of the political parties and democratic elections in former colonies. On 5 May 1975 the Governor of East Timor had called for the establishment of political parties. Two main parties emerged: UDT (*Uniao Democratica Timorense*, Timorese Democratic Union) and ASDT (*Associacao Social Democratica Timor*, Timorese Social Democratic Association). In September ASDT became *Frente Revolucionara do Timor Leste Independente*, FRETILIN. UDT, initially the most popular party, advocated democratisation, income redistribution, human rights and gradual independence with a federation with Portugal. It had support from senior administrators, plantation owners and a majority of *Liurais* and their kin. ASDT was formed by the new urban elites (mainly bureaucrats and teachers) and was Dili-based. It advocated 'universal doctrines of

by saying, 'for all intents and purposes', 'considering that ...' and, 'the misery of destiny'. I did not even want to imagine those people running Timor. I was surprised at the feverish enthusiasm of many of my friends and colleagues. I heard about Ramos-Horta,[20] who had begun to make speeches in public. He was not an idol, but I admired his courage, and his image of 'official' non-conformist had made him well-known and respected.

The freedom of choice crippled my ability to think straight and I opted for the easiest solution—to get out. I left for Australia, to find work and save some money, perhaps to return some day. Friends in Darwin helped me with all the papers there. After six months I returned to Timor to see if I could take the family with me. Justino and Borja were my most devoted persecutors for wanting to leave. I sympathised with Fretilin but was overwhelmed by worry about a future in our incapable hands. However, I gradually started to give way to my colleagues' continuous 'attacks' upon me. Chico Lopes da Cruz [21] tried to persuade me to join UDT. I thanked him for the beers and the lunch we had had at the Bacau Hotel.

I knew I was not much use. I went to work in the building industry as a labourer, earning 40 escudos a day. I became outraged that the older master bricklayers were receiving less than I was. I tried to convince them to protest but they said, 'Don't think about it, son. Look down there, see those others? They are looking for work. If we protest, we'll be sacked and they don't mind coming and collecting 20 escudos a day for cassava for their children'.

The blacksmiths were going to be sacked. We protested. I incited them to arm themselves with iron bars against the foreman if they did not get to keep their jobs. We lost the action. I felt guilty—once again. I joined Moniz da Maia, a road-building company, as an apprentice electrical mechanic. All my work-mates were Fretilin.

socialism and democracy' and independence; it carried this message together with health, education and cultural programs to the countryside and quickly built up a rural base.

[20] José Ramos-Horta was born on 26 December 1949 of a Timorese mother and Portuguese father exiled to East Timor by the Salazar dictatorship. He was educated at Soibada and the *Liceu*. He was an early leader of the independence movement and was exiled for his anti-colonial attitudes for two years, 1970-1971, to Mozambique. He saw himself as a moderate within Fretilin and the emerging movement for Timorese nationalism. He was mandated in 1974-75 to represent East Timor abroad and left the island three days before the Indonesian troops invaded. Of his 11 brothers and sisters, four have been killed by the Indonesian military. He has been a leader in the international delegation of the East Timorese resistance since 1975 and in 1993 he was awarded the Nobel Peace Prize for his tenacious efforts.

[21] Francisco Lopes da Cruz was an NCO in the Portuguese army, another graduate of Dare seminary and editor of the weekly newspaper *A Voz de Timor*. He was the leader of the political party UDT. After the Indonesian occupation he became the first Indonesian appointed Governor of Timor and eventually an advisor to the Indonesian government.

The political climate was now unpleasant. Hopes for the future were dramatised by the exodus of the colonists and a debilitated government, along with an army of longhaired soldiers mixed up with 'revolutionaries', and a general climate of dissatisfaction and instability. There was a confusion of aspirations put forward by different small circles, but they were gradually smothered as Fretilin gained ground. UDT clung tooth and nail to traditional authorities which had already lost the prestige still stubbornly being attributed to them. The civil servants were not arguing about the future of Timor; they were more concerned about the possibility of having to live without money, and most of them joined UDT. To be a civil servant meant having social status. For some, it just meant maintaining the existing social status of the family but for many it meant promotion to a secure life, money every month, a promise of a pension and, perhaps, the reward of some nice holidays that not everyone else received. Such a weak and unproductive civil service did not have much choice really! A few frustrated racist individuals joined Apodeti.[22]

People were incited to violence and I began to understand the mobilisation to action. I struggled between getting involved and keeping to the sidelines. It was not that I did not want to join in, but I could see that the situation could easily get completely out of hand.[23] Lari Sina [Abel Ximenes] insulted colonialism while at the same time protesting about the delays in getting paid. I tried to denounce the inconsistencies of attitudes like these and I stopped receiving salutes from Fretilin. They called me a 'UDT infiltrator'. Friends avoided me until I identified myself politically, in writing, and once again I was greeted and could greet others with closed fist, the Fretilin salute! At first, friends and colleagues in the UDT continued to raise their hands and greet me. Then came indifference, until finally it became obvious that we were avoiding each other. This really was not what I had wanted. UDT parents, Apodeti uncles, Fretilin children. What shit this freedom was!

Everyone was a politician. There were new politics, and what politics! The Goans said, 'Independence? In 1961, we would have been independent; there were more white houses in Goa than here'. The well-heeled Cape Verdians would

---

[22] Apodeti, *Associacao Popular Democratica Timorese*, the Timorese Popular Democratic Association. This political party was first called the 'Association for the Integration of Timor into Indonesia'. It was without doubt funded by the Indonesian government and had only about three hundred members.

[23] The political atmosphere was tense after the Portuguese revolution and an Indonesian destabilisation operation had begun in October 1974. In January 1975 Fretilin and UDT formed a coalition to facilitate national independence. Elections at village level began in mid-March and were supervised by the Decolonisation Committee of the Portuguese Parliament.

explain, 'In Cape Verde I am PAIGC but here I am UDT!'[24] The Portuguese in the colonial structure lamented, 'I am not a colonialist. I am not an exploiter. I was paid to work here!' The 25th of April had not provided any answers but had only raised questions from which we would make our own history.

I had begun working as a telephonist for Marconi, the government telecommunications centre. Ma'Huno, founding member of ASDT-Fretilin, had 'arranged' for me to substitute for him because he was going to the CP1, the army base in Aileu which in the future was to become a stick to beat us with.[25] A Portuguese official, who was also working in decolonisation matters, used to talk with Ma'Huno and another founding members of ASDT, Montalvao.[26] I stood by their side to listen.

'You should convince your colleagues to become more cooperative in the decolonisation process. Your leaders have learnt a few Marxist phrases by heart on the steps of the palace, and when they come into the palace to start discussing the program of decolonisation all they can do is spout those Marxist slogans, which don't help at all!'

'For us it is *ukun rasik an,* self-determination. This is our problem. All the rest is rubbish', said Ma'Huno.

Disillusioned, I started to wait for my political friends at the Resend Hotel Bar in the afternoons and asked Borja, Redentor and Mota, 'What do you discuss at the meetings?'

'Programs of politicisation, literacy, and so on ...'

Mari Alkatiri, a founding member of Fretilin, said angrily, 'If you want to know, come to the meetings. We're not parrots!'

I was embarrassed but I waited for them many times to come out of meetings to offer a lift to whoever needed one. I was already participating in a revolution—a revolution of my own ideas![27]

---

24 PAIGC is *Partido Africano de Independencia de Guinea e Cabo Verde*, the left-wing liberation movement from Guinea-Bissau founded by Amilcar Cabral. This is written in an insulting parody of a Cape Verdian accent.

25 Ma'Huno Bulerek Karatainu was the Deputy Chief of Staff of Fretilin. He was one of the three Central Committee members to survive with Xanana into the 1980s and became leader after Xanana was captured in 1992 but was soon also captured. He remained living in Timor, always a strong advocate for Timorese independence.

The army camp (CP1) at Aileu became the Fretilin rehabilitation or punishment camp. Those arrested by Fretilin after the civil war were imprisoned here. Many criticisms have been made about Fretilin, based on the activities that occurred here during this time.

26 Montalvao was a *Correios, Telegrafos e Telephones* employee. He became involved in civil war negotiations between the Decolonisation Committee, UDT and Fretilin. He became a Fretilin commander who surrendered and was later killed by the Indonesian army.

27 Circa April 1975 Xanana began work on *A Voz de Timor* firstly as a special collaborator then by the beginning of June as an editor. He began to publish articles and poems.

The situation had become unbearable. I asked myself what would happen if the violence started spreading. The fury of the political leaders excited everybody's spirit and so many slogans worried me. I made a conscious decision, on 20 May 1975, in front of many Timorese elders who were shedding tears and crying *ukun rasik an*, self-determination, that if I wanted to fight for my Homeland there was only one way to do so: join Fretilin! I never had a membership card, and never asked if my friends had one. Although I followed the political developments of the situation and of the parties I came to no conclusions. I was troubled.

One afternoon, like most others, I was at the Fretilin headquarters. UDT had mobilised a demonstration in Dili, an action that was provocative.[28] Chico Lopes met all the men at his house, got them drunk and then ordered them to march on Fretilin. News started spreading around the HQ that they were approaching. The women gathered stones and stood behind the trees and the men armed themselves with sticks.

I tried to convince everyone to avoid confrontation. The UDT men, dressed in traditional costumes, came around the corner of the Santa Cruz cemetery. They were screaming calling for blood and performing war dances, swords gleaming, their actions motivated by the wine. Hoarse from shouting, I kept appealing for calm. People were startled by the order, but they obeyed. The UDT people were many, too many, and they were all drunk. I phoned the military police. Those were terrible moments: the 'warriors' of UDT were past the cemetery. Fretilin people were nervous. I continued to yell for them to be calm until the military *Unimog* police trucks arrived.

The military police saluted me with the Fretilin closed fist and we avoided the bloodshed that would have been the beginning of the end—maybe even worse than the coup. Two truckloads of UDT militants from the city went past. I continued to appeal for calm. A few Fretilin, unhappy with the lack of action, went to wait for the UDT trucks in Barrio Economico where they threw stones at them.

---

[28] There was a split in UDT over the coalition with Fretilin, and UDT announced its withdrawal from the coalition on 26 May 1975. Local elections were held under the auspices of the Portuguese Decolonisation Committee and 90 per cent of the newly-elected *Liurais* were Fretilin members or supporters (Hill, 1978, pp. 122-3). UDT staged several anti-Fretilin and anti-communist rallies in Dili on 9 and 10 August and eventually a full-scale coup on the 11th. Indonesia had been directing a subversive destabilisation campaign called *Operasi Komodo* since October 1974 and was broadcasting anti-communist messages into the territory from Kupang, its campaign changed to one of political infiltration and finally to outright military provocation in the border regions.

Behind the trucks were three cars full of the elite of UDT. In one was Domingos de Oliveira.[29] Easy prey, I thought, but once again, I managed to control myself. Dr Cascais, a Portuguese lawyer who was serving in Timor as an army lieutenant, stopped the car in front of me. I expressed my unhappiness. He tried telling me that it was absolutely essential that Fretilin begin a dialogue with UDT, but he did not continue. Carvarino[30] stopped by my side. 'Don't listen to that fool. Let's go inside', he yelled at me. I was disappointed, confused and worried!

Coup and civil war 10 August 1975

On the evening of 10 August, I realised that the personnel of OPS, the Fretilin Popular Security Organisation, had begun to trust me. It must have been nearly 19.00 hours when I received a message from them: Alarico[31] was in contact with Ponciano, a 2nd sergeant in the Portuguese army, about an army uprising to combat UDT's plan to arrest our leaders. UDT were on their way, and members of the Central Committee were in danger.[32]

We ran, then set up security along the roadside. On the corner opposite the Santa Cruz cemetery, hooded figures were already emerging: Nicolau Lobato,[33] Mari Alkatiri, Carapinha,[34] Hata,[35] and others. Alarcio jumped over

---

[29] Domingos de Olivera was the Secretary General of UDT. He was one of the signatories of the discredited Balibo Declaration, 30 November 1975, that requested integration with Indonesia and that Indonesia enter Timor and pacify Fretilin forces.

[30] Antonio Duarte Carvarino, also called Mau Lear, was one of several Timorese students to return to Dili after the revolution in Lisbon where they had been studying. He was labelled a 'Marxist from Lisbon' in an Indonesian newspaper. He became a supporter of ASDT and Fretilin. Influenced by Freire and the liberation movements in the Portuguese African colonies, he was responsible for setting up some of the first schools under the Fretilin literacy program. He was killed, reportedly on 2 February 1979, after being taken prisoner during the 1978 Indonesian encirclement campaign. It was reported in the *East Timor News*, Autumn 1984, that he was burnt alive with petrol after being tortured.

[31] Alarico Jorge Fernandes, son of a Timorese mother and Portuguese *deportado* father, was educated at Soibada and the seminary. He worked at Bacau Airport as a radio operator. He became Secretary General of Fretilin not long after it was formed in Dili and then Minister of Information or Internal Affairs and Security in the Democratic Republic of East Timor (DRET) Cabinet. An anti-communist, he aligned himself with that faction of the resistance. He has been accused of the massacre of the UDT prisoners after the Indonesian invasion. On 3 December 1978, during the encirclement campaign, he surrendered to the Indonesians with three or four supporters and Fretilin's only radio. He now lives in Indonesia.

[32] The Central Committee was the 50-strong policy-making council of Fretilin.

[33] Born in 1946, Nicolau dos Reis Lobato is remembered as the first nationalist leader of the military resistance and died a hero in this capacity. His father was the *Luirai* of Soibada. Nicolau attended Soibada and Dare Colleges. He worked in the public service and then attended the

into the cemetery and fired a shot as he fell. We all rushed to Fretilin headquarters. The Central Committee members present held a quick meeting. Mari told me that UDT was planning a coup for that very night, and that the Central Committee members would have to leave the city. Beyond Becora, we heard shots being fired, and megaphones announcing the 'revolutionary anti-communist coup'. It came as no surprise to me. I knew it was a simple, logical and natural consequence of that type of politics.[36]

A handgun, a hunting rifle, and two bombs made by the fishermen of Bidau were all the protection the members of the Central Committee had. Mota Ulun, on the Becora River, became a temporary base. We had couriers running between the Army Engineering Battalion up to our base of fragile lookouts defended by bamboo bows and arrows. Nicolau, Carvarino, Hata, Mari, Alarico, Carapinha and others were all there.

Rogerio Lobato[37] arrived as a mediator sent by the Governor, Lemos Pires[38]. Nicolau set 15 conditions, including the disarmament of UDT; Timorese soldiers resuming control of the city; outside communications being

---

Milician sergeant's school and joined the Army for two years before re-entering the public service and studying economics. He was a founder of ASDT and set up agricultural co-operatives in his home in Bazatete (30 km from Dili). Nicolau was called to Dili to become Vice-President of Fretilin and shaped much of its agricultural and economic policy. His wife, Isabel Barreto, the daughter of the *Liurai* of Bazatete, was raped and shot on Dili wharf on the day of the Indonesian invasion. When Xavier do Amaral was expelled as Fretilin President in September 1977 Nicolau became Fretilin's second president. He led the resistance until his death on 31 December 1978, when he was hunted down and killed by Indonesian troops in the mountains.

34 Carapinha was a Portuguese public servant who worked for *Obras Publicas,* Public Works, during the Portuguese administration. He joined Fretilin.

35 Hata was a member of the Fretilin Central Committee. He was another who had attended university in Lisbon, but said later that he did not learn any serious political ideology—just how to paint communist slogans on the wall.

36 In the early morning of 11 August UDT took charge of strategic points in Dili including the central Police Headquarters. There was some fighting during the night and some deaths occurred. UDT forces patrolled the streets and the city was tense. The following is UDT coup leader Joao Carrascalao's signed statement about the UDT 'show of force' in August 1975: 'I decided to organise this movement who's [sic] spirit is unity, independence, and non-communists for Timor … we had no arms and so decided to dominate the police by using strategy: we know that all the police follow completely their *commandante* and we invite him to our HQ and we put him in prison there. Then we went to the police and told them that their commandant was in prison and if they didn't surrender we will kill [him] … Then the police handed over all of their guns and … 10% of them join our cause. After this we went to the Army HQ and we asked for the second in command of the Military for the Army not to interfere in our problem because all we wanted was to oblige Fretilin leaders to have talks with us without violence' (Dunn, 1996, pp. 150-1). The 'arrest' of Police Commander Gouveia has been disputed due to his later strong pro-UDT stand.

reopened; safe conduct for Fretilin negotiators; negotiations being conducted through Governor Pires as the representative of Portugal. I approached Rogerio's military bodyguard, who told me of the conditions that the Engineering Battalion of the army had requested. I convinced him to help us get some arms to protect the members of the Central Committee and asked Nicolau to authorise my plan. I met with some old army colleagues at the Taubisse army base and explained our objectives to them: to get arms for the protection of the Central Committee, the destruction of Marabia,[39] and urban guerrilla warfare. UDT had already tried to take the *Quartel General [QG],* the army headquarters, and had been forced to retreat.

The following night, Venancio Ferraz arrived with full uniforms for all of us and we had a meeting at the back of the house. We went to the perimeter of the Engineering Battalion and waited. At nine we advanced. I called the guard, identifying myself. We had to crawl under the barbed wire and were escorted to the *QG*. The Timorese soldiers gathered, enraged, having found out about the 'sons-of-bitches from UDT who wanted to assault Engineering'. They recognised me and became furious: 'Why?', was their question of anxiety, desperation and rage, amidst the slamming of heels and grinding of teeth.

I answered, 'Why don't you make a move? Why do you let UDT kill and imprison?'

The short, bald Chief of Staff appeared, rumbling with threats. I looked at Venancio and the baker from the army supply store. They were calm. Guido Soares[40] and Rogerio were there too. There was a quick interrogation and a

---

[37] Rogerio Tiago de Fatima Lobato, brother of Nicolau Lobato and later appointed as Minister of Defence in the DRET Cabinet. He was one of only eight Timorese to rise above rank of sergeant in the Portuguese army, to the rank of Lieutenant, the highest rank that any Timorese had achieved. In the days that followed the coup he lobbied the army to support Fretilin, though the Portuguese had given him the task of bringing about negotiations between Fretilin and UDT. He left East Timor with Ramos-Horta on 4 December 1975 to internationalise the issue and now lives in Portugal.

[38] Colonel Mario Lemos Pires was the Governor of Timor from 18 November 1974 until the Indonesian invasion, appointed by the Armed Forces Movement (AMF) to oversee the decolonisation process. Fretilin called him progressive-conservative. After the coup he tried to negotiate a solution to the situation and resume the decolonisation process. He convened the 'decolonisation committee' on the day of the UDT coup and contacted Joao Carrascalao and Rogerio Lobato. He and Portuguese officers tried to keep pro-Fretilin Timorese troops neutral, trying to confine Timorese troops to their barracks and to convince their non-commissioned officers that they should adopt the MFA stand of *apartidarismo*, neutrality. All foreigners were expelled on Tuesday 12 August.

[39] Marabia is about 1-2 km from the governor's palace in Dili. Radio Timor was operating from here.

Portuguese officer and Rogerio painted a picture of the future for me: 'The problem is communism!'

'But I am not a communist!'

'Some Fretilin leaders are. And Indonesia will not allow that, and will invade Timor.'

'We will respond to the war.'

'But you will be alone. Yes, you will have a few weapons, but you won't last for long. You won't have any spare parts or ammunition.'

'Then we'll use sticks and stones if we have to', I answered.

The Portuguese officer laughed and said, 'If you meet up with the leadership of Fretilin, tell them they had better talk with UDT'.

We left. A corporal approached and apologised. It was his brother who thought we were UDT and had informed on us, foiling our plan to get arms.

That same night I returned to Mota Ulun. The members of the Central Committee had moved a bit further up the mountain and they were still in a meeting when I arrived. I told them of my lack of success and the advice of the Portuguese captain.

'Are you going to listen to these guys? The colonists always think they know more than the colonised', said Hata. Nicolau ordered me to return to HQ and inform the rest of the Central Committee to come up to the mountains. The Fretilin Central Committee had decided to proclaim the 'Popular General Insurrection'. In my mouth this political directive had such a sweet and agreeable tone![41]

When I got to HQ, Borja and Juvenal[42] and others were there. I gave them the new directives. When we left, only Juvenal Inacio stayed behind. As we climbed Mota Ulun, Raul Isac, a Portuguese army sergeant, appeared: 'The Vice-President [of Fretilin] moved to Aileu yesterday.'[43] We returned to HQ—

---

40 Guido Soares was a Timorese of Ainaro descent, a former seminarian, an army officer and a Fretilin cadre who also became a minister in the DRET cabinet. He was killed, together with Nicolau Lobato, in 1978.

41 From the mountains Fretilin planned a counter attack and a call for peace talks. In a press release on 13 August Fretilin called for an armed struggle in response to the UDT coup to begin on the 15th. They called for 'a general armed insurrection against the traitors of the homeland and for the genuine liberation of the Maubere People'.

42 Juvenal Inacio, also known as Sera Key, was a Political Commissar in Fretilin and became Minister for Finance in the DRET (Democratic Republic of East Timor) cabinet. He was captured in July 1979 and disappeared. The *East Timor News* (Autumn 1984) states that he was captured in the region of Bibileu in March 1979, was first taken to Baucau (for reasons that are not clear), then, while being taken to Dili by helicopter, was dumped in the sea.

43 In the continuing civil war, bitter fighting between *sucos* of differing party allegiances had broken out in the central mountainous Maubisse-Turiscai-Same area, 50 km south of Dili, and

the sanctuary. Only the President, Xavier do Amaral's[44] bedroom was left undisturbed; the rest of the house was ours but there were about 100 men! We were apprehensive but calm. Couriers came and went, giving accounts of the situation from all over Dili.

One afternoon, a military jeep arrived at HQ. Carmo and Bosco[45] came out and asked if there was a member of the Central Committee present. Juvenal was invited to go with them and asked me to accompany him. We stopped at Montalvao's house. All the native sergeants were there and a handful of the foundation members of the ASDT. The armed forces wished to mediate dialogue to avoid bloodshed; all present had agreed but there was the need for representation of a member of the Fretilin Central Committee. I made a sign to Juvenal and asked to speak alone with him.

'You can't decide anything. I came with the directives from the Central Committee for the "Insurrection". You don't represent the Fretilin Central Committee.' Juvenal was taken to the palace where he met with Lemos Pires and 'saw' Joao Carrascalao.[46] The following day he was taken to Aileu in a helicopter to speak with the Fretilin Central Committee.

---

in other areas. Fretilin had taken over the main towns of Maubisse and Aileu, a town 20-30 km south of Dili (from where it was broadcasting) where local troops placed themselves under its control. UDT's army lacked discipline and in Same a UDT leader executed 11 Fretilin members (mostly members of the Revolutionary Brigade engaged in literacy work near Alas) including Domingos Lobato (brother of Nicolau and Rogerio). Other unauthorised killings by UDT also occurred. There is much dispute over these killings.

44 Francisco Xavier do Amaral was the founding Fretilin President and the first President of the 'Democratic Republic of East Timor'. Born in Turiscai in 1937, he was the eldest son of the *Chefe do suco*. An intellectual, he went on from Soibada to Dare and then to study at the Jesuit seminary in Macao. Stories of the 1912 and the 1959 rebellion influenced him. He taught at the *Liceu* and then set up his own school for those excluded by the Portuguese. Critical of the authorities, he gained a following. He was invited by Jose Ramos-Horta to become President of ASDT because he thought they needed an older, well-known and respectable figure to lead them. After the invasion he lived in his *suco* of Turiscai and was arrested by Fretilin on 7 September 1977 after he failed to attend the national meeting. (See footnote 82). He surrendered or was captured by the Indonesians. Used by the Indonesian government as a supporter of integration, he has only recently escaped to Portugal.

45 Fernando Carmo was co-editor for *A Voz de Timor* and a professional soldier trained in Angola. He was in the Portuguese army during the coup and was chosen by the government to facilitate between Fretilin and UDT. He was the most experienced Timorese military leader and became Deputy of Falintil. He was killed by Indonesian troops on the day of the invasion trying to save the Australian Journalist Roger East (See end of footnote 63).

Bosco is Joao Bosco Soares, an army sergeant, brother of Guido Soares mentioned previously.

I stayed by myself at the HQ. Fretilin activists had imprisoned some UDT men and a girl. I heard screams in the kitchen. I told them to untie the prisoners and said I would not permit the use of violence. It was not their fault they were UDT. The threats over attacks to our HQ increased; it was said that we had arms. The native soldiers came and went, asking for action, whispering rumours or asking for advice.

The dawn of a restless Sunday.[47] As on previous days, the pervading calm suffocated us with uncertainty. We hoisted the Fretilin flag and our national anthem, *Foho Ramelau*, was comforting to hear, momentarily allaying our fears. I was shouting helplessly at some soldiers, 'Give us weapons', when I was told I had visitors. I ran out. Pedro Melo had brought my father, my wife Emilia and the children to see me. We hardly had time to embrace before the lookout warned us, 'Trucks full of UDT soldiers are coming!'

I told everyone to disperse. Two trucks full of troops stopped. Maggiolo Gouveia,[48] the Portuguese Lieutenant-Colonel and Chief of Dili Police, stepped down, brandishing a whip and sending sparks of anger into the air. Mouzinho, Mayor of Dili and UDT Vice-Chairman, shouted hysterically while he beat a boy who dared to linger. There were three of us, including Chico Horta. Maggiolo, eyes bloodshot, fumed, 'Lower that flag! Take down that rag!'

I looked at him. I didn't move. Joao Carrascalao came over. 'Gusmão, take down that flag!'

'Take it down yourself, if you want to. This is our headquarters, and we have a right to hoist our flag here', I replied.

He took it down, and the three of us were ordered into the trucks. I waited for the insults and hostility. I looked at those helmets and unknown faces, unperturbed, but noted quick movements of closed fists. I didn't know what to think but my soul was not empty.

---

[46] Joao Carrascalao is currently leader of UDT, younger brother of Mario and Manuel, all children of a Portuguese *deportado* and a Timorese mother. He attended the *Liceu* and studied aerial surveying in Switzerland. His brother-in-law, Jose Ramos-Horta, says he was the true spokesman of UDT at this time. It seems he organised the practicalities of the coup on the night of 10 August, as his statement in footnote 36 shows. He was an outspoken critic of reconciliation with Fretilin and refused to recognise Xanana as leader until the 1998 Timorese Convention.

[47] By 15 August, UDT had arrested 80 Fretilin members. Xanana says he was arrested on the Sunday, the 17th, but other accounts note that the Fretilin HQ was attacked on the night of the 18th led by Joao Carrascalao and Maggiolo Gouveia. Several of those arrested and jailed were shot.

[48] Joao Carrascalao had 'arrested' Maggiolo Gouveia at the beginning of the coup. Gouveia then announced on the radio that he had left the Portuguese army and had joined UDT in order to 'save Timor'. He was a prisoner of Fretilin after the civil war and was executed by them in Aileu after the Indonesian invasion.

Maggiolo dragged our Fretilin flag along the road. At the sporting club we stopped and Maggiolo went to speak to the Portuguese officer. You could see the emotion, the victory in his gestures, in his voice. He presented our flag, his trophy of war, and pompously dragged it along the ground.

At Palapaco, the UDT headquarters, 'the armed forces of Captain Lino'[49] were being acclaimed. Here was UDT: all familiar faces! The important ones, the court of assimilated Timorese—the ones with the easy jobs. I was lucky to pass unnoticed because, as I entered the building where my comrades were being held prisoner, I didn't suffer the sweet punches most of them received. Friends from UDT came to ask if I needed anything. Many waved to me from outside—a great commiseration for the politics we had not been able avoid. I despised my brother-in-law when I saw him armed. It was hard to admit that we had come to this.

Punches, kicks and insults met each recently arrived 'Fretilin'. I was sweeping the floor and every time a new one arrived I tried to sweep up to him and ask for an update of the situation.

'Aileu was taken and they are advancing this way.'[50] 'The forces at the army headquarters have rebelled', and so on.

Vincent Sahe[51] and a group of young men from the CP2 army base at Bucoli were pushed inside. 'Communist', was the call behind the uncontrolled

---

[49] Lino was a Captain in the Portuguese Army and a relative of Joao Carrascalao. He, along with his Los Palos military garrison, declared themselves pro-UDT on the 13th and marched from Lautem to Bacau to Dili to help UDT.

[50] On 17 August Rogerio Lobato was airlifted to Maubisse with the task of bringing Xavier do Amaral back to Dili to take part in negotiations. Rogerio made a return trip to Aileu, a 24-hour walk, where he gained the support of the military garrison and by 19 August had come back to Dili to command the military there who had also made the decision to support Fretilin. By the 20th (the day the resistance army, Falintil, was formed) over 2000 Timorese soldiers, with their weapons, had joined up with Fretilin and Rogerio Lobato, in command of these forces, had seized control of the main arsenal. Fighting had reached Dili and the Portuguese withdrew to their residential suburb of Farol which was respected as neutral by both sides, as was the palace area. UDT was now on the defensive. This was civil war proper and it raged until the 27th (about a week) when UDT were driven out of Dili.

[51] Vincente dos Reis, known also as Vincente Sahe, was the son of the *Liurai* of Bucoli and was educated at the *Liceu* in Dili. In 1972 he won a scholarship to study engineering in Lisbon. He was in Portugal when the 25 April coup took place and returned to Dili in September 1974 with Antonio Carvarino, Maria Pereira and others, the group of ex-Lisbon students who were characterised by Indonesian press reports as the 'Communist wing' of Fretilin. He abandoned his Portuguese surname and took up his pre-Portuguese family name, Sahe. In his hometown, Bucoli, he set up political, cultural, women's and youth groups and an agricultural cooperative. These groups became the forerunners of later similar activity by Fretilin members. In 1974 Sahe moved back to Dili and worked as a science teacher and was active in helping set up the students

punches and kicks that made Sahe's body roll, but with no sound of protest. It was a UDT who explained to us that we were all there because we were communist. Sahe asked him if he knew what communism was. 'Communism is, well, ah, I'm not sure', he said and left.

Most of the UDT were drunk. After the assassination of Jose Sequeira, a popular founding member of Fretilin, we were all tense. I was not aware of anything going on when I saw two guards laughing at me. One of them looked at me through the Mauser target and pointed the gun at my chest. A comrade, who knew their Mambai language, alerted me.

'They are going to kill you and are asking themselves if the bullet from the Mauser can pierce your chest!' (I was bare-chested, as I had been arrested barefoot and without a shirt.)

'Don't look at them, please,' said my friend. I lowered my head and closed my eyes. We were at war, and I was confused that I did not feel anything and could not think about anything. I heard an agitated conversation at the door and opened my eyes slowly.

'Some others have just arrived and they are trying to convince the two guards not to kill you because they say they know you, and that you saved them from being beaten, that you freed them', my comrade whispered.

I looked over and they waved at me with smiles. I learnt a lesson that would guide me all through the war. I understood that we could love each other individually, even after all this!

As Fretilin advanced, the UDT leaders became increasingly nervous. Maggiolo's red eyes were popping out of his head as he came in, growling threats, beating the air with his whip.

'Look at this. That Arab, Mari, says he's going to destroy Dili and build houses with *palapa* palm.' He was ranting, perhaps frustrated, perhaps regretting the biggest blunder he had made in his life. Some of us pleaded, 'I am not communist; I don't know anything.'

The festive atmosphere, the elation and shouts of UDT victory during the first few days after my arrival gradually waned and disappeared altogether. Outside, signs of any movement were sporadic and fleeting.

---

union, UNETIM. He became Minister of Labour and Welfare in the DRET Cabinet. After the Indonesian invasion he went back to his home and set up *Commando Lobito*, a Regional Command, possibly the first headquarters set up after the invasion. He was elected National Political Commissar for this sector, which he named, *CASCOL* (Centre East Sector Commissarat) *Naroman*, (Tetum for 'gleam' of hope). He is spoken of as a thoughtful and dynamic leader. Some say the resistance in the eastern part of East Timor was stronger because of the structures planned and conceptualised by Sahe. It is unclear when Sahe was killed—at the fall of Matebian in 1978 or later in 1979.

We were deployed to clean latrines. We had to clean up UDT's shit with our hands, bugs crawling up our arms. Many faces were familiar. Some friends apologised to me. Some were apprehensive or ashamed or had fear written all over their faces. What contemptible politics—the politics of quarrels and telling tales on each other, of casting the first stone, of letting fists do the talking, arrests and arming oneself, responding with violence.

Palapaco was being pounded by mortar fire.[52] I picked up and transmitted information to Sahe. 'Our side is now in Sang Tai Hoo and Casa Vitoria', or 'Our side has occupied the docks'.

The corpse of Fernando, my sister Lucia's husband, was brought in. I went with some comrades to bury him under a shower of bullets. Outside, the last UDT forces were leaving. I sat down to console my sister. Captain Lino was a defeated man when I spoke to him.

It was just like a cockfight.[53] The choice of opponent in cock fighting has its rules, with the timing and the colours of the feathers being significant. Once a choice is made, bets are laid noisily. The great punters act with the weight of deliberation and a certain common agreement. As a rule the challenger is presumptuous and the other player is deeply fearful of losing but does not show it. He suspects the other could be hiding something, perhaps the true colour of the feathers. The arrogance of the challenger causes exaggerated leaps and hoarse screams of victory every time his cock strikes. The madness of his passion and the blindness of his vice only allow him to acknowledge he has lost when his opponent executes his victory dances. The jubilation of the winner, oblivious to everything else, can be quite provocative and immoral. The losers' feelings are shown by their silence and by the bowed heads of their inconsolable faces.

We prisoners were part of an extremely dangerous political game. My comrades crouched, prayed aloud and insulted our leaders: 'Have they forgotten we are here?' Then Manuel Carrascalao appeared. He was not that Manuel, affable and full of humour, that I knew. His eyes were red and he made threats. Minutes later, grenades were thrown inside the prison. I don't believe anyone was ordered to do it. They were not meant to kill us but to detain us inside

[52] For several days fighting raged in the streets of Dili and approximately 400 people were killed, fewer than in the rural areas. Two boats took over 2000 Portuguese, Chinese and Timorese to Darwin. Credible estimates of those dead range from 1500 to 3000 (Budjiardjo and Liong, 1984, p. 50; Jannisa 1997, p. 211). Atrocities were reported. Fretilin gained the upper hand and revenge actions were taken. UDT leaders were blamed for the killings in the countryside; those who were captured by Fretilin were severely beaten.

[53] The cock is the symbol of the warrior, of courage and bravery, and cockfighting is a very popular and serious sport in Timor.

while the last UDT vehicles left the HQ. All this over an anti-communist coup that now only smelt of that rotting human shit that was drying in the sun. Our revolution was one of thorns that penetrated the flesh of all Timorese.

UDT left in the direction of Moatel in the west of Dili. The Fretilin forces were advancing in that direction. I went to the Fretilin HQ to inform them of the flight of UDT[54] and of our liberation.

Days later I found out that Emilia and my two children, my father and my sisters were in the old Australian consulate. Then I heard that my friend, the loyal, unselfish and faithful Pedro Melo, had already died. I want to declare the value of our friendship: how true, frank and without self-interest it was. At times it had a dimension that exceeded the love dedicated to a woman: different from romantic love, yes, and maybe not comparable. The confidences, the discussions, the advice and the communion of happiness and sadness that we shared … all in a unique context. When you lose a friend of worth you feel you have lost half of your own self. I saw many widowers, eyes swollen by tears, swearing on the grave of their lost ones that they would never look at another woman. Only months later, absorbed in Cupid's entanglements, they made new promises that buried their earlier vows. True friends who are lost have no substitute; they are gone and only remain as a memory.

Post civil war and independence September–December 1975[55]

Now followed a period that emphasised our fragile situation in every sense. I do not contest the efforts of the Fretilin Executive, the cunningness of their decisions and their great will in the realisation of plans.

I was an activist, a friend of the members of Fretilin Central Committee. My apprehensions and observations of events were in the context of the day-to-day situation—the behaviour, revelations and tendencies of individual leaders. Our Homeland, still in gestation, was torn apart after a difficult labour.

---

54 UDT were forced out of Dili to Liquica and on 24 September about 900 people crossed the border into West Timor. All in all about 2000 refugees fled to Atambua in West Timor. Here they were kept in camps by the Indonesian authorities; many died there.

55 By September 1975 Fretilin gained exclusive control of East Timor and on the 11th the first outsiders arrived in Dili to assess and report on the territory: international journalists including a Channel 9 television crew (including Kerry Packer) from Australia, the International Red Cross, the Australian Council for Overseas Aid (ACFOA) and a doctor with a medical team. On 28 August Fretilin had appointed three commissioners to plan an economic reconstruction. On 16 September Fretilin was calling for the Portuguese authorities to return from Atauro Island where they had withdrawn on 27 August. Food rationing was organised from the Taibesse army base. The Red Cross administered the hospital in Dili and inspected the gaols. Some schools reopened and crèches were established to look after orphans.

Alarcio Fernandes and, later, Hermenegildo Alves[56] were real executioners with a frenzied thirst for vengeance. That hurt so much. Once I went to visit Fretilin's prisoners. Mouzinho was despondent and beaten. He asked me to look for his gold chain and give it to his mother. Maggiolo was quiet but sure of himself. I felt sorry for him but at the same time I admired his attitude; he was still asserting that he was who he was. He was a different Maggiolo from the one I had known before, frenzied, intoxicated with political hysteria! Now he was calm, head hung low, silent, perhaps feeling superior to his lamenting and crying comrades. Fernando Luz[57], now unrecognisable, embraced me.

'Gusmão, I didn't kill anyone, I never gave orders to beat anyone. My hands are clean, I did my duty—you understand!' Years later, in the region of Los Palos, they told me that he even apologised for arresting people! Why is it that politics makes people become obsessed with crime, and gives them such an appetite for violence?

I never wanted to go near Fretilin's prison again. Many of us lamented and shook at every scream of pain as it penetrated our eardrums. Yes, the accusations against the UDT prisoners were clear: 'They killed, they are murderers!' Maybe too clear, for they did not allow any softening of attitudes. The threat in Dili and in the interior was 'An eye for an eye, a tooth for a tooth'—and it saddened us because it was so dangerous. We were at war, and it was painful and uncontrollable. Members of the Central Committee with three or four cars were taking trips to the beach with their girlfriends. I saw box-loads of '555' cigarettes in a Fretilin member's house. I took a packet and left despondently. It must be the same in all *coup d'état* situations in Third World countries: excesses, privilege-seeking by politicians, discontent within the army, social disorder, uncontrolled paramilitary forces. But, if the truth be told, the desire for vengeance directed at UDT elements was temporary and after a while it appeared that all of Fretilin accepted that it was enough that some of the UDT had been arrested and gaoled.

I participated in a meeting with some members of the Central Committee and the majority of the army commanders (the ex-sergeants). You could feel a lot of tension in the political climate that followed the euphoria of victory and the excesses of the violence.

'I am Fretilin and I'll continue to stay Fretilin but I will not accept communism!' said Alarico Fernandes with exalted solemnity. 'I won't permit the communists to climb on my back', said Carapinha.

---

[56] Hermenegildo Alves was a part of the regular Portuguese army that went over to Fretilin.

[57] Fernando Luz was UDT Secretary General, replacing Domingos de Oliveira. He was killed by Fretilin at Aileu together with many dozens of UDT political prisoners after the Indonesian invasion.

The commanders appeared satisfied, but the meeting had not satisfied anyone. Xavier was not a president; he was just a symbol, like a flame that is not quite extinguished; not shining but refusing to go out. The sergeants were not satisfied. The military was distancing itself. Rogerio Lobato was too proud, and the military police just turned into an elite. The militias were almost out of control and wanted to impose their rule.[58]

The general population, scared in the beginning and watchful during the climax of the conflict, little by little started adapting to the new situation, forgetting the political rivalries. But UDT had created bedlam in a childish war and then run away to the other side of the border, thanks, maybe, to the humanity of our military and to the TNI, the Indonesian army, who had come in to counter-attack. There was a general mobilisation of forces to defend our Homeland which had finally become free. But free from whom? No one knew for sure. From Portugal? From capitalism or imperialism? From colonialism? Or from itself? Apprehension about the future dominated people's minds, because the real war was just beginning, and it was calling their children to arms.[59]

I took charge of producing the paper *Timor Leste*.[60] Its publication was a response to a specific political situation, a liberation movement that was too young and perhaps immature but that had come out the winner. Understandably, it had its shortcomings. Our victory had been too easy and easily-won success always has its drawbacks.

When I received a list of members of the Central Committee, to be published in the paper, I saw my name on it and immediately ran to Borja, Secretary of the Information Department in which we worked.

---

58 Dunn says that during the first few weeks of the Fretilin interregnum some Fretilin soldiers committed offences against the population but Nicolau Lobato soon attained an 'impressive standard of discipline'. He says the interregnum can be divided into two periods: an enthusiastic and hopeful period from late August until mid-October 1975 when Indonesian military operations began and the second from then a frightening period until the full-scale invasion in December (Dunn, 1996, pp. 186-188).

59 By October/November 1975 heavy hand-to-hand fighting was taking place between Fretilin and Indonesian troops. This reference to the real war just beginning signals increased fighting on the border and deeper Indonesian incursions into the north-west. Indonesian raids were made on 14 September into Bobonaro, Atsabe and Suai. An Indonesian soldier captured on the 14th said he had been inside East Timor for five days. The Indonesian news agency Antara announced at the end of September that UDT, KOTA and Trabalhista (two small political parties) formed a coalition called MAC (Movement Against Communism) and had called on Indonesia to intervene militarily to end the crisis.

60 From September until December 1975 there were ten issues of this Fretilin newspaper *Timor Leste: Journal do Povo Maubere*.

'No, Borja I don't accept it! You know only too well that I am a nobody. I am prepared to work, but not as a member of the Fretilin Central Committee. You've got to speak to the comrades and withdraw my name.'

'It was a decision of the FCC! You have no choice but to accept it.'

I had to agree. The decision had been made and it was my responsibility to respond to the confidence they had vested in me.

Our only ideology was *ukun rasik an*, self-determination. We did not yet comprehend what a grave responsibility we had assumed toward our Homeland.

Nicolau Lobato was a great leader. He deserved everyone's confidence and above all that of the soldiers. Portugal did not want to return.[61] I realised then, for the first time, that the decolonisation process was just a way of playing for time. What I had also not understood before was that we had been hurled into the pit of independence. What for UDT had been a headache, the precious escudo they needed for purchases, became, for me, of vital importance to the life of the Homeland which had come to a halt, groaning in blood. The tranquillity of Sunday markets in the interior was shattered and the shops in Dili were closed—looted, broken into because the people felt they were a colonial product, imperialist, and represented the exploitation of one human being by another. [62]

Emilia came home from her attempts to put the education services into some order and told me, 'So many colleagues, relatives of Central Committee members, have special cards and they go into shops and just pick up cloth and clothing'.

'No-one is going to pick up anything', I told her amid the crying of our children, Nito and Zeni, who did not want to see any more Atsabe potatoes, fried or boiled, which was all we received, every day, from the army rations store.

'Portugal will not return'. The phrase was the spectre that haunted everything. East Timor was ours, left to us. What I had to do was to dedicate all my strength to face that spectre.

---

[61] The Portuguese administration had withdrawn to Atauro Island on 27 August and was awaiting instructions from Portugal. Portugal did not give Governor Pires permission or instructions to return even though he repeatedly asked. He would not speak to UDT or Fretilin after they had ignored his efforts during the civil war. Fretilin kept the palace guarded and the Portuguese flag flying. The Portuguese watched the Indonesian invasion of Dili from the island and left for Darwin on 8 December.

[62] Fretilin had to change quickly from a loose political group to a de facto government and revive the fragile economy that had ground to a halt during the civil war: shops were closed, farms unattended or abandoned, and town services inoperable. By mid-October Dili was nearly back to normal but food and currency shortages were still a problem.

Maubere

MAUBERE People,
MAUBERE, child of East Timor,
tear open your belly,
your cravings,
ruts of neglect, of anguish, of oppression,
and hurl them to the wind,
to your furthest brother
in the secret places of the sacred land
of your parents, of your children,
of your grandparents, of your grandchildren …

MAUBERE People,
reaffirm, today, your wish,
your talent, your determination,
in a year of enervating dissatisfaction
coalesced from mysterious meanders …

MAUBERE People,
open your eyes, stay alert,
then you'll reach truths borders,
For enslavement is a conspiracy of dangerous illusions
when you sleep the sleep of the blind

MAUBERE People,
stir up your flesh, your body,
your spirit, your mind, your brain!
Oh! corpse of obscurantism!
Resuscitate, crush, delineate
the disguise of this conspirancy! …

MAUBERE People,
clench your fist,
shout out loud,
The hour is YOURS, MAUBERE!
And your defiance will bring down
the walls of your own enslavement! …

MAUBERE People,
confront and face yourself in the long march of liberation.
Liberate yourself!
BE STRONG! … BE MAUBERE!

Xanana Gusmão
East Timor, 1975

I went to Bobonaro to make a report on the incursion of the TNI at Maliana and I met Roger East there.[63] Both of us went to Tapo, where his white clothes attracted mortar attacks from Maliana which caused us some frightening moments as we moved down towards the line of combat. In the town members of the Education and Culture Committee were finding it difficult to get the program passed by the Regional Committee. The sergeants and the priests and sisters had formed an anti-communist bloc. I was totally inexperienced in such matters but had to mediate. The sergeants were defeated but not convinced and arranged another two meetings with the corporals. These meetings were simply attacks on Fretilin—we ran away from there!

I returned to Dili and informed Nicolau of the political situation in Bobonaro. 'Don't come to me with such stories. I know them well', he barked. 'Don't stick your nose in where it is not wanted', I consoled myself.

One afternoon, passing by the home of Xavier Amaral, I was called in. A few members of the Central Committee were there, among them Nicolau, Hata and Mari. There was a need to make a unilateral declaration of independence, and it would be made public the following afternoon.[64] It was a simple ceremony of the poor country that we were, facing a war of invasion that was

---

63 Indonesian military commander Beni Murdani led this military operation and between 7 and 8 October; his troops with the support of naval vessels attacked Batugade. Fretilin troops withdrew to Balibo and Maliana. On 10 October journalists from Australia left for the border and on the 14th Indonesian forces took Maliana. On the 16th the five overseas journalists who had witnessed border attacks were killed by Indonesian troops during the takeover of Balibo from where about 40 Fretilin were able to retreat. The Indonesians also took Sabarai and the-mountain stronghold to Tapo. An estimated 1000 Indonesian troops died capturing this territory west of Loes River. The wet season trapped the Indonesians in their bases at Maliana, Balibo and Batugade and protected the Fretilin forces. On 20 October a light bomber attacked Fretilin in Atabai and Indonesian vessels positioned around Dili harbour formed a loose naval blockade.

When the ACFOA team arrived in Dili they were informed about the Indonesian attacks on the border towns Maliana and Balibo. ACFOA reported on these military activities and the conditions in the territory sending messages to the Australian government. The battles were reported in the Indonesian press as battles between UDT-Apodeti (including Indonesian volunteers) and Fretilin forces.

Australian journalist Roger East set off from Darwin in early November with the encouragement of Fretilin leaders to set up a news agency in Dili and to find out what had happened to the five missing journalists. He was the only Australian to ignore the advice of the Australian Department of Foreign Affairs to leave East Timor. His last message sent from East Timor one hour after the invasion was never used by AAP and was printed in the *New Left Review* in June 1976. It includes his report of this journey to the border. He was captured on the day of the invasion by Indonesian troops at the Marconi Telecommunications Centre still trying to send messages to Australia and was executed on Dili wharf.

64 On November 28, Fretilin declared East Timor independent at a swearing-in ceremony at the palace in Dili. One Fretilin leader at the time said, 'It is not that we want to be independent

burning the first pieces of our Homeland. It was a ceremony we stole from the enemy and if there was any joy it was hidden in our hearts, a treasure that was hard to share. People's faces showed general apprehension that reflected the seriousness of the situation, and nobody asked about the future. We all had our feet firmly planted on the grounds of the palace garden. I filmed the ceremony. Roger East asked if he could release the film in Australia; stupidly, I said no. It was mine, a treasure stolen from the future of our Homeland—our future that was also being put in danger by 'whores' from Colmera, Dili's red light district, who sat satisfied with independence in the luxurious residences they had seized!

'While members of the Fretilin Central Committee are driving around in their cars, and are off to the beach with girls, doing nothing, my soldiers are dying at the border', shouted Rogerio Lobato, furious, in a meeting held just after independence. Although there was an element of truth in what he said, he should not have generalised in that way. I remembered getting a new car, taken from a Chinese individual. I exchanged it two days later as I felt uneasy about driving it. Instead, I asked for an old vehicle that had belonged to the colonial government.

I volunteered to go to the war, to feel the 'tears of the border'. I had seen this phrase inscribed on the helmet of the soldier who had returned from there. Some of my comrades had fallen to honour the Homeland. Sahe, Sera Key, Kruma, Ma'Huno, Fera Lafaek and I were the first members of the Central Committee to go to the war. When we arrived Hermenegildo Alves could not contain himself: 'What did you come here for? That Rogerio is a fool!'

Days later a message arrived. The first government was being formed. There were some new ministers among us. Congratulations were tenuous expressions of solidarity. The atmosphere suddenly became heavier.

'You, a minister?' Antunes asked Sahe, Sera Key and Kruma in surprise.

'Just let me touch the backside of a minister!' he joked. There was a general feeling of incredulity, combined with a feeling that we were not ready for the independence of our Homeland. I was perturbed in my spirit and this feeling stayed with me.

---

yet, or that we are ready for it. But if we are going to fight to the end, we can at least die independent'. Horta describes the ceremony: '... the most low-key, sombre and modest of any such ritual anywhere in the world ... One after another we read the allegiance to the people, the Central Committee of Fretilin and the new Constitution. A few hundred people looked on and applauded without great enthusiasm from the gardens of the palace' (Ramos-Horta, 1987, p. 99).

The next day in Kupang compromised UDT and APODETI leaders declared East Timor integrated with Indonesia and invited the Indonesians to liberate East Timor, in the Balibo Declaration dated 30 November 1975, hence the invasion eight days later. The Balibo Declaration was signed by UDT (Lopes da Cruz and Domingos Oliveria), Apodeti, KOTA and Trabalhista leaders. Many of these signatories have since recanted.

3. Invasion and occupation (1975 – 1976)

Indonesian invasion 7 December 1975

We were awoken in Loes on 7 December by a strange incessant rumbling noise. It must have been about 3.30 or 4.00 in the morning. Heavy military aircraft were passing overhead, flying east, following the coastline.[65] That afternoon, we were told to go to Command.

'Indonesian paratroopers have landed in Dili', Hermengildo informed us. There was silence for there were no answers to the many questions. The following day we were off in the old Land Rover through Railaco, arriving at Balibar at *Comando da Luta*, Command Headquarters, where we found Nicolau in command. We would look towards Dili whenever the firing of the Meriam gun and naval artillery allowed us to poke our heads over a hill or out from behind a tree. Sebastiao Sarmento[66] tried to aim at the ships anchored in the port. We witnessed days of pillage through a huge pair of powerful binoculars. The weapons of war were vomiting fire over Dili's hills while cargo ships emptied the customs house of its contents. The boats were

---

[65] The attack of 7 December 1975 began with a naval bombardment of parts of Dili and just before dawn paratroopers were dropped into the waterfront area. Shocking atrocities committed by troops on the civilian population of Dili went on for about a week and according to one priest as many as 2000 citizens, including 700 Chinese, were killed in the first few days. Tens of thousands of Dili residents and entire villages fled to the mountains behind Fretilin lines as the Indonesian troops advanced.

Dunn describes the military situation: 'The resistance put up by Fretilin in the streets of Dili was little more that a delaying tactic. But on the outskirts of town the Timorese troops staunchly held their ground, and the invasion forces were pinned down for several weeks. On 10 December a second invading force was landed at Bacau, in order to secure East Timor's second-largest town, and to gain control of the territory's main airfield … For some reason Fretilin had established only a light defence force at Bacau and the Indonesians were able to acquire control of the town … Meanwhile in the Dili area, the Indonesians found themselves pinned down on the small coastal plain between Tibar to the west and the rugged hills projecting out to Aria Branca to the east. With field and naval guns they pounded the Falintil positions in the mountains to the south, but the Timorese were continuously on the move, and sustained relatively few casualties during this early period' (Dunn, 1996, pp. 258-9).

Fretilin troops amounted to about 20,000 men (2500 regular troops, 7000 second-line reservists and 10,000 with previous military training) armed with a recently augmented arsenal of modern NATO weapons. They were able to put up substantial resistance for the next three years. By the end of the 1975, 20-32,000 Indonesian troops were stationed in East Timor.

[66] Sebastiao Saramento, from Soibada, was a former Catholic primary school teacher, Portuguese army sergeant, and a Fretilin sympathiser. He was also the brother-in-law of Maria Goretti Joaquim who was kept prisoner and raped by high-ranking Indonesian officers in Dili and disappeared. He was the Commander of the 2nd Brigade in Falintil and a military advisor to Nicolau Lobato.

filled, load after load, the cranes cramming those metal Indonesian bellies! An interminable line of people streamed upwards. I saw no fear in their exhaustion. I saw resignation in their eyes, and anguish that must have been torturing their souls, but they knew to smile, as if somehow it would relieve their suffering.

Sera Key and I decided to go to the hospital in Dili. We searched all the wings but there was no trace of our families. Friends and acquaintances said they could be at the old Australian Consulate again but others told me, 'No point trying, Gusmão. We recently escaped from there and near by at the intersection of the Taibessi army base it's hot'.

I looked at Sera Key in silence and accepted the situation. In reality, at certain moments, words have no meaning; they just hurt even more and emphasise your powerlessness.

The enemy was trying to advance westwards and was already in Taci Tolu. Nicolau told Fera Lafaek and me to go to Tibar to help maintain the morale of the forces. One day Hermenegildo returned from Balibar to the front at Loes and informed us, 'The enemy is about to take the crossing to Aileu'.[67]

Fera Lafaek and I immediately felt as isolated as if abandoned. That afternoon we pulled everything from the old *Unimog* troop carrier and arrived in Aileu that night. *Comando da Luta* had already moved to Maubisse so we kept on going in that direction.

Nicolau remained calm, sure of himself, although worried. In my eyes he only sinned from being too personal in decision-making but that was understandable. On the one hand the situation of the war demanded a strong grip of command and on the other we were too inexperienced to help him. On 31 December we escorted him to Same in the south-east—the *Firaku* [people of the east] forces wanted to go and fight in their own regions. There was news that all the UDT and Apodeti prisoners who were still left should be eliminated. I should say, nevertheless, that the *Firakus* freed a lot of the UDT prisoners, taking them along with them to their areas.[68]

---

67 Aileu, a town 20-30 km south of Dili, was taken in February 1976.

68 This 'news' concerns some Fretilin leaders who decided to eliminate UDT prisoners as they were forced to retreat from further Indonesian incursions. About 150 UDT and Apodeti prisoners whom Fretilin leaders took to the mountains with them after the invasion were killed, reportedly on about 25 December. These included Major Maggiolo Gouveia, the former chief of police, Vitor Santa, a former senior administration official and Osorio Soares, an Apodeti leader. It is unclear who ordered the killing. Xanana suggests earlier that Alarico Fernandes, the Minister for Internal Affairs and Security, and Hermenegildo Alves were responsible. The orders did not come from Nicolau Lobato, who was probably distracted, having just learnt of his wife's murder and his missing son.

At night Sera Key confided in me, 'Do you know, Gusmão, they would not even permit us to see our prisoners. My two brothers are being held there. I accept that my older brother might have carried arms and killed someone. I can't ask them not to kill him. But the youngest one is 'slow', he doesn't even understand what he does and everyone knows that. I want to save him. I want to save him from paying for something he didn't do or, if he did, he did it without any consciousness. I asked them to save him, said that I would be responsible for him, but they wouldn't accept it.They didn't even take into consideration that I am a member of the Central Committee and I was appealing for a brother who I know is innocent. But that is the struggle and these are the sacrifices we have to accept.' He had a dispirited look about him but he was calm.The first time I had seen Sera Key leave a meeting in Xavier's home I could not believe that he was Fretilin. 'Hey mate, you're here too?' I greeted him.

'Are you here because you're sick of the UDT guys as well?' he asked, justifying his delay in choosing a political party.

The enemy was already half way between Aileu and Maubisse. Nicolau said that members of the Central Committee should choose their own direction. He did not hide his irritation at seeing some members of the Central Committee inactive, parasites who were dependent on him but who suffered hardships none the less. Sera Key and I went to ask for roast corn from the people while the Committee of the area occupied Chinese shops and ate their fill. They were in their kingdom.

I chose to go to Manatuto and Fera Lafaek joined me. Montalvao made up a third. We travelled through Turiskai. Xavier was in his kingdom leading a carefree life under the feudalistic care of his brother. They had milk, meat and eggs. It was so difficult to climb the seven heights to get to Fahi Nehan.[69]

This was my first immersion in the belly of my Homeland! I experienced an atmosphere I had never known: welcoming fogs took us into their cool embrace and imparted a soft hue to the ochre-brown earth that sustained and gave life to enormous *ai bubur*, eucalyptus trees. I learnt to truly appreciate the songs of my Homeland one night in an old hut, harmonies disappearing out into the cold darkness, the old men and women competing with the passionate but not yet tempered voices of the youth. I celebrated my first real encounter with my pure mountain origins, genuinely pure, by eating *koto Moruk,* bitter bean, and drinking *daulorok,* palm wine, to which the suffocating smoke of the fires lent a human breath. It was a bitter delight to find an identity amongst the crum-

---

[69] The 'seven heights' is a chain of seven mountains and Fahi Nehan is a small town between Same and Turiscai on Mt Laquebur between 1000 and 1300 ft. The chain includes Mt Querelau at 1600 ft and Turiskai on Mt Aibali at 1550 ft.

bling explosions of war, a war that had pushed me into this open space of the Homeland, confused, tired and searching for my place to fight.

I went to Laclubar, Cribas, Marabain and Manatuto to command a platoon of archers. All the people within the limits of those tilled fields, so close to the sea, had surrendered. The fields and the sea constituted life in Manatuto and the history of my people was repeating itself, as under Portuguese colonialism and Japanese occupation, they could not free themselves from a complex of cults and their transcendental way of living. This was manifested by the indolent slowness of their buffaloes, the lazy cries of the sheep grazing with no water on the tilled planes, the smell of the sea breeze inviting relaxation, and an exaggerated belief in their prayer, 'Colonel Saint Antonio! Save us from the war'![70] Only a few hamlets had moved further up the slopes away from the enemy. We had fewer than a dozen arms and were ashamed to be from Manatuto.

The majority of the few of us that were 'enlightened' were young students from the student union, UNETIM.

'Being Fretilin doesn't meant necessarily assuming Fretilin ideology', I reasoned, as I tried to make a decision about the politics of party membership cards. This had made Manatuto a Fretilin 'fortress', a place where they did not hesitate to burn Apodeti's flag.

At a meeting in Barique in April 1976 it became obvious that the military had an aversion towards those of us who were politicians. Concepts (new to me) were the basis of arguments. Silence and an obvious dissatisfaction characterised the climate of argument and debate.

'Imperialism, social imperialism' was the reason the politicians gave for rejecting the request for help to the Soviet Union.

'I don't want to know if it is imperialism or social imperialism. I don't care if the help comes from America, the Soviet Union, China, or wherever. All I need is help. Isn't that what we need?' yelled Xavier, dazed and defeated.

Outside the meetings, the soldiers avoided the politicians. 'If they don't decide to ask for help, they'll see what is going to happen', said the soldiers. They deliberately said it out loud as they went past, as if we were not there.

Returning from the meeting, I heard there had been a successful capture of arms in Baucau. I went to *Lobito*, the Regional Command and Commissariat and asked Sahe for some arms.

---

70 Saint Anthony is the most well-known and patronised Catholic saint in East Timor. Statues of him are placed at each corner of the rice fields to protect them and he is called upon at planting time to ensure good rainfall (if the rains did not come he was dunked). In indigenous rituals Saint Anthony was also invoked before battles to bless the combatants.

'It's propaganda that we had to make up', he confessed. He gave me *Historical Materialism* but I informed him I had already heard enough 'isms' in Barique.

Soibada: Historical meeting

A historical meeting took place in Soibada in May 1976.[71] It was historical, because we finally established an organised structure for the struggle and defined the activities of the resistance. That meeting was the true pillar of the fight for the freedom of the Homeland. But all histories are complex and enriched, I think, by acts originating from internal struggles about ideas and concepts.The soldiers had separated themselves from the politicians; Alarico aligned himself with the soldiers. At the meeting in Barique, many soldiers had been appointed to the Central Committee. We all knew that this was a way of avoiding a rebellion of the soldiers against the Fretilin Central Committee which would drag with them the military commanders.

Hata, Carvarino, Sahe and Nicolau deliberated about the nature of the state. Xavier defined it as 'eternal, coming from God …' Anibal,[72] behind me, whispered: 'What are you writing? They are defining Marxist concepts.' Alarico

---

[71] A Fretilin conference was held in Soibada from 20 May to 2 June 1976 which included a cultural festival. Items on the agenda included: change in military strategies toward more guerrilla warfare, a tightened-up political organisation, and maximising food production. The territory was divided up into six sectors, supervised militarily by a commander, each then divided into smaller political and military units. Falintil troops were further divided into *Forcas de Intervencao*, intervention forces, and smaller units or *Brigades de Choque* or *Brichoques*, shock brigades. A *Commisario Politico,* political commissioner, was in charge of social and political activities in the *Bases Vermelhas,* red bases or *Bases de Apoio*, support bases within Fretilin-controlled areas. Each region had its own regional secretary and regional commander. The regional secretary was responsible for organising food production, housing, education, health care and political courses. There were conflicts in the leadership over combining a long-term war with a political revolution to overthrow colonial and feudal traditional structures.

The Indonesians had declared the Provisional Government of East Timor on 18 December 1975 in Dili. On 31 May 1976 an 'Act of Free Choice' was conducted in Dili by the 'Regional Popular Assembly' which petitioned President Suharto for integration with Indonesia. The Act fell far short of UN conditions for a vote of this kind and the UN chairman of the Special Committee on Decolonisation declined the invitation to attend, as the UN had not been involved in the proceedings. In June 1976 a massacre of some 2000 people occurred in Lamaknan/Lakmaras. On 16 July the Indonesian Parliament passed a bill incorporating East Timor into Indonesia. Behind Fretilin lines life was easier: food was still adequate and people were united together. Food was not a problem until 1977 when Indonesian troops began 'search and destroy' missions to the mountain regions with the deliberate aim of destroying food crops.

[72] Anibal de Araujo was a Fretilin Central Committee member, who surrendered in 1977. By the beginning of 1979 he was assumed to have 'disappeared' (*East Timor News*, Autumn 1984).

surprised me. I did not want to believe what I was seeing and hearing. 'I declare here, before you all, that I accept Marxism as the only way of liberating our people from the exploitation of one man by another', he said.

And with that declaration he left the meeting and Soibada, taking the radio. The soldiers did not indicate any consternation and, considering the situation, that worried me.[73]

Xavier, failing to deter the revolutionary avalanche of minds, limited his participation to saying, 'Comrades, the session is open', or 'Because of the late hour the meeting is closed.'

After the celebrations of the 20th of May, the Fretilin anniversary, he escaped and sought refuge in his kingdom. The soldiers did not appear to be surprised and that intrigued me. It was obvious that Xavier had lost control because he knew so little about politics. Nicolau was on the other side, the soldiers continued to form a separate nucleus and the majority of us, the members of the FCC, were unpoliticised.[74]

4. Resistance and learning to lead (1976–1978)

First command and reporting

I was transferred to the Viqueque Region to support Solan, a Fretilin adjunct from Los Palos. I had never participated in organising anything, never spoken to the masses. I would learn. The enemy had regained all of the Bacau-Viqueque line. At the beginning of July I was nominated Vice-Secretary of the region and I was told to go to the eastern section. I protested because I still needed to learn from Solan.

'Go and make do', was the order.

Six extremely difficult months followed, with me having to rely completely on my own resources. To the north were Lari Sina, Mau Hodu[75] and

---

73 Alarico surrendered or was captured by the Indonesian forces about 18 months later, 3 December 1978, with three to four others, and more importantly with Fretilin's only radio, mentioned here.

74 It may seem strange that members of the Central Committee of a left wing political front could be unpoliticised. Fretilin was originally a front that sought to encompass many political ideologies and many members of the resistance forces did not understand or agree with its increasingly radical left wing ideology, especially the ex-Portuguese army soldiers, many of whom come from strong Catholic and politically conservative backgrounds.

75 Mau Hudo or Jose da Costa was a resistance fighter who was stationed close-by to Xanana from July 1976 in the Viqueque Region, through to the fall of Matebian. By June 1990 he had become the Vice-Chairperson of Fretilin, much admired by the younger generation of resistance. Constancio Pinto said, 'I really admired his courage as a fighter and his sharp mind as a political theorist and strategist. Mau Hudo was a very quick thinker ... [he] put a lot of hope in young

many qualified young members of the student union UNETIM, and the No 2 Training Centre in Bucoli where politics were discussed. Ma'Huno had been transferred to the Los Palos region and he had crossed the enemy line, the Baucau-Viqueque cordon, with me. I accompanied him to Uatu Karbau before he crossed into Iliomar. It was market day in Uatu Karbau. The Zone Secretary asked me to speak to the people because I was 'his' Vice-Secretary. Ma'Huno, very much in his own style, said that he was from Los Palos. I said I was not prepared to talk and asked to be excused. The other zone Vices of Baguia (associates of Lari Sina) came in speaking in 'isms' to impress me. I did not even understand what they said. From then onwards I promised myself I would never speak in 'isms' to the people (even if I ever got to understand them). I convinced myself that the political workshops should not be so refined.

These were the first steps in my political apprenticeship. I did not have an HQ and I was travelling from village to village, visiting our forces, covering all the *sucos*. In Uatulari they were difficult people with undisciplined forces who were not in the line of fire. Adelino Carvalho, a Fretilin *Liurai*, was ambitious and unhappy because he had not been appointed the Secretary of the Region of Vikeke. He undermined our efforts to organise and had his own militias. Uatulari and Uatu Karbau also had Apodeti *Liurais* who were products of the 1959 Rebellion.[76] Ossu was divided in two and threatened further still by infiltrators put in place by the enemy. Our commanders constantly arrested the Apodetis and I kept freeing them. Finally they got tired of arresting them because they realised I would just set them free again!

In December there was a meeting west of Venilale at CASCOL, the Centre East Sector Commissariat.[77] The reports of the other members of the

---

people ... encouraged people to support the resitance with material aid, and he urged us to continue our efforts to bringing together more groups in the underground movement' (Pinto, 1997 p. 121). He was captured Jan 1992 and underwent what is euphemistically called *pembinann* or 'guidance'. In March 1993 he remained on the list of untried detainees during Xanana's trial. He played a big part in the planning of the August 1999 ballot and was killed in the mayhem that followed. He is believed to have been shot dead while searching for his family in West Timor.

[76] The 1959 rebellion (see footnote 18), instigated by a group of Indonesian officers, had created long-term bonds to Indonesia which resulted in these *Lurais* joining pro-integrationist Apodeti (see footnote 22) in the 1970s.

[77] By the end of 1976 a series of Catholic Church reports estimated 100,000 East Timorese had died as a result of the invasion, 80 per cent of the territory was not under the direct control of the Indonesian military forces, and support for integration was declining because of the violations of the occupying forces. By early 1977 Indonesia had reportedly lost 5000 troops.

The 1978 article ,'Timor's Arithmetic of Despair', listed 60,000 dead, and 125,000 passing through or living in squalid refugee camps, while Indonesian officials estimated that there could be as many as 100,000 people still hiding in the mountains (*Far Eastern Economic Review*, 29 September 1978).

Central Committee filled days but when it was my turn I apologised and spoke for ten minutes. Sahe said, 'You've done a lot!' I was extremely shamed; I felt that Sahe should not have spoken to me like that and was hurt by his cynicism. That night I expressed my displeasure and offered to resign from the Central Committee, but I had been wrong about him.

Sahe said, 'You misunderstood, Xanana! I knew very well you weren't prepared and that you had never worked with the masses. I wanted to encourage you and affirm that you had performed well considering all the difficulties. Theory comes from practice and if you continue working as you are you will more dynamically assimilate the theory', he explained. This principle has always stayed with me in relation to my subordinates.

I was really struggling in my region but at the meeting at CASCOL Sahe's self-sacrifice impressed me. The people adored him: his simplicity, his patience in educating the cadres, his soft way of criticising their mistakes, his calmness in facing situations. It made him an exemplary teacher of what a leader should be. He knew how to listen and that was important for me. He knew that my theoretical knowledge was zero compared with the youths who came out of the courses of political education he administered. Carvarino, however, was the opposite. He was a mocker and unapproachable, wheras Sahe received opinions and afterwards debated them. But counter-revolutionaries were displeased with these methods and the resolutions of the meeting. Sahe's understanding attitude allowed me to continue in my own way: less routinely, less dogmatic and less in the revolutionary style. Although I acted with a certain independence I did not shirk maintaining discipline. I avoided rest at the HQ and in setting this example was able to exert discipline and could demand responsibility from my own subordinates.

Revolutionary arrests, violence and betrayal

From the Bacau region (the eastern part), we heard news of the counter-revolutionary reaction of Aquiles Freitas[78] and Ponciano who was considered a 'hero' of the UDT counter coup. Lari Sina informed me that Adelino

[78] Fretilin dealt severely with traitors, but from all reports dissents were surprisingly few until a serious division developed in the leadership in 1977 (Dunn, 1996, p. 269). Aquiles Freitas Soares also went by the name of Magli, the son of a Luirai of Letemumu of Kelikai. He was a Portuguese army officer and a Fretilin commander. After the invasion he maintained his own loyal army platoon in the border area. He was a great soldier and the Indonesian forces on the border areas were fearful of him. He did not agree with UDT's policy of integration and was a supporter of independence but he did not fully accept Fretilin's ideology either. He was suspected by Fretilin and because of his strong position was a threat to their hierarchy. He was jailed and killed by Fretilin because he was seen as a reactionary.

Carvalho, of Uatulari, and Fernando Sousa, of Uatu Karbau, were part of Aquiles' network which had branches that reached into Iliomar. He said Adelino was an enemy who made organisation difficult. Although he undermined the population and defied instructions I did not see him as a reactionary. I only understood the word 'traitor'. At that time, at least, I did not accept that they were reactionaries. Nevertheless, I promised to help dismantle the network, arrested Adelino and sent him to CASCOL. This was also an opportunity to dismantle the structures created by Adelino, in which the chiefs he had appointed were the traditional village chiefs and the secretaries of the *suco* were the old *suco* chiefs. I was able to sweep away the 'feudalist oldies' and call on the youth of the Uatulari and Uatu Karbau and *sucos*. Lu Olo[79] was appointed in Ossu and was supported and influenced by the western side, directed by Solan and assisted by Sahe.

Aquiles and Ponciano, before being escorted to CASCOL, along with Fernando Sousa and Adelino, asked for me to intercede on their behalf to the Commissariat.

'We know we are going to be killed. Please ask the Political Commission to let us stay here with you. We'll work for you, be your escort, and we'll do anything you order, but please don't send us there. We've erred, that's true, but give us another opportunity. We're not traitors. We were only telling people not to force us to close our left fist and to attend Marxist courses.'

Father Luis Costa was also going to be escorted to CASCOL because he was considered a reactionary too. 'You know, Gusmão, I knew so and so', he reminisced, full of enthusiasm. He spoke of my old seminary colleagues who were priests, like Cosme Cerejeira who was said to have left the priesthood to take on a wife. They confessed to friends with families, 'You're lucky mate! You've got a generation that will remember you. My family line ends with me.'

'This person won't last long as a priest', I thought, seeing the shine in Luis' eyes.[80]

I had written to Sahe to inform him about 'my' prisoners. On my first trip to CASCOL I took with me Fernando Sousa, who was to become Secretary of the Uatu Karbau region. Aquiles and Ponciano had complied with the popular revolutionary law. Some *Liurais* from Uatu Karbau, accused of involvement in the reactionary movement and imprisoned, were released as in Uatulari. But for Lari Sina in Baguia and Quelicai it was either black or white and some victims of the revolutionary violence were nationalists.

---

[79] This nurturing by Xanana of the young Lu Olo paid off; he is one of the current commanders in Falintil.

[80] Xanana was right; Costa reportedly ended up living with a woman in Dili.

While I was a member of the Central Committee I was not tolerant of revolutionary violence. The concept of violence did not please me, and I did not apply it. I began to see the art of persuasion and conciliation as important political principles basic to me.

In May 1977 a meeting was held in Laline. Xavier was summoned several times but did not want to come. He was quite happy in his kingdom and did not want to go to any more meetings. The meeting was a historic occasion because Marxism was acclaimed.

There were sensitive changes in personal and political ideology: Domingos Ribeiro, Joao Bosco and Nascimento seemed sincere about their political turnaround. During that meeting, Nicolau and Joaquim Nascimento gave their coffee plantations to the state. Hermenegildo Alves, an incorrigible drunk, said in a low voice but loud enough for everyone to hear, 'Any day now, the state will get my wife's gold earrings too'. During the breaks, Eduardo dos Anjos, the inveterate bohemian with whom I had spent a good part of my youth in Dili, beer-drinking and partying, was still the attraction, telling endless anti-revolutionary jokes, which did not amuse the Department of Political and Ideological Orientation (DOPI). Sera Key debated issues, making an effort to demonstrate his abilities as a political theorist. In fact, he was the only one who livened up the meeting, until all the political commissars were told to sit around the same table and get organised. After that there was no more debate.

At the end of 1976 I managed to get hold of a copy of the *Thoughts of Chairman Mao* and it was the only personal property I carried around with me. I read and reread it, trying to understand Mao's simple way of describing complex things. I tried emulating Sera Key as a political theorist, but not simply to debate. Through Mao's explanations, I tried to understand our situation better, because it was difficult to spend hour after hour just listening to dissertations on unknown concepts and then trying to retain anything.

Hata asked me, 'Where did you read all that?'

'Comrade Commissar, don't play around with me.'

'Don't think, Xanana, that we are all well-versed in theory. In Lisbon, I spent most of my time with the Portuguese Communist Party painting slogans on the walls!'

I was shocked to hear his admission and it damaged the 'halo' I had conferred on all those university student activists. I began to understand the childish behavior of de Cesar Mau Laka[81] and a few others.

[81] Cesar Mau Laka went to university in Lisbon and joined Fretilin on his return. Apparently he returned to Dili at the height of the 1970s fashion of espousing left wing ideology and ideas of free love.

Sahe called me over. He offered to help me during the breaks to understand some of the concepts better. From then on I learnt a concept that would help me immensely during the rest of the struggle. It was a sure method of analysis and forecast of the situation, a way of seeing things objectively and of calming the conscience. It was the concept of analysis of the current state of affairs: the dialectic of reality.

Soon, the enthusiastic environment of the 'political school' was riddled with all sorts of strange behavior. At mealtimes Nicolau stopped talking. Carvarino retained his mocking look of triumph—he took pleasure in hurting others.

'No-one prays to thank God for this food that the people have sweated to collect', Nicolau said. I understood how he was upset because although he was a Marxist he also continued to be a religious person.

DOPI met interminably and the escorts would send us far away so that we could not overhear the arduous, passionate discussions. Nicolau stopped going to the meetings. He said he was sick. We could feel something was not right but none of us knew—only DOPI knew what was going on.

There was a simple commemorative ceremony on 20 May, the anniversary of Fretilin, which I also filmed. At lunch Nicolau hardly touched the food. In the afternoon he called me and asked, 'Do you want to go with me?' His voice was sad. I would have sworn he had been crying. Sera Key joined us. We walked three kilometres from the meeting place. When we arrived, Nicolau opened up. 'I don't want formalities here among us. Let us spend these hours talking comrade to comrade, friend to friend. Please help me, I need to relax. I'm going through a crisis; don't ask me why. Call me Nicolau instead of Vice-President—you can't imagine how much you'll help me. Let's not talk of war, let's not talk of politics, let's talk of happy things. I want the warmth, the heat and honesty of friendship.' Some said Nicolau had become insensitive, hard and imposing! In Soibada a year ago, I had had a conversation with him about family issues, his murdered wife and his missing son. Here again was the human face of a man who made politics, of a man who commanded a war, of a man I had admired and respected since that meeting about the post-coup negotiations with UDT in 1975 in Mota Ulun, when his brother Rogerio was acting as the negotiator between the Portuguese and Fretilin. Rogerio had been sweating like a pig when he climbed up from the river to where we were. From afar we could hear him complaining, yelling and carrying on. Nicolau waited until he had approached and finished with his complaints and then said, 'I'm not your brother! Keep your distance and salute me because I am the leader of our people!'

In groups we studied the 'strategic questions' of Mao and a change of war theory. The theory excited us in the planning of ideas and in strategic thinking, but it was a theory that required a heavy loss of life. To understand the scientific truth of war, as Mao himself said, 'All war is specific to a time and place. All war is evolutionary, in the unfolding of the war itself'.

We passed a resolution allowing individuals, under certain conditions to marry twice. Sera Key asked me to accompany him to Cribas, where his wife's family lived. 'Are you going to get married again?' he asked me.

At the Soibada meeting a year before Cesar Mau Laka and Solan had tried to influence our thinking about 'free love', mostly to justify the behaviour that some had brought from Dili and which was being spread in those hamlets so full of girls. I had a serious talk about the problem with Sahe and his wife, Wewe, my very dear friends, whom I will always remember. In the region where I was working, if I had managed to earn the trust of the elders and the people, it was due to the puritanism that Sahe and Wewe taught me to practise.

'No, I'm not', I replied.

'I am not getting married either', said Sera Key.

We were aware that a hard and prolonged war was waiting for us, particularly from the concepts we had learnt.

We returned to our region and were shaken to learn of Xavier's treason—even though I was not surprised![82] Treason was a new phenomenon, yes, but I remembered what Eduardo dos Anjos had said in Balibar, the day after the invasion. He had met Xavier coming down to Dili. He said he wanted to go and 'speak with the invaders to ask them to retreat immediately!' Eduardo managed to convince him to stop such strange and daring behaviour!

Sera Key returned after a meeting in Aikurus and informed us about the Bakau-Vikeke to Tatuala cordon. The cordon would mean we would now only be one sector—*Ponta Leste,* East Point Sector. From that moment, I was responsible for Unit Two, an amalgamation of the eastern parts of the Baucau and Vikeke regions. Sera Key was perturbed. Pedro Sanches, the Commander of the *Ponta Leste* Sector, (the old *Concelho* of Lautem) had been named an 'agent of Xavier'. Afonso Savio, Pedro's brother, and the Regional Commander

[82] This was a serious division within the leadership of Fretilin. Xavier do Amaral was deposed as President in September 1977, charged with treason and placed in custody. He was accused of planning secret negotiations with the enemy, plotting to seize full power and creating divisions between the military and civilian sections of the resistance, of not paying enough attention to the war and behaving like a traditional feudal lord. He and a number of his collaborators were expelled from the Central Committee in the subsequent purge. In early November Nicolau Lobato was elected second President. On 30 August 1978 Xavier was captured or surrendered to the Indonesians during the battle for Remexio. (See footnote 26.)

accompanied Sera Key to the North-Centre Region. Sera Key was confused. He had placed a lot of confidence in Afonso and could not bear to think that Afonso as well as all the other staff in his sector could belong to Xavier's network. Afonso was very sad when he felt the change in Sera Key's attitude. He knew of the accusation that hung over his brother.

'You've got to resolve it', I said to Sera Key. 'You know him', I continued. 'You've got to trust him and before you accuse him you've got to think hard. It is my principle not to accept accusations unquestioningly, when I know the staff member well. I'll investigate but continue to utilise him, testing his loyalty and firmness.'

Sera Key told me about the atrocities committed in Aikurus. In the beginning he had been petrified, but afterwards had convinced himself of the need for 'revolutionary violence'. All kinds of torture were practised: burning coals were thrown on people's stomachs who were then left to rot. I could not believe my ears. Sera Key had changed; he had accepted violence and had become convinced of the need for it.

'You are the only one who knows your man. You are the one who understands the situation in your sector. Only you can make the most appropriate decision', I advised Sera Key.

I reminded him of the Aquiles affair, the violence used in the Baukau Region and of the arrest of Adelino Carvalho, Fernando Sousa and the others, the *Liurais* in Uatu Karbau. I reminded him of the three people in Iliomar, also involved in the Aquiles case, who were arrested in Baguia and sent to Uatu Karbau to await their return to Iliomar. The three people, Francisco Hornay and two companions, had cried as they begged not to be handed over, as they would be killed. I demanded that the Secretary of the Iliomar area, Commander Lere, not mistreat them before they were handed over to a member of the Central Committee. Once they had crossed the Uatu Karbau/Iliomar line the three were beaten to death. I told Sera Key I disliked vengeance and that in the region I supervised I would go in person to attend to cases of 'reaction' and 'treason' so as to prevent confessions being extracted by the infliction of pain.

'But this is a problem of national significance that relates to national security', Sera Key asserted.

Afonso Savio was arrested. All the members of the former executive were called to Unit Two Headquarters in Matebian. Adao Amaral, Jose dos Santos, Pedro Sanches, Gil Fernandes, Raul dos Santos, Victor Gandara were all detained. Sera Key, Ma'Huno and Txay conducted the interrogations. On the third day I could go on no longer and I asked that the investigation be interrupted for a meeting of the four Central Committee members.

'I cannot accept this violence. I cannot accept that a member of the Central Committee would inflict torture in this way. You are acting in reaction to insults and influenced by emotions because you feel betrayed by your staff. I cannot accept that Adao Amaral and Jose dos Santos should die under torture. Look at the physical and psychological state of Pedro Sanches. When he is in pain he says 'yes' and afterwards he declares that he only said 'yes' because he could not bear the pain any more. I won't let this happen here in my unit. Take them and kill them in your own unit!'

Sera Key had never been confronted like this before. He looked at me, incredulous. The meeting was interrupted.

The following day Sera Key summoned me to another meeting.'We are leaving today to control the situation in Unit One', he said. That was my wish. I handed over Pedro Sanches to the care of Edy. Edy was a corporal of the Indonesian Navy who had been captured in Matebian and I had looked after him. He was now working at our HQ. Pedro Sanches' body had been burnt and his breath smelt nauseating. We feared for his life. The others, Gil, Raul and Victor, started working at the HQ after an investigation that I conducted.

There were new arrests in Unit One: Jose de Conceicao, Dinis Carvalho, Nurse Sarmento. Andrade Sarmento, the first person Pedros Sanchez had mentioned to stop being tortured, was the one who suffered the most. A short time after that there was a meeting of the Commissariat with all the executive to explain the general political situation after dismantling Xavier's network, and restructuring the activities and placement of cadres.

At a meeting of the five members of the Central Committee, including Solan who came from the Centre East Zone, I was assigned to Unit One (including Loro, Lore, Moro, Los Palos and Tutuala) as the Political Representative, the one responsible for politics, and Ma'Huno was assigned as the Commander of Comdop, Operational Command, responsible for all activities. I asked to change with Ma'Huno because we had both been stuck solely in the one area for so long. But I was told no, because I did not know the personnel and did not understand the language. We all moved to Unit One, Solan because he was *fataluku*, from the far eastern part of Timor and wanted to be in familiar surroundings again. Sera Key and Txay went to say their goodbyes over three nights of modern dancing and parties at headquarters. I was somewhat put out by this because at my previous headquarters I had never allowed such a thing. Dances were only allowed on national days and in places where the population was concentrated. From Sahe I had learned discipline and self-sacrifice, and also to avoid any path that might lead me into some marriage. Female activists who went around the villages choosing modern instead of traditional dance had been punished.

Sera Key returned to Matebian, where the Sector Command was going to be established. He asked me to order the return of Pedro Sanches, Raul, Gil and Victor Gandara for a new investigation. Dinis and J. Conceicao took turns in accompanying me on my visits. I freed the rest of the prisoners. I employed all the mistrusted staff and we overcame the atmosphere of tension, discontent and mutual distrust. As usual I only rested two or three days at the unit HQ and the rest of my time was spent out touring the region.

A famine raged, affecting everyone. People from the far east of the island were forced by enemy incursions to go through to the west of Lore.[83] Food had been abandoned in the hurry to leave. I organised the forces and we offered security to the population for five days to go and retrieve the food and animals they had hidden. We repeated the operation and our forces advanced a little closer to the Muapitine Line. On the second day Commander Latu Aca arrived. His horse was burnt. 'The enemy must be on our rearguard', I thought. The people became restless.

---

[83] In May 1977 Fretilin reported heavy bombing which signalled the beginning of the campaign of annihilation, 1977-79. The main casualties of the operation were civilians who had to make the awful choice between staying in the mountains to starve or surrendering and entering concentration camps. Falintil encouraged the civilians to surrender because of the increasingly difficult food situation. Thousands 'reported' themselves and in the resettlement camps malnutrition and enforced sterilisation were widespread and many with Fretilin associations were shot or tortured. By September 1977, 15,000 new Indonesian troops had entered East Timor for a new military offensive although the wet season of 1977-78 took some pressure off Fretilin.

A letter from a priest in Dili in November 1977 read: '[The war] continues with the same fury as it had started. The invaders have intensified their attacks in the three classic ways—from land, sea and air ... From last September [1977] the war was again intensified. The bombers did not stop all day. Hundreds of human beings died every day. The bodies of the victims become food for carnivorous birds (if we don't die of the war, we will die of the plague), villages have been completely destroyed, some tribes (*sucos*) decimated ... and the war enters its third year with no promise of an early end in sight. The barbarities (understandable in the Middle Ages, and justifiable in the Stone Age), the cruelties, the pillaging, the unqualified destruction of Timor, the executions without reason, in a word all the "organised" evil, have spread deep roots in Timor. There is complete insecurity and the terror of arbitrary imprisonment is our daily bread (I am on the persona non grata list and any day I could disappear). Fretilin soldiers who give themselves up are disposed of—for them there is no prison. Genocide will come soon, perhaps by next December. Taking advantage of the courage of the Timorese they are being recruited to fight their brothers in the jungle. It is they who march in front of the [Indonesian] battalions to intimidate the targets'.

It was 4.00 in the afternoon and the chief of a village had invited me to share in eating some meat that was being cooked. I was already chewing the first bit when the chief spoke. 'Kaka', he said, using a name which showed affection and respect, 'do you know what meat this is?'

He pushed forward the cooked head of the dog that he had hidden behind himself. 'Dogmeat', he said.[84]

My eyes nearly popped out of my head. I stopped chewing.

'Dear Kaka. Do you know why I ordered to have this bitch killed? She had a skin full of sores and her eyes were full of pus', he continued in an apologetic attitude that was somewhat betrayed by the bright stare he gave Adao. I saw the trembling of his repressed laughter. I felt sick. Then we saw the commander appear with his distressed horse.

'The Comrade Commissar has asked for your urgent attendance at the HQ of the Luro Zone. He's getting married tomorrow and it won't do it if Kaka isn't there', he said. It would be a day and a half trip. I turned around to the chief. 'Please, next time kill me a fat dog!'

I left the chief behind, laughing at the trick he had played on me. I arrived at 11.00 the following day at my HQ where I changed into civilian clothes, but somewhere in the surrounding fields I had lost the heel of my left boot (Portuguese army issue). And so without my heel I limped along through this hard and prolonged war. By midday I was at the HQ of the Commander of the Luro Zone.

'This is a surprise', I said to Sera Key.

'You know, Xanana, the decision was difficult, but it's difficult continuing this way and for how long will it go on?' he answered.

Some of the population in Muapitine and at the foot of Mt Paitxau had not surrendered and refused to march west with the others. They had an executive body. Mau Velis, one of the executive, had maintained contact, through Mehara, with Joao Branco, an ex-member of the Central Committee and the Commander of a sector that had surrendered. Mau Velis wrote me a letter asking me to not 'be like the others' and proposed a meeting. The 'others', members of the Central Committee, did not agree to the meeting but I gave instructions to the commanders in Lore to maintain the connection. Shortly afterwards I met with Mau Velis, initiating a number of clandestine activities.[85]

---

[84] Eating dogmeat became common when there was no other food to eat.

[85] Xanana refers often to this organised clandestine group of Joao Silvestre Branco, Mau Velis, Miguel Santos and the resistance of Muapitine, Mt Paitxau and Mehara who had come to remain in an occupied region. These areas are in the extreme eastern tip of East Timor. Against the wishes of the Central Committee Xanana had secret meetings with these leaders and later they offered him much support. Joao Branco, the ex-member of the Central Committee and the

Every so often I went to stay with Sera Key in Matebian. Once he was very despondent and frustrated. Kilik, the Commander of the sector was not helping him: he did not study the 'strategic questions', would not discuss military problems and surrounded himself with an insolent silence. I knew that Kilik was a private man and proud, one who had difficulty accepting the opinions of others. You needed to be tactful when dealing with him and Sera Key promised to try a different approach. Months later, Sera Key called for me to come again to his HQ. 'Anti-social, rude, that's what that man is. I came here to alleviate the tension', he yelled by way of a greeting. 'The guy boycotts all my plans', he continued, nervously rolling his moustache, a tic of his which appeared when he was thinking or agitated.

We had a meeting, where it emerged that seven years before, in 1970, Sera Key, then an army instructor, had yelled at the young recruit Kilik in the mess, who felt insulted.

How can you keep the desire for vengeance deep within yourself for seven years for such an insignificant reason? 'Because Comrade Commissar is white!' Kilik said. His desire for revenge was fed by racism!

We sorted out a solution for that problem which improved the relationship between the two of them but for me it left in the air questions about the mentality and the consciousness of people.

Simple people are so practical! Problems resolved with a punch means time is not wasted nurturing cynicism, false attitudes and ridiculous ideas. How is it that educated people acquire new ways of wrapping up their egos and new ways of externalising what they carry deep within themselves? During the war this kind of competitiveness became a great indicator of such false attitudes.

In the second half of 1978 I did get married. It was generally accepted that it was going to be a long, hard war. Would I be able to keep up the puritanism that I had undertaken (and of which I was proud because it had been an important factor in gaining political trust in difficult regions)?[86] In the meantime Ma'Huno was left to take care of his baby after his wife died.

---

ex-commander of a surrendered sector, was killed by the Indonesians at the end of 1979, together with a group of 40 others.

[86] The resistance had now accepted that it was a going to be a long hard war and temporary measures, such as puritanism, were being abandoned. Many thought they would never be able to resume relationships with partners from previous marriages and it was accepted that people could remarry.

Bombardment

Months later, we would begin the march to Matebian.[87] I still carry in my eyes those vivid scenes of courage, self-abnegation and the will to fight of those people. Happiness and enthusiasm took the place of the doubts, the worries and the belief that more sacrifices were waiting for them in Matebian.

We had a meeting with the entire executive in the eastern part of Matebian to find solutions to the problems created by the first arrivals from the east at the foot of Matebian. The tension increased. Some cadres in Baguia and Laga were still dissatisfied. They demanded the re-arrest of those 'implicated in the reaction [treason] of Xavier'. They claimed such people should not continue to be part of the resistance and, if necessary, should be killed. This was the first serious challenge I faced. I was the target. I asked Sera Key to let me assume the responsibility and told him, 'You would have to arrest me first!'

I still maintained the contacts with Branco and agreed to meet him in Home. Adao Cristovao showed up and a few others and I asked them to take the old people, the ill and the weak who were finding the trip to Matebian very hard. It would be one less burden for the war effort that had now taken on new proportions.

I returned and went straight to the Commissariat, already moved to Uada Boro. They did not agree with my suggestion to leave the old people behind. I always got irritated with decisions 'from the top' that did nothing to help the real situation on the ground. This was what prevented me from becoming a leader tied down to an HQ, receiving only written reports. I preferred to go out and get to know the reality, to see and appreciate it so as to understand the dimensions of that reality and to test the degree of dedication and initiative of the cadres. I regretted moving all those people to Matebian where it was impossible to cater for them. Matebian was literally full and problems arose everywhere between the recent arrivals and the residents.

Sera Key called me, despondent again. 'It must be about differences with Kilik', I thought, 'or on how to proceed with the defence of Matebian.'

---

87 In May 1978 a new Indonesian military operation, the Skylight Offensive, was launched under the command of General Yusuf, Commander-in-Chief of ABRI, in preparation for the visit of Indonesian President Suharto in June. During the next six months Fretilin's military position was weakened and later that year they were forced out of Remexio and Railaco. Fresh troops, supported by US-supplied aircraft, destroyed Falintil positions in several encirclement operations. One report noted that as many as sixteen Indonesian battalions were employed on the ground, while the civilian population living behind Fretilin lines was bombed intensely, causing heavy casualties.

In September 1978 Xanana supervised a march of the population, fleeing the bombing campaign from his region in the far eastern tip along the length of the Legumau range, taking the old road constructed during the WWII Japanese occupation which connected Luro and Baguia.

'I entrust you with a case so you can resolve it.' he said to me. 'I've been here all this time waiting for you to arrive.' It had become general knowledge that his wife had been kissing another cadre in the past few months. I punished the woman with six months forced labour in an area where she was forbidden visits from her husband. 'You were too hard towards us—poor her', he lamented.

Soon the enemy advanced and I was sent to the west of Matebian.[88] Explosions, death, bombardments, cries and retreats. But the people were calm: maybe resigned, maybe truly prepared for us all to die there. Our forces retreated and the enemy infiltrated. One dawn I was awakened by loudspeakers from the Indonesian forces, calling my name: 'Vice-Assistant Xanana, there is no need to continue fighting. Tell the people to surrender!' They had moved in from Uatu Karbau during the night and occupied a strategic point.

Solan and Olo Kasa came to replace me. I returned to the eastern part of Matebian. Uada Boro had been taken. Sera Key was alone. No one, not even the commander of the sector, was with him.

'I apologise to you; I went to get her', Sera Key said, trying to explain the presence of his wife. With a few assistants we went to set up our command near Uai Bitae. We had lost the North, Sesugua and Nalidole. I visited all the front lines engaged in combat. There was no room for the people. There were bombardments, explosions, deaths, blood, smoke, dust and interminable queues of people waiting for their turn to try to get a bit of water for the children from a few springs. There was no crying. Dead bodies were everywhere, but strangely they were not rotting, they dried! The nights were warm and the fog did not dissolve; it seemed that it was afraid to lift because of the interminable battering of artillery from the land and sea.

Kilik, the commander of the sector, remained with his family. There was total lack of control. The commanders of the companies were the only ones responsible for a determined resistance. I met Ma'Huno in a shelter, still confident. He was worried about his second wife who had gone crazy. I had told him not to marry so suddenly, just to try and arrange a mother for his son, but he would not listen.

The fighter planes were sowing the seeds of death all day long. We were suffocating under that Matebian sky which stayed stubbornly clear.

---

88 By the end of 1978 Fretilin's defence in the eastern sector was concentrated in the Mt Matebian region, the last support base of the resistance. The Indonesian military launched a scorched earth policy to destroy any food crops in the region, followed by a campaign of intensive air and sea bombardment. The base fell on 22 November 1978, and great numbers of East Timorese civilians and Falintil troops were killed.

I went to meet with Sera Key. 'I am going take a company and move east. We are going to attack Los Palos which I think has been left with little defence. The terrain around there is very exposed and open, good for guerrilla attacks upon the rearguard of TNI.'

'But how are you going to get back in?' he asked.

'I'm not leaving to get back in, I'm leaving to break this siege!' I screamed at him. Once again I regretted not just having taken the decision alone. I had spoken to two of the local commanders and both agreed with the plan. The people could not retreat any more. We were encircled. I went to see the sector commander again. Kilik had finally shown up! A last-minute decision was made to send two companies to try to break the siege but I knew they would never make it. Two days later we met and decided to give up the defence of Matebian, to tell the population to surrender. One company for guerrilla action would be under my responsibility in Ponta Leste and all the other forces and cadres would go to the Centre to strengthen the national base.

The meeting-place was bombarded. I saw death with my own eyes. A deafening explosion had been just a few metres ahead of us. Pieces of burnt, dirty flesh were plastered to the stones, the trunks of the trees embedded with sharp edged metal that had dismembered the bodies of my *Companheiros*. I, who used to yell for others to find cover while looking after other fighters, now suffered a terrible fear of aerial attacks. This event profoundly marked my attitude for the rest of the war.

That night, we went into a cave.

'Are you taking your wife?' Sera Key asked me.

'I don't even know where she is'.

'Morally, you've got to communicate your decision to her. We are taking our wives', he said, without conviction, pointing at Olo Kasa and Solan.

'Morally, I should not even meet with her; as a matter of fact, I don't even know where she is.' I farewelled them.

It must have been 11 o'clock at night on 22 November 1978, when we started descending the east face of Matebian, a little to the north of Baguia.

The following day we grouped at the south-west base of Mt Legumau. Assisting me were Txay and Kilik. Hodu and Ruak[89] were among other cadres who had been selected by me for future activities. The first directions were to

[89] Taur Matan Ruak is the current military commander of Falintil. He was still at school when the invasion occurred and joined the resistance as a young man. In 1983 he was assigned a command in the Ponta Leste sector and between 1984 and 1986 served as military advisor in the Western sector. He was promoted to Deputy Chief of Staff and between 1986 and 1993 he was responsible for all Falintil commando operations. He was elected to the leadership on the accidental death of Konis Santana in March 1998.

divide ourselves into small groups; take off our uniforms; hide the arms; keep in touch with what was going on; make contact with the people in the area. There was a three-month deadline for the change in tactics. I chose Holly Natxa from Sakalo, Konis Santana[90] and two of his brothers.

'We are going to try to get to your areas as quickly as possible. We have to contact Mau Velis', I told them.

5. The Long Walk (1979–1980)

Suspicion, chaos and surrender

We reached the coast of Muapitine without too many problems. On the night of 7 December, the third anniversary of the invasion, we traversed the plain in the direction of Mehara with Mau Velis. We met with Miguel, the *Kepala Kampung*, the Indonesian-appointed village head, who would join Falintil with his forces in 1983. For a month and a half I travelled through the hamlets, making contact with the people, with the *Hansips*, the civilian guard, and the youth. I was learning about a guerrilla war that would serve as the base for an organisational structure of the resistance. I had a meeting with Joao Branco at Migel's house and we settled a few ideas on the continuity of the struggle.

In February 1979 I summoned Txay and Kilik so we could assess the situation. They did not agree with my plan to traverse the northern plains because they thought I had prepared all this to deliver them to the TNI. These suspicions were so hard for me to accept in such a difficult situation! The commanders who were supposed to be in the Centre Region joined me. They had found chaos and suspicion when they met Hermengildo Alves, Secretary of the Vikeke Region, and in the Centre in the area south-west of Bibileo, so they had returned.[91]

Solan and his sick wife, Olo Kasa and his weak wife, Sera Key and his wife, with their escorts, were all in Builo but isolated from each other and abandoned by their forces. Sera Key recommended to his two commanders that the forces that had returned from the Centre Region, and those that could not get

[90] Nino Konis Santana became the military leader of Falintil on the capture of David Alex, until his accidental death in March 1998.

[91] In December 1978, Alarico Fernandes, the Minister for Information and Internal Security, announced over Fretilin radio that he and some of his comrades had broken away from the Central Committee. The circumstances under which he was captured by, or defected to the occupying forces are unclear. With his capture Fretilin's only direct radio link with the outside world was cut.

Surviving Fretilin leaders and Falintil troops in the east set out to reorganise their forces. Search parties to find surviving resistance fighters in other parts of the country were sent out. The first two parties never returned. The third and forth groups returned, but they had found no other guerrillas.

through, be put under my charge. He would go to the Centre to try to find the Resistance Executive. I left Txay and Kilik and went in a westerly direction to try to manage the forces. Hodu and Ruak were south of Legumau, Mauk Moruk in Saelari and Alex[92] was also there. They were brief encounters. Commander Lay Kana, in Sesugua, was the best commander in the area at the time. In Uaibobo I met Olo Gari and Fera Lafaek and in Builo, Sabika and others from Uatu Lari.

I recommended to everyone that we wait for reorganisation. We learned that Solan and Olo Kasa had been captured. When I returned to Saelari I learned that Lay Kana and the bulk of his company had been enticed by Lari Sina and Olo Kasa to surrender as they had done in Quelicai. Lari Sina, in collaboration with Iswanto, the Indonesian Commander, had begun to infiltrate our forces. In Saelari I had ordered them to surrender, with directions to maintain contact with us and also to make contact with the resistance in Dili. They did not manage to accomplish this because they too were massacred, as were Lay Kana and his company.[93]

Confusion reigned and my spirit was shaken! More than shaken, just about beaten. I did not want, above all else, that cadres should begin to surrender behind my back like Lay Kana. Kilik was confused; he wanted to look after his daughter who had just been born. He asked me if he could be exonerated!

I summoned all the cadres, placed the problem before them and tried to convince them that if they wanted to surrender they should not do it behind our backs (as Lari Sina and Iswanto had enticed them to do), that they should do it in coordination with us. What I asked of them was that I at least be able to choose and keep the arms we needed so that we were not left with inoperative and non-automatic pieces.

This discussion took place in a tense atmosphere. Alex and Kiby Sama added comments in an air of patriotic passion. In the meeting with the soldiers

---

92 David da Costa, known also as David Alex Daitula, was a Makassae born in Bualale-Quelicai in the late 1940s. He did military service in the Portuguese army and worked as a civil servant in Dili in Finance. He joined Fretilin and Falintil during the 1975 coup. He was an escort to Antonio Freitas and was based in Baucau when it was invaded in December 1975 and in 1976 became a commander of the elite companies until Mt Matebian fell at the end of 1978. David Alex became the Deputy Chief of Staff of Falintil troops after Xanana's capture. He was injured and captured by Indonesian troops on 25 June 1997. He is thought to be dead.

93 Dunn explains: '… the brutal treatment of those members of the resistance who surrendered provided the independence movement with a good reason to keep fighting on. Some were shot shortly after capture, more than a 100 members of Fretilin, with their families, being disposed of in this way at Quelicai in the central eastern sector. Others were tortured' (Dunn, 1996, p. 282).

they demonstrated that they were still prepared to resist. This was a moral victory. I could not take control of some of the arms because they were in the possession of the soldiers who were not obliged to follow our political directives, but I trusted Alex, whose forces were complete. Some cadres and commanders still surrendered. I indicated to Ruak and some cadres to go to the other centres to find the Resistance Executive.[94]

Disillusionment and devastation

I went to Laleno and called another meeting. Before the arrival of the cadres I called for Dinis Carvalho and ordered him to collect some 30 automatic arms and munitions and to hide them secretly in the Mehara area.

Txay had returned to Lore. As soon as I had left the East he and Kilik resolved to go their separate ways without studying or debating the points that I had left them to study concerning the reorganisation of the forces and associated activities. Ma'Huno had returned from the Centre Region to Ko'oleu. 'I will not surrender', said Ma'Huno. 'In Ko'oleu they will not find me, no matter how many battalions they have'. But I had begun to have real confidence that they were determined to continue the struggle. The soldiers would not even permit the cadres to talk about surrendering; they did not want to hear any explanations of that kind. The guerrillas of the East were apparently the most exposed to the enemy because almost all of them regularly kept in contact their families.

Sickness and Nicolau's death

I returned to the west of Matebian, climbing into the hills. Sad silence, desolation. Grass was spreading its cover over short cuts and paths, struggling to smother the cabbages and potatoes which were the only signs a human hand had ever been there. Every ridge, every stone, every brook and tree had witnessed tremendous suffering.[95] Our group of seven marched on in silence. All the scenes of the last months rushed back into our minds. We could hear the voices of the dead, those same voices that created the sensation of respect felt when entering a *Lulik* house. Matebian was our Great Home because the entire population of Ponta Leste had relocated there during the massive operation of annihilation. The fine rain and thick mist made us sweat beneath our uniforms.

---

[94] Taur Matan Ruak notes that he was requested in early 1979 to go and find Falintil survivors in the central part of East Timor and that he and his men were betrayed and captured at Mt Bibileo in Vikeke. 'ABRI surrounded us and we were trapped. I surrendered to ABRI on March 31 1979'. After 23 days he managed to escape and rejoin other Falintil forces.

[95] The image of natural elements playing silent witness to events when the people can no longer speak or can no longer be heard is a traditional Timorese symbolic expression of immense suffering. There is one myth where the stones actually sing.

More of the resistance forces of the Commanders Kali Sa, Ko'o Susu and Mau Kalo had come under the control of the Indonesians. The forces of Uatu Lari, which I had known in 1976, were still pigheaded and undisciplined. 'Brother, those of us that wear the *langutim* are still here and those that wore pants and spoke of politics like the flowing of Ue Bui River are today living in the towns.' [96] This was the welcome of those comrades who were such a headache three years before. The feeling of repulsion towards political cadres and the indoctrinated commanders, who preferred to accompany their families to the towns took a long time to extinguish and often made it difficult for the activities of the few political cadres who remained in the armed resistance.

I ordered Commander Olo Gari to go to the other centres to see if he could find any sign of resistance. I took some cadres and a company back east to take part in a meeting on the reorganisation of the forces. On the march we were either fighting or caught in rain. I was already unwell and physically weak. By the time we reached south of Legu Mau we had run out of food. On the third day, two platoons deserted. The others looked at me, waiting for an order to turn back, clearly not prepared to put up with hunger and marches into unknown areas. I asked for five volunteers and continued marching. I was the only one who knew any short cuts. All around us the countryside had changed, so different from when there had been people living there with their vegetable gardens, animals, houses and villages.

We arrived in the Iliomar area and searched for food but there were only *ai bubur*, eucalyptus trees. When we returned we had less than ten *kuan* tubers to show for our unfruitful search. Commander Zei Moto had gone to hunt for game but had come back with only *hudi kain,* banana tree stalks. Two pots were steaming to cook the food. When I chewed the first bit of *hudi kain*, I said to him, 'We're all going to die if we keep eating this mush—even the pigs wouldn't eat it.'

He watch me pour away the contents of my plate, then swallowed up the remains of black water tinged with purple, smiled and winked.

I had a meeting in Lore with Ma'Huno, Txay and other middle-ranking cadres. Kilik did not show up. Defining military areas and restructuring the locations and activities of the resistance forces were the most urgent matters. I told Dinis to go and get the arms hidden in Mehara.

'You ordered that arms be hidden? Without our knowledge? We, members of the FCC?' protested Ma'Huno and Txay.

I would maintain this practice for the rest of the war, without fail, in my relationship with the Central Committee and cadres of the middle ranks. In

---

96 The *langutim* is the traditional, native loincloth worn by *Firakus* (those from the east). The Ue Bui is one of the biggest rivers in East Timor; the reference to it means that politics was being spoken about very often.

practice, political trust can only be acquired from dedication, a spirit of discipline and the initiative and willingness to accomplish the best.

I was physically exhausted. I had contracted chronic malaria of the worst kind, at least three attacks a day which devastated me. Every tremor left my jaw and neck cramped and an infernal fever followed. Before each attack my stomach blew up until the skin of my belly hurt.

I went to hide in a small thorny wood in Mota Ulun with my assistant Virgilio and two boys, one of whom, Sabalae, suffered the same illness. The three of them went out one day looking for buffalo. The hunting would have to be far away so as not to give away our presence. Sabalae and I gathered some *kaleik* and tried to prepare it—we had nothing to eat.[97] In the afternoon we put it into water. 'It will be better in a couple of days', we said, satisfied that we knew what to do. In a couple of days there was only a mess; the *kaleik* had gone off, mostly washed away by the water. That night the three returned with plenty of meat. An old woman was called to treat me with prayers and sprinklings of water. 'The bitter corn is only for him', the old woman ordered Sabalae, giving him the flowering stalk and teaching him the prayers for the ritual of sprinkling the water. We did not follow any of her instructions.

Holly Natxa arrived and we left the following day for Dili. On the way I found out that Ruak had escaped from Ossu where he had been taken with Sera Key but had been captured in Bibileu. Sera Key and his wife were captured, sick, abandoned and betrayed by the last forces from the East Centre sector which had also surrendered.

Olo Gari had returned. Even in the areas of Turiscai, where he had engaged in battles with the enemy, he had not found any evidence of forces or people in the bush. I then sent Ko'o Susu to try again in the areas of Laleia and Manatuto. Ma'Huno had regrouped and was again in Ko'eleu, and Txay had also retreated.

The trip from Kakavei, Los Palos, to Mt Laleno, which should have taken half a day, took me three days with constant stops to relieve the attacks of fever. From Mt Laleno we went on to Sakalo. I looked pregnant with a belly so swollen that it that could not inflate any more—it was full of air. I met with Holly at his parents' place; he had brought six cartons of resoquina, the malaria drug. I wanted to take advantage of my convalescence to see our connections in Dili and prepare a good number of the cadres there in political theory. After taking the resoquina I was in full recovery; the fever stopped even although I was still very weak.

---

[97] *Kaleik* is a wild fruit from the trepaderia tree. It is a big climbing creeper plant with huge seedpods and fruit that is poisonous. It requires a long preparation consisting of soaking the fruit in running water for day to get rid of the poison.

I was informed by Dili that there were forces in Dare and in Tibar, that Nicolau had fallen, that Cesar Maulaka was around the South Centre Region, in the area of Alas, but much of the information was contradictory.[98]

We were betrayed and at dawn were attacked. Three of my comrades fell; I escaped with only my gun. My feet hurt but I reached Mehara. The propaganda from TNI was that I had died. Even the corpse of one of my *Companheiros* had been taken to the town to prove to the people I was dead. I agreed with my companions that we too should spread the rumour that I had died. We moved to the south coast of Maupitine. It was my idea to force members of the Central Committee to realise that the situation demanded that they take more responsibility and for the middle level cadres to understand that they had to think hard and face the situation. Very few were behaving appropriately, with the majority more inclined to search for their families again.

The three companies in the forest of Lore were destroyed and the survivors regrouped in their different areas. We continued with the strategy of concentrating our forces just as we had done during the earlier period when we had functioning support bases but now there was no theoretical basis to it. Our dispersion was imposed by the enemy and was not a strategic plan but a simple reaction to enemy assaults.

I was left in the care of a family in that area where the commander continued to be the connection between the West and the East. Part of the East and the North was left to the care of Konis' group, who were located in Tutuala. My 'death' changed nothing; on the contrary, it caused more division amongst the cadres, especially after the middle-ranking cadres insisted that those more senior (at the time Ma'Huno, Txay, Kilik and Bere Malay Laka) meet, study the problems and make a decision. Ko'o Susu returned and informed us that

---

98 Although President Nicolau Lobato had been killed on 31 December 1978, Xanana had not learnt about it until now because of poor communications and his period of illness. Indonesian forces had located Lobato's camp and he was killed in the ensuing engagement. According to press reports from Jakarta about 20 Fretilin leaders and troops were killed with him. General Yusuf himself at once flew to Dili to inspect the embalmed body of the fallen Timorese leader, which was photographed with the triumphant Indonesian officers. Carvarino, the Vice-President, took over from Nicolau but he too was killed on 2 February 1979. It meant the end of the first generation of Fretilin leaders.

During the first half of 1979 Fretilin forces were in poor shape. There were many more captures and killings, and several hundred of the demoralised troops who surrendered were reported to have been shot after they had been taken into captivity. In light of this most chose to fight on and along with Xanana the guerrilla campaign shifted towards the east. When the wet season set in at the end of 1979 the remaining units of the armed resistance regrouped and resumed their attack,s usually in the form of ambushes in the Ermera-Liquica-Aileu-Dili area, and major operations took place in the eastern section.

he had encountered elements of the population and forces in the areas of Uai Mori and Laline.

Now fully recovered, I called a meeting in Iliomar in the forest of Lore. We had been sent pamphlets with a photograph of Nicolau's body. It only confirmed the information received from Dili. Ma'Huno would not believe it was Nicolau as there was something wrong with the colour of the corpse's skin in the photos, but we did not know at the time that Nicolau had been embalmed. Kilik was of the opinion that we should not inform the people or the forces, to avoid any more low morale. It was how we had also handled my 'death'. At this meeting we established the structural bases for an organised resistance based on an intimate bond between guerrillas and the people of the temporarily occupied towns.

It was also decided that I would go as far as I could to try to contact anyone from the Fretilin Central Committee. The sector was left in the hands of Ma'Huno, while Kilik and Bere Malay Laka took command of the forces, so I began a new journey to the west of Matebian. I had to endure a month and a half of kidney pain and daily fighting. I could not sit down nor remain standing, and I could not bear to lie down. I used to roll around on the ground as if possessed. How I cried! Many were the times I wanted to commit suicide. I could not stand the terrible pain, the horrible discomfort. I used to drink huge amounts of tea made from leaves or peelings or roots. The sympathy in the eyes of my warriors offended me. I avoided the impotence of their words. I tried all possible and imaginary cures. I put up with hot tins and boiling steam from tubers and leaves heating my anus. The explanation was that I was suffering from a 'woman's sickness'. Vanquished, beaten, I carried my steaming *asa loki*, a cure, around in a pouch. Not that I really believed that the remedy would enter through the intestines and warm up the kidneys or anything else inside the lower back area. I just knew I needed to believe in something to keep on living.

Empowerment

In May 1980 I went through the Central East Region with 60 armed men.[99] I gradually got better along the way but it was a difficult march. In the west of

[99] Xanana crossed the Baucau-Vikeke cordon to make a general assessment of the whole territory and by the end of 1980 communications had been established between a number of surviving units. More than 100 Timorese deserted from both the 744 and 745 Indonesian Battalions and from the *Hansips*, the civil guards. This new addition of troops boosted the capability of Falintil, and in 1980 it launched two daring attacks, one in January not far from Dili, and an assault on the capital on 10 June.

Matebian, where there was still a lot of food, the forces were not prepared to withstand hunger and fatigue. Often at nightfall, I would leave them down by some river bank because they refused to move any higher to spend the night. Only the *fatalukus*, disciplined men hand-picked by Dinis Carvalho, would follow me without a word of protest. I had bawled the others out so many times, at meetings, showing them the way back. Then they would slowly catch up to us again and feel too embarrassed to talk to me. After we had made peace with one another, the complaining and lamenting started up again.

I also implemented the plan to secure an organisation of the people that we convened all the way from Venilale to Vemase.The old men embraced me crying. 'Son, carry on the fight! Don't ever surrender! You are our only hope!' The guerrillas were moved by this and swore to die for the Homeland. After that they were examples of self-denial, discipline, sincerity and solidarity to all the Falintil fighters. They were nearly all killed. Right now there are only three or four survivors of that group which we baptised the 'National Unification Detachment'!

Back in Remexio we stopped. Ko'o Susu continued south towards the border areas with half of the troops. I stayed with the other half. I needed to prepare myself for the Conference on the Reorganisation of the Struggle, planned for between October and December.

6. Decision to take up leadership (1980 – 1981)

Decision and support

After gathering more information supplied from Dili, I decided to take up the leadership. Ma'Huno was more senior, a founding member of the ASDT. But I knew him well and thought it would be irresponsible to agree that he should lead the fight just because he was the veteran.

I called Holly and Ko'o Susu. I explained the issues to them, asked for their views and pointed out my reservations. 'You can count on us to help in whatever way we can.' They shook my hand and I, crying, felt the heavy weight of responsibility on my shoulders. I became 'Commander of the Fight' to all my warriors. For them, my decisions and even just my words took on a new importance, becoming 'The Commander of the Fight's decisions' and 'The Commander of the Fight says'. And they did their duty, those brave selfless *Companheiros*, with a consciousness that they had been born to die for their Homeland, under my command.

'*Maun Boot sa'e, ami sa'e; Maun Boot tun, ami tun.*' 'Older brother climbs up, we move up; older brother climbs down, we climb down.' It was a simple concept of duty, a generous offer of their lives! Never betrayal! If it was 'easy' to decide to assume command of the struggle, I was totally conscious that the decision had been the most difficult I had ever thought of taking. We sought refuge near Lacluta. I would have to study; I would have to demand of myself some notion of revolution, of war.

I took stock of the revolutionary process. At the meeting of the Political Committee in Aikurus, Hata took on responsibility for the ideological training of the Fretilin Central Committee members, and I so much wanted to be involved. I remembered the nightly talks that Sahe and I used to have in Makadike/Uatu Lari in August 1977, when he would help me out with political theory, and we would prepare for the time when a revolutionary party would be formed. We would be Maoists. At least they were Maoists, and considered the communist parties of the Soviet Union and Western Europe all social-imperialist. Sahe also admired the 'purity' of the Albanian revolution and the internationalist militancy of the Cuban revolution. He asked me that night, 'Would you agree to join the Party?'

My ideas still muddled, I said 'No'.

He looked at me, shocked. 'Xanana, I would have expected anything but this of you!' Then I explained to him what I was prepared to be a militant but not a member of the Central Committee. I was not ready.

Study and preparation

Now my head was burdened and I was still not ready. But I had in my hands a duty to fulfil: to carry out the work of my predecessors. I could not conceive of liberating our Homeland without liberating our people. This was the supreme objective. I spent my nights studying by the light of candles made from the wax of those Timorese bees that once had been introduced to me as 'our forces' by the *Luliks* of Sananain. This was where we used to gather before attacking Manatuto and from where we were chased by tanks and mortar fire. I found those beehives on the same branches as I had seen them before. It was revolution and war and I would have to dominate a little if I wanted to accomplish anything. My capacity to direct would depend on my capacity to understand and this would depend on my dedication to study. My dedication would depend on the environment in the camp.

We were 20 or so in a camp with Second Commander Jony because the other half had left with the First Commander Ko'o Susu. Later the Nahak Company joined us from Dili. Security was perfect. The total silence was a sign of solidarity from my warriors, who understood that if their 'big brother' was tearing at his hair, it was because he was finding it hard to understand some concept or other; if he cried, it was because he was asking himself 'Why did it all come to this?'; if he asked for stronger coffee, it was because he wanted to spend the whole night studying; if he was up and walking around, it was because he was tired; if he asked for cigarettes, it was because he had smoked all his ration. 'Why must it always be me?' I thought. I did so much wish that at least one member of the Central Committee was still alive on one of the two borders

I sent points to the East so that all were studying and preparing themselves for the conference. Ko'o Susu had returned with some hopeful news. He had found some forces and middle-ranking cadres. He had contacted the population of Same and they helped to establish the connection with the surviving forces. Supported by the Nahak Company and some Mambai people, he returned to his mission of contacting people with a summons to the conference. In October I made Holly Natxa go to summon the cadres in Ponta Leste.

First National Conference for the reorganisation of the country

In January 1981 only the first group arrived with Hodu. I asked him if they had studied and discussed the points I had sent him. 'We met one day in Legumau for that reason but …' he lamented. How could I conduct a meeting without any of the participants being prepared? How long would we have to talk, while the enemy was already bordering us? The centres had stopped being a secure zone. Kilik and Olo Gari accused me of having fled Ponta Leste for fear of the *battue*[100] and demanded that I send them arms for them to mount a stronghold in Matebian, 'offering me' machine guns in exchange.

I tried to overcome that situation. During combats and marches I began to write two reports, *Homeland and Revolution* and *Themes of War*, to facilitate a more methodical study of our processes. I had assumed command of the struggle on the grounds I was the Commander of the Falintil. Before my arrival we had small discussions at the centres and I noticed I did not have the same military thinking as Kilik, who was more attached to the thick Portuguese military manuals. It was difficult for us to agree. I understood then why we had not been able to guarantee, on the ground, a better defence of Matebian, why the attempt to have a base in Matebian had failed and why the forces in the Lore Forest had been driven away. It was because there was no command during that difficult period. It could not continue this way, I thought. I should secure the command of Falintil to avoid the ongoing application of wrong methods of war. There were so few of us left that we should accept experimen-

[100] *Battue* is a method hunters use to beat out game from the undergrowth, and refers to Indonesian military operations which used these tactics.

tation. The few successes and the enormous failures of the first three years were sufficient evidence for us to profit from some correction to our thinking.

Ma'Huno arrived with the second column of officers. His salute took me by surprise. In a few months I had forgotten what he was like! At night, or in between my attempts to organise my thoughts about our revolutionary process and our war, I would go and spend some time with the cadres who, excepting Mau Hudo, were all from the East. I was saddened by their completely changed attitude towards me. My brothers were abandoning me. My *Companheiros* were keeping me at a distance. I cried so much while I was talking to them, while I was asking them the favour of not spoiling me, of not feeding in me the presumption of power, of not planting in my soul the seed of ambition, and of not kindling pride in my spirit and satisfaction at being leader and Commander of the Falintil.

In March 1981, the First National Conference for the Reorganisation of the Country took place. Today in Cipinang, 13 years later, I am still learning with the same spirit of the struggle, with the same will to win and with the same consciousness that I am just serving my Homeland. [101]

[101] The conference resulted in a total overhaul of organisational and political structures. Falintil units would now be mobile and the clandestine organisation inside the strategic camps and in population centres supported the armed resistance. At the top level, the resistance was now to be led by *Conselho Revolucionaria Resistance Nacional*, the National Council of Revolutionary Resistance (CRRN), and at the lowest level were the *nucleos de resistencia popular* (nuclei of popular resistance), set up to maintain links between the resistance movement in the bush and the clandestine network. Xanana was elected National Political Commissar, President of the CRRN and Commander in Chief of Falintil.

MESSAGES FROM A NEW LEADER

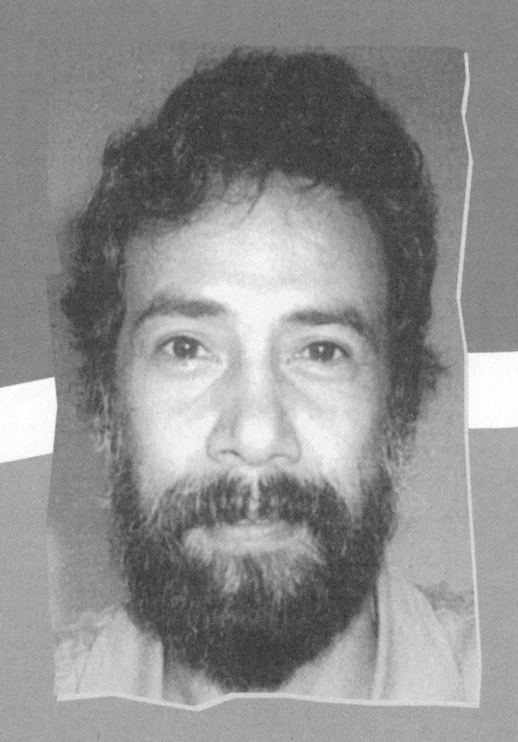

1982–1986

CRRN Salute

The National Council of Revolutionary Resistance Salutes the Fretilin Delegation of External Services

In this message Xanana reaffirms the continuation of the resistance and their need for support from the political diaspora community. He addresses all those members of the Democratic Republic of East Timor (DRET) government declared on 28 November 1975, nine days before the Indonesian invasion. He writes as President of the National Council of Revolutionary Resistance (CRRN), the resistance structure inaugurated at the March 1981 Conference when he was officially declared leader of the resistance (described at the end of the Autobiography). He personally and passionately salutes members of the DFSE, the external delegation of Fretilin established in Lisbon in support of the internal resistance forces.

Comrades, Members of the Revolutionary Government of the Democratic Republic of East Timor, Patriots of East Timor!

On behalf of the members of the National Council of Revolutionary Resistance, and all military and civilian personnel; on behalf of the glorious Falintil and of the heroic—the one thousand times heroic—Maubere People, I salute, with great personal satisfaction and confidence, the members of the External Delegation of the Revolutionary Government of the Democratic Republic of East Timor who are engaged in arduous work in the diplomatic field. I also salute, with joy and eagerness, all the children of East Timor who from afar have continued to follow with sadness and pride the heroic deeds of their brothers and sisters.

We have taken, without pomp and ceremony, another huge step towards the victory of the Maubere People, a certain and inevitable victory rooted in the unshakable determination of the heroic and beloved Maubere People. This victory rests upon the sacred gift of those children who have given their lives defending their Homeland and is cemented by the generous offerings of the fertile blood of its heroes.

For seven long years, East Timor has been devastated by the horror of a genocidal war, sustained by the bloodthirsty clique of Suharto. For seven years the Maubere People have been decimated by their Indonesian executioners, but have also proven to the world their indomitable will to defeat the barbaric aggressor and affirm their strong and total repudiation of this military occupation by Javanese colonial expansionism.

Hundreds of thousands of patriots have given their lives for our Homeland: from the heroic members of the wise, intrepid and glorious Fretilin Central Committee, notably our beloved comrades, Nicolau Lobato, Mau Lear and Bieky Sahe, to the valorous Falintil guerillas; from the tens of thousands of Fretilin cadres to the popular masses: the elderly, children, women, men, adults and youths who have not refused the sacrifices required of them.

Today we continue to witness, in the concentration camps and in the mountains of East Timor, magnificent examples of patriotism and self-abnegation by the children of this land, fully conscious that their deaths will consolidate our march towards victory.

Upon the mantle of blood that covers the sacred soil of our beloved Homeland, and upon the ashes of its martyrs, the Maubere People, its armed resistance and leadership, after a difficult and painful period of campaigns which destroyed our support bases, have again raised the armed resistance.

A handful of East Timor's best sons remained resolutely intent on fighting to the last man and overcame a long and critical period of two years of disorganisation. Coming from all parts of the territory, they met in March 1981 for the first National Conference. Here the nation was reorganised, the liberation forces restructured and a new leadership appointed.

Today, the liberating fire of our guns has been reignited throughout the whole territory and our political presence has expanded deep into the concentration camps, guaranteeing organisations of solid popular resistance. In summary, we have moved onto a new level of political and military control of the country.

The Maubere People are politically, morally and militarily prepared to resist for as long as it takes to expel the criminal and barbaric foreign occupier from their Homeland.

The murderous Indonesians, committing all sorts of barbarities in East Timor in the most abominable ways, have no restraint to their fury in exterminating the Maubere People. The vandal aggressor tries in vain to hide from the world thousands of instances of exile, imprisonment, torture, massacre, persecution and constant threats. Yet all of this constitutes eloquent proof of the ever-increasing rejection of the new occupier of our Homeland. The Maubere conscience and their mortal hatred of the enemy increase and consolidate as the repression intensifies.

The constant political and military actions of glorious Falintil which Jakarta's criminal soldiers are increasingly impotent to prevent, let alone put an end to, have become an enormous headache for their generals. The present situation is one of instability for the enemy and insecurity in the villages controlled by the aggressor. This situation means we have developed a position of strategic counter-offensive.

Comrade Members of the Revolutionary Government of the Democratic Republic of East Timor, Patriots of East Timor!

We know how much you worry when you think of our beloved Homeland! We know how much you worry about the future of our beloved People! Whether in friendly or foreign countries, carrying out the work of the struggle or in other circumstances, we know that your thoughts are with us, certain that you have confidence in the vital and inexhaustible strength of the East Timorese People who have found new ways to struggle for our liberation.

We appreciate your tireless efforts on the difficult task of changing world public opinion in favour of our struggle. We know of your efforts to solicit, from friendly countries and governments, from natural allies and the anti-colonial nations, lovers of peace and progress, the necessary support to demand that Jakarta's puppet government implement immediately UN resolutions on East Timor. We follow, whenever the difficult circumstances of our struggle permit, your efforts to guarantee and consolidate our victories in the diplomatic field against the barbaric aggressor.

Shoulder to shoulder, united by the same faith in victory and the same sacred objective of liberating our Homeland and beloved People, let us continue to carry out our tasks on the various fronts of the struggle with increasing commitment. Let us remove all obstacles, overcome the increasingly great difficulties and let us always confront new demands because the struggle continues, harder and without truce, in the villages and mountains of East Timor and on all fronts!

Homeland or death!

To resist is to win!

President of the Council [CRRN]
Kay Rala Xanana Gusmão
Commander-in-Chief of Falintil
CRRN Headquarters in East Timor, 13 October 1982

Message to the 37th United Nations General Assembly

This is an edited text of Xanana's first message to the United Nations, and he takes the opportunity to fully report on events in East Timor since the invasion. This translation was reproduced in the Spring 1983 edition of the East Timor News.

Mr President and distinguished gentlemen. Forgotten on the map and blockaded by the most powerful nation in ASEAN, East Timor has been devastated by an extremely hard war since 1975. There have been seven long years of Javanese colonial expansionism, resulting in an unjust war against the incomparably heroic Maubere People.

It is with pride and great satisfaction that our voice of resistance can today reach your world organisation. The 37th ordinary session of the General Assembly is now taking place. Today, we take this opportunity to address the distinguished gentlemen taking part in this meeting, regarding the true facts and the bitter reality of the sacrifice that the Maubere People undertake.

Mr President, distinguished gentlemen. In September 1975, Indonesia began border violations and then increasingly occupied villages along the frontier. The invading forces brought in artillery by land and sea, along with tanks and aircraft. The invading forces continued their criminal actions and in this period did not even spare the lives of five Australian journalists who accompanied the glorious Falintil in their mission to stop the aggression against their nation.

On 7 December 1975, the bloody regime in Jakarta sent their paratroopers and marines to Dili, where they massacred many patriots and another Australian journalist in taking the capital of the country.

With the extreme arrogance that characterises imperialist aggressors and their lackeys, the 5000 generals of Jakarta dared to think they would win lightning control of the country within 48 hours.

In January and February 1976, new contingents of paratroopers were dropped successively in Baucau, Los Palos, and Suai. Despite this, the Maubere People, to the surprise of the shameful and cowardly aggressors, proved to the barbarous invaders that they did not understand Maubere consciousness and the patriotism of the East Timorese population. This patriotic consciousness of the people was immediately and magnificently revealed, when they spontaneously climbed the mountains of their country, and with genuine zest, unequivocally, resolutely and totally energetically repudiated the presence of the new expansionists.

We defeated the incompetent Portuguese colonial government that collaborated with internal reaction, then ran away. The people of East Timor refused to accept the new foreign domination. Whole villages, threatened by the powerful aggressor, moved to the mountains of their violated land, including the old people, the diseased, the children and their possessions. Following this initial phase of spontaneous resistance of the masses of East Timor confronting the powerful bellicose invaders, the popular, organised resistance developed under the clear leadership of the central committee of Fretilin.

The glorious Falintil combated the enemy offensive while the people of East Timor actively participated in the resistance war, whenever possible, with traditional weapons. Because of its superior numbers and weapons, the enemy was able to control the villages of the north coast, whose population were prevented from leaving. The enemy also cordoned off the corridor Dili-Betano and Baucau-Vikeke. A few villages fell under the control of the Indonesians, who repopulated these villages with people captured during military operations. They then moved to control the corridors Dili-Bobonaro and Lautem-Los Palos.

The powerful enemy, who came full of force and pride, began to find a series of obstacles affecting his ambitious design of annexation, faced with the determination and courage of the armed Maubere People who inflicted heavy casualties on their enemy and repelled them with tenacity when they raided Maubere bases. Poor planning by the militarist Jakarta regime confronted by the tenacious resistance of the Maubere People, left them trying to find something to justify their weakness in the light of Indonesia's anxiety to impose domination.

Two years later, they sent 50 battalions, with berets of all colours, from commandos to infantry, from paratroopers to marines, and with a whole diversity of material, from AR15 and MU2 and Golachenikov [rifles], from light Herstal to heavy rockets, mortars, cannon and bazookas, to tanks and armoured cars and helicopters, anti-guerrilla aircraft and ships. They began the strategy of destruction of the support bases, where the popular resistance was consolidated against the invaders.

These same bases allowed the population, which at that time could be estimated at 80 per cent of the total population of East Timor, under Fretilin control, to live in security and tranquillity. We recall with revulsion that in 1976, with only 2 per cent of the population under Indonesian control through the force of the gun, a fantasy act of integration of East Timor was signed, as 'the way chosen by the Maubere People!'

So with this powerful military capacity, the invaders made a very big military operation starting from the south zone of the border region in September 1977. Only in November 1978 was the vandal occupier able to overturn the last remaining organised resistance of the Maubere People on the edge of the island.

This was a painful period for the Maubere People. With their land burnt, their houses destroyed, their possessions plundered, their animals machine-gunned, the Maubere People, in their great and heroic march from the defence of their country, also saw their children, their invalids and their elderly form a human column to be massacred by the constant bombardment and aircraft gunning. But these people were ready to die for their sacred native land! Disembowelled bodies, bodies blown to pieces by bombs, human bodies in unrecognisable shapes, burnt by napalm, innocent children riddled by assassins' bullets from aircraft guns, held in the arms of their agonised mothers, without burial, red paths of blood created by the survivors in the travel to safety marked the signs of pain and suffering and of the mortal hatred of the enemy—this was the heroic image of that difficult and pitiful period.

Finished and sick, yet determined and fixed in their goal, the Maubere People had to accept to enter into the control of the aggressor, as a condition to develop a new form of resistance.

The little Indonesian soldiers also did not escape from many human and material losses. Not satisfied with their successes, they increased their criminal bestiality. But thousands of patriots continued to reject enemy control and were aggressively massacred when captured. Throughout the territory the most inhuman spectacles were witnessed, such as the cutting off of sexual organs, tongues, lips, ears, fingers, arms or legs, or victims screaming horribly after their abdomens were ripped open and who were then either burnt alive or tied to tree trunks where they were left to rot in the sun or rain. Women were stripped and sadistically violated, then beaten until they died in an orgy of blood and crime. All this because they were identified as Fretilin and didn't want to surrender!

These spectacles aimed to impose an acceptance of control and avoidance of the possibility of desertion. But nevertheless, the badly treated population, violated and oppressed, once more began to rush back to the bush.

With the control of the population established, the enemy then concentrated, first of all, on the extermination of the wise, intrepid and heroic Fretilin Central Committee, the clear-sighted vanguard of the Maubere People, then to annihilate the heroic combatants of Falintil. These operations continued until

March 1979, when they achieved success by concentrating all their effective troops available at that time in the central region of the country.

Meanwhile, in the eastern sector, the surviving members of the Central Committee of Fretilin, together with dozens of staff, forces and population of the resistance, continued to organise. In the centre and border regions, after the death of the heroic members of the Supreme Direction of Struggle, the majority of the forces were manoeuvred by the capitulators and traitors of the nation. Under their direction, many of the armed forces surrendered to the enemy, crying without hope for the destiny of the nation or people.

This shaky period in the national territory which saw the destruction of the resistance bases passed. The staff, forces and population in the eastern part then went looking for their brothers, who were fixed and determined to maintain the armed resistance. After two difficult years, after two years of adaptation, after two years of correcting the mistakes, the inevitable happened: a reorganisation of the country and the forces and the formation of a new leadership occurred for a new and strongly increased national resistance!

In 1979, meanwhile, the enemy decimated the people in a new wave of massacres. The prisons filled with hundreds of patriots. In all villages there were, and still are, prisons and each day five to ten people are tortured—burnt with cigarettes, systematically subjected to high-voltage electrical shocks—the human victims of the *nangala* knife-killers. Some extract fingernails, squeeze testicles with pliers. Under the table where the red beret assassins sit, the victims have their toes pressed by weights. All this is for interrogation, in order to find out about the popular organisation in the concentration camps. And then comes murder—mass execution by firing squad, being bludgeoned to death in front of the grave they have first dug themselves, being drowned in drums of water head-first—and the dead person's family are told by the authorities that they 'have gone to Jakarta to study'.

Then, as if this was not enough, the women of the resistance and the wives of those massacred are taken at night time for interrogation. They must accept, under threat of death, to amuse the *nangala*, the police, the *Koramil*, the *Kodim*, because these women are accused of having contact with Fretilin.

Fighters and staff of Fretilin, when captured, are interrogated to obtain statements about the conditions of the resistance, under the most abominable tortures, after which they die. They are then tied to a car that tows their dead bodies along the ground around the village while the population are forced to watch and 'welcome the visit of Fretilin'. Women captured in the bush are subject to criminal action. They are stripped, their heads shaved and made to pass between the queued population who are forced to denounce them. Anyone who doesn't want to look at the unfortunate woman and doesn't want to laugh at or insult her, is immediately hit, arrested and killed, after being accused of being Fretilin. In the concentration camps, the population live in terror and panic, day and night.

Any car noise in the village, the approach of the occupying force, or any element who asks for an address—all are signs of imprisonment, a prelude to torture or to death. It [1979] was a year of terror and intimidation! We need not refer here to the thieving practices of the soldiers against the population, the rape of the women, the massacre of many husbands who fearlessly spoke out against the rape of their wives and the massacre of the many women who resisted the threat of rape. Because of all of this, the Maubere People once again became conscious that they should fight; that they should resist in order to be victorious over these foreign invaders …

Humanitarian aid from international organisations was totally controlled by the occupying authorities. The food was used to supply their troops in operations against the Fretilin fighters. The clothes and medicines were sold in *Kooperasi* [shops] by members of *Kodim* (who ended up owning practically all the commercial enterprises) and also from the houses of the officers and sergeants of *Koromil* and the police, before they could be distributed in the concentration camps.

It was a year of much suffering for the Maubere People. They were like captured animals, without agriculture, without clothes, without houses! When the famished and diseased population went to the bush for food they were killed when they were seen by Indonesian soldiers, on the pretext that they were contacting the guerrillas of Fretilin. The enemy used the difficult conditions of life of that year to establish their system of collaboration. Using the food and clothes from the international aid organisations for payment, they established a spy machinery to hunt Fretilin in the concentration camps. The collaborationists compromised and became loyal to the Indonesians. They denounced without any cause 'suspicious elements'. The terror increased as did the insecurity of the population at the same time as the famine also increased. Deaths were frequent and disease threatened the population with extermination.

However, the actions of the heroic combatants of Falintil never ceased. With each success of the liberation forces, the enemy answered with reprisals against the population in the concentration camps. In some places large numbers of people were massacred. Disease and famine in 1979 were worse than in the three previous years. In some *desas* [Indonesian villages] which had a population of 400 to 600 people, only five to eight families remained alive at the end of the year.

In 1980, the whole country lived under a new wave of massive killing. But the enemy was impotent to really control the population of East Timor. The threats, the persecution, the torture and the prisons only increased the hatred for and repudiation of the occupier. These increased in direct proportion to the repression. The people's patriotic consciousness was repressed, but it never wavered. It revolved around the centre of the Maubere People, who consolidated in clandestine organisations that were primary and vital necessities for the struggle. The Maubere People were reinvigorated, rising to the needs of their struggle. They knew better their mortal enemy. They improved their new form of resistance, which was adequate to the new condition and situation which became more and more threatened by the enemy. The Maubere People regained their commitment for the liberation struggle of their country!

... The enemy became a more aggressive and furious killer. But they were unable to stop the clandestine organisation of the popular masses, which increased in breadth and depth.

Finally, the enemy reached the conclusion that what they had done in 1978 had only made the Maubere People transfer its support bases from the mountains to the villages. In Jakarta, however, the carnivorous Suharto and his corrupt generals did not realise this great truth: 'It is the people of East Timor who wage war for its own liberation and Fretilin is the blood that circulates in the veins of the old and young in East Timor. So to exterminate Fretilin, it is first necessary to exterminate the Maubere People.'

Meanwhile, Yusuf [the Indonesian Minister for Defence] and his assassin friends racked their brains to review the measures and counter-measures which failed to impose their colonial domination over East Timor. Their executioners were working in the dark in our country.

They asked Fretilin if they had seen Fretilin and Fretilin responded that they had not seen Fretilin!

Aware of its incapacity, the enemy adopted another method of terror and intimidation—exile! Tens of thousands of patriots have been forced to leave their houses and their crops and whole families have been sent to Atauro Island and various other places in the country. There, facing miserable conditions of life, they die each day from disease and famine in their dozens. To avoid prolonged opposition, the enemy has not improved the inhumane conditions—the barracks and dormitories in which they crowd together the sick, the elderly, men, women, children and babies, the small amount of rotten corn, the forced labour and the stealing by the repressive authorities, who seize money or objects of value taken by the people to help them survive their exile, to buy food and clothes, etc …

Only a small number of those who are accused or suspected of being Fretilin because they have family members in the bush have returned to their homes. If they have been allowed to return, it is because the enemy has made sure that their brother, father, son or husband has been killed by the occupying forces. Some of those released from exile have disappeared on their way home.

Another subtle method of elimination is called 'mobilisation', or *TBO,* of the suspected or persecuted person, who is forced to accompany the aggressive forces into the bush. Then they are raped or massacred, and when the operation is over, the people are informed that they ran away in the bush or were killed by Fretilin.

In this way they try to turn the population against its own armed forces—something they can never do, because the population is familiar with the assassins' practices and because of the existence of the clandestine resistance organisations in the concentration camps.

We do not want to forget that many Timorese people who are armed by the enemy to fight against their compatriots have also been persecuted, tortured and massacred.

Another year passed, and the carnage by Jakarta took a new face in order to 'finish the war' that had lasted so long and had demonstrated the enemy's military and political incapacity. This led to more violence and intensification of the war. Using the excuse of carrying out military exercises, 6000 more soldiers were sent to East Timor, besides the battalions that were already there. With paratroopers and marines (who quickly tired of looking for Fretilin), with tank and naval bombardments, with helicopters and aircraft flying over, shooting into suspected areas considered Fretilin refuges, the new offensive began.

A big weakness surrounded this theatrical operation classified as *perang terakhir*—the so-called final or decisive operation, by the impotent Jakarta generals, which took place in the middle of 1981.

Finally, the enemy had opted for the *Timorisation* of the army to complete the war. Seven years ago, the enemy started the war using paratroopers and today they give the war to the sons of East Timor. They arm the Timorese, pay them in order to die instead of Indonesian soldiers and reward them with mountains of inflationary rupiahs whenever they present the occupying authorities with the heads of the resistance fighters. These heads are often taken from the bodies of the undefended population in the bush, as well as from guerrilla fighters who have been killed.

To encourage these Timorese to commit these crimes, they announce that for every head of a Fretilin leader the prize would be many rupiahs, a good house, travel to Indonesia, food and so on. Today, because of this, in the bush of East Timor we see the sons of the same country kill each other, while the Indonesian soldiers give security to their authorities who carry out reprisals, torture and massacres against the Maubere People.

The last big attempt of the impotent enemy to silence the armed resistance of the Maubere People was the mobilisation of the total male population, from children of 12 years of age to old people who were forced to take part in the so-called clean-up operation throughout the whole territory (the 'fence of legs', 1981). The enemy had some victories in the central region of the country as a result of mistakes by the resistance fighters, rather than the capacity of the enemy. But the enemy could not suffocate the resistance, which was essentially a big defeat for Indonesian strategy!

Following Yusuf's strategy of genocide and indiscriminate massacre that his executors practise against the old, the children, the pregnant women and the guerrillas, armed or unarmed, the population gave one of its greatest proofs of the highest expressions of patriotism and of its conscious participation in the liberation struggle, by leading their resistance compatriots through the 'fence [of legs]'. They hid small groups of guerrillas among them, thus helping many captured people waiting for death. They led the enemy far from the places where their brothers were during the day and night. They led their sons through this great human wall.

In other regions, neither resistance forces nor the population suffered any defeats. In the central region where the populations from the border, centre and coasts were forced to concentrate, the little enemy also converged from the three parts of the country and forgave nobody. The bastard Indonesians, killing machines for the genocidal Suharto, captured, killed or wounded people, thirsty for blood, and once more bathed in the heroic blood of another 200 patriotic martyrs.

At the present time, the barbarous occupiers seek to continue the war with a structure of 'civil defence' based on the shaky foundation of their political and military capacity to control the population. Today, they have quickly resettled the zones in the interior of the country. They thought this strategy would decrease the resistance of the heroic armed Maubere People. Against all their expectations, this year has witnessed many political and military successes for the glorious Falintil.

The extreme political and military incapacity of the enemy was shown by their own Colonel Daurem, the chief of the carnage in East Timor, who had been apprehensively meeting with the local authorities, asking them why they had not exterminated Fretilin. He handed over to them the war the Indonesians had brought. He gave them the responsibility for the defence and security of the concentration camps. 'The war is handed over to you. You must help the *bapaks* [Indonesians] to win the war and defeat Fretilin!'

Some of the more daring said that they should mobilise the population again, leaving just the old people and babies. The unfortunate Colonel, oppressed by the awareness of the inevitable political and military defeat that would result, replied quickly, 'We don't agree. If we did that, the whole world would know and Indonesia would be condemned for this again!'

With the image of the shameful defeat of its retrograde colonial expedition in its mind, the Indonesian aggressor continues its criminal actions.

Many soldiers, sons of our Indonesian brothers, who refuse to fight in whole companies when sent to the bush, see out the time required for the operation and avoid, when they can, contact with the glorious Falintil. They sadly declare they did not come to East Timor for war. They say they were lied to by Suharto who told them that in East Timor there was no more war.

It is not uncommon for an Indonesian battalion to trick the occupying authorities in the villages because these authorities insist they should continue to fight. The soldiers know it is impossible to exterminate the Fretilin guerrillas, so when they see evidence of their presence in guerrilla camps, they nevertheless do not find the guerrillas who have dispersed to reappear in military operations in the villages.

Some Indonesian companies were punished, by being forced to remain for half a year in the bush, because they were not aggressive, because they had become aware of the just struggle of the Maubere People!

... Suharto's party won the elections again. In East Timor under the threat of weapons, all the population voted in favour of Golkar. East Timor and Irian Jaya, by a curious paradox, were the 'most dear provinces' of Suharto and the best supporters of Golkar!

Mr President, distinguished gentlemen. On the blood-covered ashes of our Homeland, the Maubere People have again developed the framework of the resistance! With hundreds of thousands of lives given for the integrity of the Homeland, the Maubere People, linked with its armed forces and led by Fretilin, have erected a new barricade of defence against the criminal occupation by Indonesia.

Under very difficult conditions for fighting, the Maubere People are determined to resist to the last man. Blockaded, small and undefended, the Maubere People have decided to defeat the powerful enemy. The armed struggle has spread all over the country. The gunfire of liberation lights up again in every part of the country and the action of the glorious Falintil, from Tutuala to the border, is creating great instability for the cruel, barbarous and bloody enemy. The cowardly occupier of our country is making propaganda, claiming that we are only 50 in number, or that we have only 20 guns and that we are only 100 fugitives. We affirm that we are not many, but also that we are not just a few—*we are an entire people at war!*

And our creed is: *Homeland or death! To resist is to win!*

Mr President, distinguished members of the UN General Assembly. The people of East Timor have repudiated since the first hour the annexation of their country. The people of East Timor continue to repudiate, today more than ever, the illegal and cowardly occupation by the anachronistic assassins in Indonesia.

We strongly and energetically accuse the participation of American imperialism in the war of genocide in East Timor, by giving arms to Indonesia to carry out its crimes against the undefended Maubere People. We have captured weapons from the aggressor's army which were recently manufactured in North America. The equipment bears the brand of NATO. The Reagan government gave military aid in tens of billions of dollars for the continuation of the war of aggression in East Timor. This support was obtained by the *sharan* of Indonesia, Mohammed Yusuf, who went to the United States for that purpose. Suharto was warmly received by Reagan who expressed his desire to continue the support for the politics of genocide of Jakarta, with a bombastic eulogy of Suharto, the prominent assassin of South East Asia.

We also accuse the governments of Australia, New Zealand and Japan and other capitalist countries as accomplices in the extermination of the Maubere People. In defence of their monopolistic interests, they support Indonesia militarily, economically and diplomatically, in its continuation of its crimes in East Timor, and in its continuation of the practice of genocide which has resulted in the extermination of more than one third of the population.

We remind the Australian government that we do not forget this act of 'gratitude' to the people of East Timor who, abandoned by the Portuguese colonialists, helped Australia against Japanese imperialist aggression which made our country the stage of war and destruction. The death of many sons of East Timor, our fathers and our brothers, in their active participation in the guerrilla war against the Japanese aggressors is repaid today with the scorn of having our struggle considered as an 'internal matter of Indonesia'!

We remind the Japanese government that we still carry the scars of the injuries caused by the massacres, tortures, imprisonment and violations of all types and the ruin of our country caused during three years of occupation by the criminal and vandal assassins. Today these scars have become ulcerous. In the United Nations the Tokyo government supports the extermination of a whole people who were decimated three decades ago by the Japanese. The Japanese people present to the world the wounds of Hiroshima and Nagasaki. The Maubere People drink the pus of the wounds caused by the Japanese aggressors in the very recent past. Today, you forget to cure these injuries.

Very distinguished gentlemen. When we hear of the massacres of 1600 Palestinians in two of the concentration camps in Beirut, we see immediate repercussions all over the world, causing repulsion and indignation. We look sadly at our soil covered with the bones of tens of thousands of compatriots of East Timor. The blockade that the barbarous aggressor imposes on us impedes the civilised world from knowing the murderous practices and assassinations of the genocidal clique of Suharto. Whenever a foreign delegation comes to our country, the barbarous occupier convinces them of 'peace and tranquility' in our country, hiding the guns and sending the soldiers out of sight ...

We affirm our solidarity with the heroic and sacrificing people of Palestine and our total support for the right of our brother people to their Homeland, where they can live in peace, security and stability, and we want to express our great admiration for their brave heroism and the determination of their liberation army in their defence against the aggressive vandalism in Lebanon by the Zionist executors and assassins, Begin and Sharon ...

We are in solidarity with the people of the West Sahara and with the people of Namibia in their struggle for independence! We are with the brother people of Cuba and Nicaragua against the imperialist threat ...

We are side by side with the brother people of Angola and Mozambique who are the targets of attack of the racist government of Pretoria. We support the just struggle of the people of El Salvador for their liberation. We finally express our gratitude to and our solidarity with the three brother countries of Indochina ...

The fight continues, harder and without truce, in the villages and mountains of our Homeland!

CRRN Headquarters in East Timor
14 October 1982

Commander-in-Chief of Falintil
Kay Rala Xanana Gusmão
National Political Commissioner

A History that Beats in the Maubere Soul

Message to Catholic Youth in East Timor and Students in Indonesia

This message, written on the 12th anniversary of the foundation of Fretilin, responds to a document sent to the CRRN nine months before [7 September 1985] from Catholic youth inside East Timor and those studying in Indonesia. This delayed reply illustrates the difficulty of circulating information within East Timor, closed since 1975. In this message Xanana outlines a political and cultural foundation for the struggle and the policies and rationale for resistance from the older generation of fighters to the new generation. This message comes at the beginning of Xanana's restructuring of the resistance and can be seen as a call for unity and a common platform in the subsequently difficult period

A central debate in this message is of the current political options of independence or autonomy for East Timor: if independence is a realistic possibility or if special autonomy is a more pragmatic approach. The UN General Assembly Resolution 37/30, concerning East Timor [November 1982], requested that the Secretary General initiate 'consultations with all parties directly concerned, with a view to exploring avenues for achieving a comprehensive settlement of the problem …'. Indonesia and Portugal were the only 'parties' consulted, and although Portugal maintained it was committed to the Timorese taking part in the consultation process, the Timorese were never consulted. Indonesia argued that the conflict was an internal affair (and rejected Resolution 37/30) but the Secretary General's representative persuaded the Indonesians to meet with their Portuguese counterparts. A meeting between the Portuguese and Indonesian Foreign Ministers was mediated by UN Under Secretary General of the United Nations, Rafeeuddin Ahmed, in New York on 24 September 1985 and was the first formal contact between the two countries since the invasion. The second phase of talks Xanana mentions here were not held for another seven years, again in New York in September 1992, and 'resulted in an agreement to hold substantive discussions at the level of Foreign Ministers.'[1] The third round of talks occurred in 1998 and ended in an agreement to hold a consultative ballot in August 1999 under UN auspices.

Introduction

The National Council of Revolutionary Resistance received your documents of 7 September 1985, in 'response to the Appeal of the Leader of the Dili Diocese'. On behalf of CRRN and the glorious Falintil, as well as on my own

[1] UN Secretarial working paper on East Timor, July 1994.

behalf, I express our profound esteem and congratulations to you on your energetic and courageous stance at this historic time of vital importance to our thousand-times heroic and beloved Maubere People! I address myself today especially to you, Beloved Youth and Maubere Patriots, for you are the vigorous blood of our people and the promise of the future of our beloved Homeland, East Timor.

In this bloody journey of our people your participation in the struggle for national liberation is a moral duty and, above all, it is a political and historical obligation. The struggle requires morality and all of us who possess foresight, who can think methodically and act according to our principles, have a duty to understand and interpret objectively the aspirations of our beloved Maubere People. It is political because any analysis and considerations that come out of that interpretation should faithfully reflect and be derived from a core of political options that fittingly represent the aspirations of our people, the people we are part of, the people whose children we are. This moral and political duty comes not only from current events, but from a history and long tradition of independence struggles. We have lived this history and today, more than ever, the sovereign will of the people needs to be defended in strong and ongoing action with all the strength we possess.

Ten years of enormous sacrifice have passed—ten years of interminable suffering that should be, for all Maubere youth, a theme for profound reflection, just as it has been for you, Beloved Youth and Maubere Patriots. These years have formed the basis of a set of principles that interpret and dignify the patriotic consciousness of the people of East Timor. Ten years of tenacious resistance by our people to the vile aggressions and the criminal occupation of our Homeland are, for the *guerilheiros* (many of whom are your age and have never sat on the school bench), the political basis of their motivation and their firm determination to die for their Homeland. These last ten years have provided for you, young students of East Timor, as you have demonstrated, the moral strength for your political decision to resist, and I hope that you continue to become stronger in a steadfast defence of the rights of our people.

Why do I recommend to you a steadfast spirit of combat?

In the conditions of our struggle (and yours also) you will face, without fail, overwhelming threats of persecution and much deception. This may make you feel like giving up the struggle, destroying your Maubere consciousness and putting an end to all that you have courageously built. I have confidence that you will not quit in the face of all these difficulties and I trust that you will never waver in the face of this pressure. We know that you have succeeded already and that you will continue to succeed!

I add to your document, Beloved Youth and Maubere Patriots who are studying inside or outside our Homeland, and I am going to refer in this message to some relevant questions you sent for consideration so that we may clarify these points and create some foundations for our undertaking that has only one object: *independence for our Homeland and liberty for our people*!

I. Autonomy or Independence?

There are people who worry about the total extermination of our people, asking if this will happen and searching for an answer. Many minds are troubled by the countless difficulties that surround the armed struggle in East Timor and are overwhelmed by the feeling that independence is impossible for East Timor. Their views on this war are taken from the examination of the 'current state of affairs in South East Asia'. This 'current state of affairs' presupposes that:

— Indonesia is not going to leave East Timor;
— the countries of the EEC and ASEAN and the USA and Australia will accept autonomy as the first step in a solution for East Timor;
— the Portuguese would accept the solution of autonomy as a compromise that preserves Portuguese culture.

How then do these people conceive a 'special autonomy' for East Timor?

According to what we understand, those seduced by the theory of introducing a (nothing more than illusory) process of autonomy in East Timor claim the following conditions will apply:

— Portuguese may be spoken freely;
— Tetum can be spoken;
— natives would hold positions of power;
— security would be handed over to the (murderous) 744 and 745 Battalions;
— only Catholicism, not Islam or Protestantism, would exist.

These conditions assume the following:

— **historical identity:** the possibility of speaking in Portuguese would preserve the sacrosanct inheritance left by Portuguese colonialism;
— **cultural identity:** the possibility of cultivating Tetum would create the illusion that the people of East Timor are outside the Great Republic of Indonesia;
— **ethnic identity**: the 'halting' of the practice that *transmigrasi* and the *Gubernor*, the *bupat* [regional administrator], the *camat* [administrator], etc., would only be Timorese;

— finally, that Jakarta would give greater freedom of movement to the ordinary people, not to mention the 'ambitious projects of economic autonomy'.

However, before we can assess these options we should look at other issues that will make our subsequent reflections clearer.

A. The War in East Timor

1. The war in East Timor is not a mere claim for minor or major autonomy within the context of the nation of Indonesia. The war in East Timor is not a civil war inside a state, in which one sector of the population intends to impose their demands, through armed means, on another. We have nothing, absolutely nothing, to do with the government in Indonesia, not in any political, economic, religious, cultural or ethnic aspect of that Great Nation of Indonesia! If, by God's will, all the current dictatorships of the world were overturned by democratic forces in their own countries and Indonesia were the only one capable of maintaining this system of government interminably, may the great Allah help them, because it is not up to us to respect him in the strict sense of the word.

2. The war in East Timor is a conflict between aggressive Indonesian forces and the resistance of the Maubere People in this continuing and barbarous occupation. A central issue is to understand up to what point the two forces can and should consider the end of the conflict.

East Timor is not an Indonesian province but for the last ten years has been a militarily occupied territory. The armed struggle maintained by Falintil is only the violent manifestation of the resistance of our people. The armed resistance directed by Fretilin is only one aspect of the popular resistance and it expresses the strength of the national and patriotic consciousness of all the children of East Timor. The war in East Timor is therefore an appropriate response to the violation of internationally proclaimed principles, which secured the people of East Timor the right to be free and independent.

3. The invasion of East Timor is a violation of the principle of the inviolability of national boundaries contained in Chapter IV of the Charter of the United Nations. This principle also states that the territory should be decolonised as has occurred in other cases throughout the world. The annexation by force of East Timor is a violation of the principles that regulate the process of decolonisation in Resolution 1.514 of the General Assembly of the United Nations, which defends either a plebiscite or the vote of an assembly elected by universal suffrage to determine the political future of a colonial territory.

The continued military occupation of East Timor is a violation of universal principles and international law that affirm every people has the right to self-determination and national independence.

The continued and illegal military occupation of East Timor is a betrayal of the character and the spirit of the movement of the non-aligned countries.

The continued Indonesian military presence in East Timor and the barbarous repression exerted over the Maubere People flagrantly disrespect the resolutions issued since 1975 of the General Assembly of the United Nations and the Security Council. This presence and repression blatantly challenge international public opinion and the world community of nations.

In summary, the criminal military occupation of East Timor is an abusive violation of the Declaration of Human Rights, including the rights of the Maubere People to choose their own destiny.

It is on the basis of these principles that regulate the international relations and harmony amongst peoples, that the efforts of all children of East Timor must keep alive the aspirations of our fearless people! These principles should direct our thoughts and activities to respond, tit for tat, to the dirty manoeuvres attacking the character of our struggle. The objective of these manoeuvres is to weaken our determination to ensure the free exercise of the Maubere People's right to manage their own destiny.

Many will be overwhelmed by the terrifying vision presented solely to the people of East Timor if the foundation of our struggle is not properly established. This vision is that the use of force is mightier than those of reason or the rule of law; that crime and injustice are capable of overturning the determination of our people; and that the Maubere conscience can be bought off for a few rupiahs, or a few cars, incorporated in the illusory delights of 'autonomy'.

We would insult the river of blood that continues to flow into the soil of our Homeland in defence of a universally recognised right, if we do not search for the foundation of the character of the resistance of the Maubere People and try to understand how it is that our people have tolerated such huge sacrifices. If we remove the political, juridical and historical scope from the struggle of a people who want to free themselves from a perpetual colonial slavery (to which the military expansionists from Jakarta and their accomplices condemn them) and if we reduce our interpretation of the heroic resistance of our people to the extermination of the forces that oppose them, we would be paying respect to the use of force and crime, of genocide and unreason. If this were to be our interpretation of the rights for which our people have accepted and will continue to accept all sacrifices, then it would negate the great difficulties that surround our struggle; it would become the fruit of moral and political impotence, and it would demonstrate not only irresponsibility as well as a political emptiness, but a profound lack of conviction in the true aspirations of our people. Those who are frightened by the difficulties are not capable of faithfully interpreting the legitimate aspirations of our people; those who waver before the difficulties do not comprehend the great strength of our people and have not as yet drunk from the cup of determination of our people. Our people have given magnificent lessons in this respect.

Our people resist because they reject integration. Our people resist because they want to live free and independently. Our people resist because they want to be masters of their own destiny. Our heroic people will continue to resist to achieve their sacred objective: national independence.

B. Independence: a Right that cannot be Disputed

1. Yes, independence for the people of East Timor is a right that cannot be disputed—just as the independence of the Great Nation of Indonesia cannot be negotiated and the independence of countries that exist today as part of the world community of nations is not disputed. If this right exists, then this right is inviolable. If justice exists, then let justice be done. If principles exist, then we should all respect those principles.

If justice is accepted, if principles, laws and rights are accepted, but at the same time they are abused, how can one understand the validity and applicability of this justice, these principles, these laws and rights? Is it the case that justice is applied only through the use of force, to subjugate the weak? Is it the case that the principles can be disparaged when an expansionist power has the audacity to do it? Further, is it the law that the small and the weak can be totally subjugated by the strong and the powerful?

Does it also follow that 'rights' benefit only the big and the strong and were not established to defend, in the case of East Timor, the people who demand those rights? Does it follow too that the respected freedoms of the West are called 'justice' when supporting the extermination of a people? Is it the 'law' to deny the right of a people? Is it a 'principle' to be a fervent accomplice in crimes? Is it right that Australia preserves good relations with Jakarta in exchange for the exploration of the Timor Gap?[2]

---

[2] The negotiations over the Timor Gap were concluded three years later with the signing of the Timor Gap Treaty by Australia's Minister for Foreign Affairs, Gareth Evans, and Indonesia's Minister for Foreign Affairs, Ali Alatas, on 11 December 1989. This treaty split the continental shelf between Australia and Timor for the purpose of gas and petroleum exploration. The Indonesian portion was handed back to the Timorese early in 2000.

If the answer is 'yes', then we can say that rights should be understood as the rights of those in the world who can profit from the selling of arms to Indonesia to massacre the people of East Timor. That law should be understood as the capacity of Indonesia to subjugate our people through the show of force; that principles simply support Indonesia by maintaining economic relations with them and that justice is only a beautiful word that can be ignored at will, such as when people turn their backs on the crimes committed in East Timor by the murderous forces of occupation.

But beyond all this, the people of East Timor have not let themselves be intimidated and we are convinced that the right of a people to independence cannot be disputed. It is a right and we are prepared to pay the price that is necessary for it.

2. We understand, however, that the rights of our people to independence should respect the rights of neighbouring countries. We understand that the rights of our people end where the rights of neighbouring countries begin. Yes, in this we agree that safeguarding the interests of each side and the rights of each party should be discussed.

Beloved Youth and Maubere Patriots, we all understand that because of the geo-political position of East Timor, the independence of the Maubere People cannot endanger the peace and stability of our neighbouring countries. We understand very well what this means. It means that the political system put in place in East Timor cannot affect the interests of ASEAN, Australia or the USA. We acknowledge that East Timor is not just part of the whole world, but more particularly part of this region. With this in mind we are disposed to make more compromises beyond the one we made regarding having a democratic, representative-type government system in East Timor and we will follow an economic policy and treaties of cooperation that will not only permit foreign investment of capital (from Australia, Japan and Indonesia itself) but, internally, the development of a mixed (private and public) economy; and that political independence in East Timor will be regulated by the principles and the character of the non-aligned movement, rejecting any form of foreign domination.

We are prepared to be open to concessions of a strategic character and to safeguard the interests of the USA, Australia and ASEAN itself. We declare that we will ensure that these interests will be secured by political mechanisms and guarantees that contribute to the peace, cooperation, understanding and dialogue between East Timor and its neighbours.

But people who think that 'autonomy' is possible tell us, 'But Indonesia would not accept this. But the free world is also not interested in independence for East Timor! The EEC, the USA and Australia look favourably upon the solution of 'autonomy' as a first step to preserve cultural, ethnic and religious identity in East Timor.'

Beloved Youth and Maubere Patriots, I am convinced that between the spectres of our difficulties, which would deny the inalienable rights of our people, lies only one choice: our total extermination. This means that Australia, the USA, the countries of Northern Europe and Portugal are satisfied to secure good economic relations and deep friendships with Indonesia. Our extermination would demonstrate to the world that, 'We die standing', in the words of our very own beloved Monsignor Martinho Lopes.[3]

3. It is a history that beats in the Maubere soul that guides our actions. Certain people with some amazing vision of 'special autonomy' for East Timor say that this is not an important question that needs to be discussed now. In other words, they say that the little people should not be concerned with this question and emphasise that it is only a first step in a 'history that can take many turns'. For us, Beloved Youth and Maubere Patriots, our history belongs to our own people and it is our own people who make our history. Any history that presents Portuguese colonialism as good and says that we should be grateful to the Portuguese is a false history. The history of our people was made with life and blood sacrifices by our people repudiating foreign domination. Any history that speaks of the people of Timor as 'obedient and faithful' and loyal to Portugal, its Motherland, is fabricated and imposed. Some intellectuals today want to see a mention of the people of East Timor 'choosing integration' and receiving the favours of 'special autonomy' written into the history of Indonesia. In the past, our history had the stamp of the Portuguese escudo; today some would like to see the history of East Timor wrapped up by the rupiah.

Beloved Youth and Maubere Patriots, the history of the people of East Timor is a history of blood, of weakness, of difficulties, of civil resistance! The people of East Timor continue today to determine the course of their own history with the words of their own historical existence written in their blood!

Beloved Youth and Maubere Patriots, we have to avoid the confusion that some are creating. Our history is a real fact, lived dramatically; it is a history that beats in the Maubere soul which guides our actions, a history sustained with great suffering from our people. The history of our people also records the

3 Monsignor Martinho do Costa Lopes was the first indigenous leader of the Catholic Church in East Timor. He was Apostolic Administrator of Dili from 1977 to 1983 (See also page 157).

immorality, the political unscrupulousness and the irresponsibility of governments that could stop the extermination of our people. Indonesian history illustrates that they had to resort to arms to expel Dutch colonialism and the history of the people in East Timor follows that same path in order to expel the Indonesian expansionist colonialism. History should not be understood as a random product of chances; history is made and lived. The people of the Philippines applied themselves to bring down the corrupt and despotic Marcos regime; the history of the Philippines cannot attribute the collapse of Marcos to some circumstantial explanation alien to the will of the Philippines people. For that history to be authentic we must emphasise the prolonged struggle of the Philippines people that led to the flight of Marcos! Obviously, we should take into account the favourable circumstances as well as the unfavourable, in determining moments of the struggle, but if the people of the Philippines had not confronted the difficulties peculiar to their own struggle they would not be capable of living in a democracy with the freedom for which they struggled.

Beloved Youth and Maubere Patriots! We should reject false theories that declare 'the future will be determined by God' or that 'in the course of history things will sort themselves out'. These false theories can captivate many unwary people and subjugate the weak of spirit. If rights exist, if principles exist and if justice exists, history cannot express the opposite of the desires of the Maubere People. History cannot condemn our people to extermination. History cannot simply be a witness, impassive and serene, to the genocide that is carried out in East Timor by the barbarian Indonesian occupiers. 'The future will be determined by God', said Mario Carrascalao. You all have learned, Beloved Youth and Maubere Patriots, that God only helps those who help themselves. God only gives grace to those who work at it and he denies his blessing to those who hope to obtain graces without applying themselves to their own development and to the realisation of their ideals and objectives. In the past, many of us went to our *moromak china* [religious Chinese fortune teller] to find out our exam results while the *chinas* studied and passed their exams with very good marks! Why is it that Cardinal Sin of the Philippines, Bishop Tutu and the bishops of Chile did not just support their people from behind, waiting for history to one day solve the socio-political problems of their countries?

I am certain that God will turn his or her back on our people if we simply entertain ourselves by learning the *Pancacila* by heart. It will not be too much longer before some also learn the Koran by heart in the hope of earning a few more rupiahs. Better, they think, to have an 'economic autonomy' within an improved integration into Indonesia that holds an immediate promise of the possibility (since it is said that politics is the art of the possible) of a few more material advantages. In being mollified by the tune of the 'autonomies of the possible' they do not know that they are sacrificing the Maubere consciousness of our people, sacrificing the history of our people simply for the well-being of a privileged few. They will betray the struggle of our people; they will debase the blood spilled by our people and they will deny the sacrifices of all those who fought to defend the inalienable right of the people of East Timor to live freely and independently.

4. The sacrifices taken on by our people are too heavy for us to consent to such acts of treason. The sufferings have been too great for us to permit these fanciful wanderings. Repression was of such a magnitude, the crimes committed in such proportions, that we should not consent to our people continuing to be eternally enslaved! I believe that you, Beloved Youth and Maubere Patriots, are conscious that we cannot allow this injustice to prevail over human rights or brute force to be imposed over moral principles.

The Falintil guerrillas, your blood brothers and children of the same Homeland, prefer to die fighting rather than to consent to what cannot be denied, rather than to betray, and vilify the blood that covers this sacred and beloved Homeland. In the name of these courageous *aswains* [warriors], I have the utmost confidence that you also, Beloved Youth and Maubere Patriots, will not accept the offer of a golden prison in exchange for the fundamental freedoms of the people of East Timor!

C. The Armed Struggle and the Politico-Diplomatic Struggle

Some people believe that the armed struggle pursues an objective exclusive to those in the bush. When some people refer to the armed struggle, they give the impression that they want to remove it from the fundamentals of that armed struggle. As I have told you before, the armed struggle is no more than the extreme expression of our people repudiating the colonial presence. The people of East Timor were forced to offer armed resistance because Indonesia attacked us with so many battalions and its entire war arsenal. We believe that those people who think differently from us do so because they think that independence is an objective only the guerrillas pursue. These people see the continuous brutality of the occupying assassins; they even suffer the continuing repression that the Indonesian bandits exert over a defenceless population and feel in their bones the suffering of the Maubere People penned into concentration camps.

If those people once understood the true character of the struggle and had a true perception of the situation, then today they would not disdain that foundation, which is the real motivation of the Maubere resistance and if they are ignorant of that character it is because they do not allow themselves the labour of profound reflection.

So then, Beloved Youth and Maubere Patriots, I am certain that you understand, as you have already demonstrated in your letter, that it is our people who struggle; that it is all the people of East Timor who resist the barbarian occupation of their Homeland. I am certain that you understand the true character of the criminal repression of the occupants and the continuous popular rejection of the barbarian presence and that you understand also that the armed struggle is the most important aspect that cannot be disconnected from the resistance of our people searching for their independence. The position you affirmed you have taken in your letter is integral to the ten-year popular resistance. The realisation of the youth is a logical consequence, natural and necessary, of what our people want, of the will of our people and of their desire to live freely and independently. You cannot assign to the armed struggle an objective any different from that which the people of East Timor pursue; we cannot define our stance separately from that objective. When you defined your position you went to meet the will of our people; you reaffirmed yourselves as children of this heroic people who have struggled for their independence. While the guerrillas affirmed their determination to continue to defend the rights of our people with the barrels of their guns, you have affirmed your determination with a different type of arms, and you can continue to affirm your tenacity in the battle beside our people and your people against the enormous atrocities of the criminal occupant, affirming the sacred objective while you still have a drop of blood running in your veins—the *independence of our Homeland*.

1. Those who waver can only see the difficulties in terms of the Indonesian battalions which keep coming, described in the rich expression 'continuous invasions': 'the continuous invasions of battalions and armaments and the continuous invasions of transmigrants! Difficult, very difficult ...'—said without strength, defeated and incapable. Never underestimating the might of the human and military power of the Indonesian invader, and the continuing assistance of western nations to improve that might to massacre our people, we reaffirm that the battalions have never scared us, and even less so the threats of Beni Murdani. If the war in East Timor were going to be judged only on the inequality of the forces, then long ago, or better still since 7 December 1975, we would have all agreed to defeat. I believe we can affirm, ten years after that fateful day, and after successive operations aimed at exterminating the guerrillas in the last seven years which have always failed, that it will not be easy for the Indonesian battalions that continually invade our Homeland to exterminate the Fretilin fighters! The Falintil do not underestimate the Indonesian military capacity, firstly, because we are so fully aware of their capacity, but also because Falintil never overestimate the aggressor's soldiery on the battlefield. Falintil are prepared in all ways to continue to inflict as much damage as possible to the Indonesian battalions who come to die in East Timor continually.

We know that we are not capable of expelling the occupier by force, but we affirm that it will not be easy for Beni Murdani to reduce Falintil to dust with his battalions. Because Fretilin are aware that this armed conflict can be prolonged indefinitely, thereby forcing our people to make even bigger sacrifices, they see dialogue as the right way forward, not only to put an end to the war but also to put an end to the suffering of our people. In dialogue you can debate and determine how East Timor can contribute to the peace and stability of the region or, in other words, how it can guarantee that the interests of neighbouring countries are respected while at the same time the Maubere People are guaranteed their legitimate rights. I believe that we are all in agreement that unless there are negotiated solutions which respect the interest of all parties, then the war will only continue to sow the seeds of destruction of our Homeland and will only hasten the extermination of our people while it will continue to cost Jakarta great expense and the death of its soldiers.

The Indonesian generals, surrounded by the gigantic populations of their country, affirm that if an Indonesian soldier dies, a thousand others will take his place; in the battlefield, however, every Indonesian soldier prefers life to the prospect that in place of his dead body a thousand will replace him. We know that the Indonesian generals have come to realise that in East Timor it is the whole people who resist. And while western countries consent, we are certain that Indonesian generals will continue to pursue their murderous will to exterminate the Maubere People.

2. These other people think they understand the superiority military power of the aggressor of our Homeland just as they also understand that political and diplomatic factors will determine either autonomy or our total extermination. They say Portugal does not have representation (either in Jakarta or East Timor) for it to change anything; Australia's position is clear, and the West is not interested. They suppose that our initiatives and the postures that we assume as well as the condemnations, whether by organisations, entities or friendly countries, and the appeals that organisations, entities and other countries send on our behalf in favour of our struggle, are not considered, and we assume that these same people do not attribute any importance to the growing spirit of solidarity surrounding our struggle. These people focus on the force, the crime, the injustice, the unreason, and instead of acquiring a stronger will to struggle, a stronger determination to fight, they let themselves be reassured by the promises of autonomy, presenting it as if it were the only concession that could be expected from all-powerful Indonesia.

Fretilin and the people of East Timor have learnt to make war during war, and principally we have learnt from our own mistakes to make the most diverse of plans. In the realisation of these mistakes, Fretilin have not simply adopted a policy of adaptation but corrected, in certain aspects, their line of political orientation. This correction was aimed not only at giving the resistance struggle, be it armed or passive (and I do not agree with the definition of passive in describing the participation of various political forces and sections of the population inside enemy zones, which I think should really be called active), a truly national character, but also incorporating the defence of our people to live freely and independently while contributing to a solution which safeguards the interests of our neighboring countries, and considering ASEAN itself, Australia and the USA.

Beloved Youth and Maubere Patriots, I think that you also do not put the political focus of the struggle of our people for its liberation in the confidence of the USA, Australia and Western Europe to agree to pressure the Indonesian Government for 'autonomy', but in the stance adopted by Fretilin for:

— non-exclusive representation of the Maubere People, defined in principle in the political sphere as multi-party;
— a disposition to dialogue that opens possibilities for agreement concerning political, economic, cultural and technical cooperation, with Indonesia itself, so as to dissipate all that can threaten peace and stability in the area—this peace that we all desire;
— a disposition to make more compromises that in the long term would contribute to that peace and stability.

So, Beloved Youth and Maubere Patriots, I believe that all of you understand that Fretilin's stance is a political attitude, a demonstration of goodwill to resolve this conflict through dialogue and understanding, by co-operation and by good neighbourliness, between East Timor, Indonesia, Australia and other nearby countries, including Japan. The change from the previous political radicalism should be acknowledged in the political arena and you should acknowledge in the political arena the principles today defended by Fretilin: political pluralism, mixed economy and non-alignment. You should also acknowledge in the political arena our intention to respect the interests of ASEAN, Australia and the USA. I think you would agree with me that aside from the armed struggle, we are also developing a political policy with the view of trying to assure the world we will contribute in whatever way is necessary to peace and stability in the region while at the same time our people can assert their right to live freely and independently. We place our good intentions to the world in the diplomatic arena, assuring everyone that we all act in good faith and with responsibility, and that the credentials for this political responsibility are these last ten years of blood! And in the diplomatic arena we will continue to battle so that the free world acknowledges this reality and so that everyone will realise that just solutions are solutions that respect the interests of all those involved and all interested parties. We have a few friends, it is true—our duty, our task, is to give them the capacity to promote and defend the just cause of our people with the objective that these few dedicated and faithful friends can in their own way make the sceptics and indifferent aware. We can only count on the people of the Third World, the small and weak people—people like us who have struggled for their liberation, because to these people our cause is also their cause. And, above all, we should persist in the struggle, because nothing can be achieved without hard work, without diligence, without vicissitude, without sweat, without tears, without blood!

Your own document is enveloped within the plans of the resistance of our people. I believe also that you, like me, will reject the idea that the political struggle be circumscribed by the manipulations of those who desire the death of our people.

3. Others suggest that in the political arena we cannot do anything: that the world has turned against us, that Indonesia is against us, that Indonesia gets everything, and is supported by the EEC, Australia and the USA etc, etc … We recognise that we cannot really influence the EEC, and we cannot expect that the USA will lift a finger to stop the continuous wave of terror and crime exercised over our people by the murderous forces of occupation. We also recognise that we cannot influence the government of *Senhor* Bob Hawke. We realise that these all-powerful of the world, the EEC, Australia and the USA, hold in their hands the destiny of the world's people. We cannot say to Australia, for example, that the people of East Timor would reject the idea of Australia exploiting the Timor Gap because *Senhor* Bob Hawke, in recognising Indonesian sovereignty over our Homeland, gave our oil Indonesian citizenship—we cannot even propose, let's suppose, to Japan that it can come and fish in our territorial waters, because in recognising the integration of East Timor Tokyo turned our maritime platform into another Indonesian citizen!

And if here, on our doorstep, we cannot influence anything, we have even less influence when we set our sights on Europe or the USA, firstly because being so far away they can simply distance themselves from the problem, while all the time some governments keep on handing Jakarta new material with which to massacre our people—and others because they are interested in Indonesia exterminating our people.

We have all noticed, Beloved Youth and Maubere Patriots, the great difficulties that are associated with the resistance of our people, in that we cannot even offer what is ours; we cannot even invite these countries to invest in our land because they have bought it directly from Indonesia in exchange for good relations. While we are not scared by these difficulties, there are some who are terrified by this complicity in the extermination of our people: of the complicity of Australia and of other countries, including Portugal. I almost forgot Portugal. Portugal is irresponsible because during the last ten years it has been the principal support of the genocide practised in Timor; Portugal which is more interested in coming out with its honour intact, and which is trying to superimpose that honour over its obligations concerning the rights of the people of East Timor, in spite of its platitudinous declarations of 'goodwill'.

However, we should all possess the conviction that in spite of the factors repeatedly being mentioned by some media and experts of the 'Indonesian phenomenon' which emphasise the great capacity of Indonesia (member of the UN, fifth-most populous nation in the world, member of the OPEC, co-founder of the non-aligned movement, No. 1 member of ASEAN, very important member of the Islamic Conference, etc, etc) we should realise that if the people of East Timor cannot influence Australia or the EEC or the USA, then Indonesia cannot guarantee that it can influence the whole world either. We believe that in spite of the great capacity of Indonesia, those countries that are lovers of peace and justice will understand the struggle of our people for self-determination and national independence. In spite of all this, we can be confident that the Australian people, the American people and the people of Western Europe, as well as the peoples of the Third World, will continue to support our struggle and will not permit crime to win over reason, and will not allow the complicity and indifference of the governments who insult the rights and principles for which millions of people the world over have given their lives!

Therefore, in the diplomatic arena as well as in the political arena, we will continue to be firm in the position we have already taken, for we believe that if democracy in the Philippines has not changed the face of ASEAN, neither will a pluralist political system affect peace and stability in the region. Even so, the people of East Timor are prepared to maintain intact the interests of the

USA and Australia and Indonesia by signing accords of cooperation and peace treaties. Beloved Youth and Maubere Patriots, I have the profound conviction that the position you have assumed is just a first step in the difficult process of the defence of the inalienable rights of our people.

4. Only an immoral policy can justify the subservient nature of some western countries to the Jakarta government. Bill Hayden, intimidated by the attitude of Jakarta to the controversial article in the *Sydney Morning Herald*[4], placed the Telecom contract, worth millions of dollars, above the freedom of the Australian mass media. In such a trivial matter, in which Australia has chosen the path of submission to Indonesia, we can have no expectation that Australia will not continue to sacrifice its principles and would attack Indonesia over the question of East Timor. And even though *Senhor* Bob Hawke has 'called attention' to the different nature of the two governments, we are sure that if Mochtar's[5] screams become just a little bit more irritated, then *Senhor* Hawke will hasten to limit the freedom of the press in his own country, so as not to add to the susceptibility of the regime in Jakarta. We also make the commitment to refrain from making a single unfavourable comment against the Grand Nation of Indonesia, according to the principle of non-interference. But not even this commitment would be enough for Australia because we anticipate that Canberra is prepared to convince Australians to submit their freedoms to the whims of its powerful and important neighbours. It seems incredible, but the reality as we understand it, as we feel with our own flesh, is that Australia shuts its eyes to the crimes committed in East Timor! And we have no doubt that at the next Labor Party Conference, *Senhors* Bob Hawke and Bill Hayden will do everything in their power to ensure that the Labor Party recognise, as legitimate and legal, on the basis of the principles of democracy and freedom, the criminal military occupation of East Timor—and will use the expression 'the full and authentic Indonesian sovereignty over East Timor by the will of its own people' which is more to do with the pressing necessity of maintaining good relations with Jakarta! Then Mochtar will not sulk and force *Senhor* Bill Hayden to run to Jakarta and apologise! The Maubere People expect from these two gentlemen anything but a principled position worthy of Labor officials, anything but a position based on morality

[4] Reference to a front-page article by David Jenkins in the *Sydney Morning Herald*, April 1986, criticising Suharto.

[5] Mochtar Kusumaatmaja was the Indonesian Minister for Foreign Affairs. He represented Indonesia at the UN-sponsored talks between Indonesia and Portugal that first took place on 24 September 1985.

and justice, on law and international norms. The Maubere People only ask (if they have the right to ask anything of the defenders of the Indonesian criminal occupation) that the blood that has been spilt in defending their Homeland not be insulted (as it was two years ago).

However, even in the face of these events, we know our determination to continue to fight for the rights of our people is unshakable and this is reinforced all the more by the people of East Timor choosing their path: Homeland or death! All those who fight for national independence! If East Timor has to become a 'burnt land' after 'the vultures of Java come to graze' over our corpses (and the expression is not mine) and the countries of the EEC and the USA and Australia can breathe more easily after the removal of the stumbling block from their relations with Indonesia, congratulating Jakarta for having, with incomparable heroism, freed humanity from a pest (called the Maubere People), then we will all accept this today and let it become a lesson to all small and defenceless people. This would be a lesson that justice, law and rights and principles only exist for the big and powerful to entertain when it does not affect their interests; a lesson that in the end everything—force, crime, aggression—is acceptable and everyone must be prepared for it! Only the people of East Timor, small and defenceless, poor and weak, have no resources other than to count on their own strength to secure a dignified death—a death, an extermination, desired by Australia, EEC and the USA, and planned previously by Portugal in secret agreement with Indonesia, that same Portugal which today appears to have a manifest lack of interest in the case.

II. Homeland or Death!

I believe very strongly, as you do, that autonomy is a mirror illusion. I also believe that it is inappropriate to debate point by point all the aspects of this supposed autonomy. Ha! 'Special autonomy for East Timor', in the 'Great Indonesian Nation'. But I would like to refute some of the principal aspects, and consider those points on which we should remain firm in the defence of our rights.

1. What do we understand to be our historical identity? The historical identity of the people of East Timor is not a simple effect of the colonial system, in our case, Portuguese colonialism. Portuguese colonial domination is a phenomenon that must be taken into account, in truth, since European colonialism, or, better said, the colonial possessions determined the appearance of the new states that emerged after domination of one people by another was ended. The phenomenon of colonialism is only a complementary aspect of the new era of liberation of peoples and the formation of new nations.

The historical identity of East Timor dates back to long before the arrival of the Portuguese. If it had not been for the intrusion of Portuguese colonialism, the people of East Timor would have followed their own path; they would have created a socio-political structure defined by the essence of one people and one nation. With the arrival of the colonialists, this march was halted because the necessity of exploring our wealth caused a war of pacification[6] that put a stop to the struggles between the diverse kingdoms, each one wanting to take a position of ascendancy and domination over the others. The ascendancy of one of these tribes would have determined the formation of a great kingdom—the embryo of the Maubere Homeland!

Though the future of our Homeland and our people was smothered by the colonial presence, this fact must be taken into account only up to a certain point, since against a common enemy, an aggressive intruder, the march of our history did not change direction, but simply gained new character. We say 'new character' because if we put aside the tribal fights, the kingdoms together formed an alliance to expel the foreign oppressor from what was already being considered a common Homeland: this new character united the common aspirations and the will of all. It is out of this common character that an understanding that this piece of land is ours was generated. A feeling was generated in all the kingdoms of a common heritage, and the notion that we were all equal to, while at the same time different from, the Portuguese who wanted to dominate us. And it is because of this, because this character gave all the kingdoms a common motive, a united cause in the civil resistance against Portuguese colonialism, that I say we should consider it a common Homeland.

This prolonged struggle of our ancestors speaks for itself as a definition of our historical identity. In spite of the Portuguese domination, the East Timorese people did not lose their awareness that their history was being subjected to, made dependent on, an exterior force more powerful than themselves. In their life-style and festivals, our people did not evoke the arrival of the Portuguese, but remembered, through the tales of their elders and the past generations, the blood ties between the different kingdoms. The people of East Timor were never totally subjugated by the foreigners and always rebelled against those who stopped the free course of their history. The proof of this is that only in 1912 was East Timor practically beaten by the colonial power. The war of opposition to Portuguese domination and the particular presence of colonialism were the other two factors that assured the continuity of our own history and the unique identity of the East Timorese people.

---

6 The 'Pacification Wars' took place between the late 1880s until 1912, including 'The Great Rebellion', 1910–1912.

This identity carries on, perpetuated by ten years of blood spilt by the Indonesian military occupation. This Maubere awareness has never been quelled, either by the *palmatoria,*[7] or with colonial laws, but these things forged and created foundations for our historical identity. This Maubere consciousness, the historical identity, proper and genuinely Maubere, does not bow before massacres, persecution, banishment or torture. It is for this identity that the struggle is affirmed, with blood and death. The Maubere People accepted all the sacrifices demanded of them and will continue to accept what is necessary to preserve that which has been so zealously sought and guarded under the protection of the people's *luliks* [sacred objects] and constantly relived through the oral tradition. This is a sacred patrimony, a sacred heritage that our ancestors were able to bequeath and leave to us: *the consciousness that we are a people and that we are making our own history!*

Consequently, Beloved Youth and Maubere Patriots, it is simply wrong, inappropriate and alienating to think that the historical identity of the People of East Timor could be maintained within the Great Indonesian Nation, and that ties could be maintained with the old colonial power which has, in so cowardly a way, abandoned us and left our people to the plight of extermination. It is wrong to think that the people of East Timor can be compensated for genocide with promises of the 'preservation of their historical identity' by Indonesia agreeing that 'in East Timor Portuguese can be spoken' or that instead of the *lagu-lagu* [Indonesian songs] the Maubere consciousness could be put to sleep with *saudissimo fado*![8] We energetically repudiate that the struggle and the suffering of our people can be limited to 'the preservation of the Portuguese culture' and it is our repudiation that constitutes the principal defining aspect of the Maubere People's historical identity.

A people who were enslaved by Portugal and kept in complete underdevelopment for centuries cannot tolerate a Portugal which today demonstrates such indifference and lack of interest in the genocide committed here, considering that to speak Portuguese in East Timor is more important than our fight to live freely, independently and in peace. We have heard rumours stating that the previous Portuguese government (the socialists)[9] felt shocked with criti-

7 The *palmatoria* was a Portuguese device for physical punishment, used by striking the palm of the hand. It has been described variously as a short whip, a cane and a flat piece of wood with holes.

8 *Saudissimo* describes a particular emotion, with no direct translation from Portuguese, of a nostalgic longing for a return to former days and *fado* means fate or destiny. These themes are expressed in the popular plaintive Portuguese musical genre also called *fado*.

9 Parliamentary elections in April 1983 had brought socialist Mário Soares back into power as Prime Minister. In parliamentary elections in April 1976, the Socialists won a plurality of the vote, and Soares, their leader, became Prime Minister. The country experienced severe economic problems and in mid-1978 Soares was dismissed.

cisms of them from Fretilin and that this fact was impeding 'contact' with Fretilin. We only regret that Portugal feels victimised by the accusations of Fretilin. Innocent Portugal could not accept that it was criticised for what it confirms itself: inability, and what its eminent politicians do not want to admit, lack of interest and an extremely weak position as administering power. In spite of this, there are those amongst us who think we should preserve the Portuguese language in autonomous East Timor as a basis of the preservation of our historical identity. Such an identity would only remind the children of our children that East Timor was first colonised by Portugal and in this way is different from the Great Indonesian Nation!

When it is mentioned to those people mollified by the fanciful idea that our historical identity can be preserved by freely speaking Portuguese—that Portugal has responsibility in the matter of East Timor—these people lament, 'It is a pity Portugal is so far away! It is difficult, it is difficult …'. The fact that Portugal is so far away just means that they think that their responsibility is far away as well. Should the fact that the Portuguese are so far away mean that the rights of the East Timorese people are out of the reach of the hands of Portuguese politicians and government? I think it is wrong to be taking into account distance in relation to the responsibilities of Portugal, while at the same time asking for 'the concession to speak Portuguese' in East Timor. In the end, we could hypothesise (correctly) that the problem of 'distance' expounded by those considering the possibility of 'autonomy' is simply one of money: escudos have a very long 'distance' to travel while the rupiah can arrive weekly on a *Garuda* plane. If we are correct in our hypothesis, then the historical identity being promoted is false; no more than a naïve cover-up! Beloved Youth and Maubere Patriots, we should stand firmly and not permit the alienation of the struggle of the thousand-times heroic people of East Timor!

Our struggle is difficult, our path is full of obstacles and it is only through total confidence in the strength of our people irrigated by their own blood, strengthened and fertilised by fallen bodies and with an always-renewing faith that we can (if we all put our shoulders to the wheel) guarantee our people the realisation of their objective: securing our own historical identity!

2. Those who think that 'special autonomy' for East Timor can be based on the three levels of identity—ethnic, cultural and religious—are blind. They are being blinded by an idea that in the puppet government, of the *kabupaten* [regions] and *kecamatan* [administrative units], etc., they think they will be the only ones to benefit from the Indonesian rupiah. You said, Beloved Youth and Maubere Patriots, '… the People of East Timor do not struggle to get a house, food, clothes and other material goods from Indonesia.' Our people may be illiterate but they know their own conscience better than many engineers, doctors and educated people who only have the eyes and conscience to read the million digits on the inflationary rupiah! 'Yes, [the Maubere People] struggle and sacrifice the lives of their children because they want to be free and manage their destiny. In other words, the Maubere People know the "why" of their own struggle!' Yes, Beloved Youth and Maubere Patriots, the people of East Timor know that they can be free and independent and are capable of developing the many different aspects of their own identity with all their energy. They know they are capable of constructing their own future.

We should not let ourselves fall for the illusion, as some people do, that under the status of autonomy (special or not) we could demand an end to transmigration. Those people think that half an island made up of less than 400,000 inhabitants could stop a plan supported by many western countries. Beloved Youth and Maubere Patriots, I introduce to you one example among many that you know, to illustrate what a future East Timor would be like under 'autonomy'.

By the middle of 1977, in much of Tutuala as well as in the eastern *suco* of Loikero/Mehara, the population had been captured. Before this and the operation to capture the population, the occupier had created a lot of propaganda by taking photos in which clothing and food were being distributed (as were many pamphlets about it). To top it off, the occupier said that Jakarta would distribute clothes and food to those that would surrender and that Fretilin had nothing to give. In the photographs it appeared as if they distributed everything the people needed but in reality there were just a few dirty rags and some rotting corn for the people, who did not even want it. The people of Mehara and Porlamano had finished the food taken from the jungle and because they had been prevented from maintaining their own vegetable gardens, they met and decided to make a petition to the occupier reminding them what they had promised and that they had not yet received any food or clothing. They communicated this to Los Palos, and the commander of *Kodim* immediately travelled to Mehara with Claudio Vieira and Luis Monteiro acting as faithful interpreters. The commander ordered the population to gather and ordered the local company to encircle the people with their guns pointing. Standing at the front and with one machine gun on either side ready to fire, the commander yelled, 'I know that you are politicals and that you like to play at democracy. Democracy exists in the jungle; here democracy is what you see. You don't yet know what the TNI can do. Now I want you to speak; now make your demands!' The terrified people did not utter a word, and only under threat of being shot down did the local chiefs dare to speak but now it was to apologise and to 'explain that the people were stupid and spoke without thinking'. Like a rabid dog, the official Indonesian assassin still harangued the people: 'This is the first and only time that this happens. The second time you will see what happens to you!' Not long after this, seven people in Mehara and five in Porlamano were assassinated because of the distrust caused.

Beloved Youth and Maubere Patriots! The illusion of a special autonomy will come crashing to the ground; what happened in Mehara happens in the whole of East Timor and it will be too late for those people who believe in false propaganda to reconcile their thinking. Why do I say that it will be too late for those people? Because it is those people who feed these illusions. They should reconcile their ideas and reconsider their weaknesses now because we, Beloved Youth and Maubere Patriots, all of us in the jungle and all of you who are studying, will not betray the immense sacrifices of our people for a few photographs in which a few crumbs are distributed to slaves!

3. You do not study just to secure a few rupiahs in your pocket for the future while your people suffer from hunger and disease and are assassinated in a cowardly way! You do not study to be Indonesian *pegawai* [public servants], Timorese *bupat* [regional administrators], or anything else, while our people struggle to free themselves of the eternal chains of colonial slavery. Your educational development should have the objective of serving your Homeland! Your development should be regulated by knowing that is our duty to understand better the struggle of our people. It is your duty to interpret the struggle of our people with objectivity and strength. It is your duty to act in order to defend in all circumstances the aspirations of our people. So you will continue to demonstrate that you are the children of the heroic people and you will continue to fulfil your duty as the children of East Timor and our beloved Homeland!

Unfortunately, many of those that are capable of understanding the supreme aspirations of our people, abandon our people for cars, houses, rupiahs, *gudan-garam* cigarettes and *super-mi* noodles. Others are learning to pronounce a few Bahasa words to pretend that they were born in the same cradle as Suharto; some after being 'promoted' to the echelon of *jutas* [millionaires] have the obsession of becoming *Gubernur* of bags of rupiahs. They are failures. They are people without ideals, without objectives, without soul. They conceive of freedom in bowing down, stretching out their hands for the rupiahs of the oppressors of our people. They conceive of the Homeland in the leaves of the 10,000-rupiah notes they receive. They conceive of the people as *kartu penduduk* [identity cards], which give them all they need at the expense of our people. They are the bastards of the criminal occupier; they are people selling themselves and worst of all, selling off our Homeland and our people.

But, Beloved Youth and Maubere Patriots, the youth is the promising force of our people; the youth is the hope of constructing our Homeland; the youth is the guarantee of the future of our nation. You are this force; you are this hope; you are the guarantee. Our people's eyes rest on you; our elders, our fathers, are giving you the duty to continue this struggle. Many young people have already given their lives for this struggle. Very many of our *companheiros,* young like you, have fallen beside our parents. Many others of a young age—some students and some not—continue to participate in the struggle of us all. Children of two, three, four and five years of age are already working for the resistance of our people—many of them have suffered imprisonment, torture, banishment and threats! Many of them bear these atrocities with heroism, and are not fooled by the sweets which the criminal occupiers offer them to buy information about their parents, their relatives and colleagues! They are living examples of courage, living examples of the struggle, living examples of a conscience that is transmitted from parents to children—from the massacred parents to the orphans who survive—this conscience runs in the Maubere blood in our veins, impregnates our flesh and penetrates our bones and our innermost being!

This patriotic torrent cannot be extinguished; on the contrary, it will increase incessantly. Five- to ten-year-old schoolchildren in our Homeland know as much as the adults about the subordination tactics of the enemy, of counter-information, of bribery and about the persecution of the clandestine organisation. These children, born during war, make war; a war that is not just of their parents, a war that is not just theirs—a war, a resistance, of an entire people against a foreigner occupier! I know that you are persecuted and spied upon, but I also know that you have experienced in our Homeland a richness, painful at times, but not small, marked by unmeasured euphoria, by the happiness of having been able to do something right under the noses of the enemy who persecutes you and who would not leave you in peace, by the feeling of exhilaration that 'the Maubere can do more than the stupid Indonesians'. Some have been asked more of than others; however, the experience of each of you, in spite of this variation, has the common element of the fulfilment of duty! I have visited many concentration camps and I can assure you that the continuity of our efforts in the struggle of East Timor will never end while the murderous forces of occupation remain in our Homeland. From the elderly to the children, from the women to the youth, all participate vigorously, demanding that the guerrillas not surrender because it would, according to their words, be 'the end of us all'.

Beloved Youth and Maubere Patriots studying in Indonesia and East Timor! I know that you know all that I am telling you because you have always been part of it, from the joy of success achieved through hardship, from a trusting smile to encourage a *companheiro* in difficulty, to the tears caused by the vicissitudes imposed by this repression. Your document dated 7 September 1985 is significant because as the rest of the world celebrates the International Year of Youth with festivals, demonstrations and ovations, there, in Indonesia, young Mauberes celebrate the year by taking a patriotic and political position of great profoundness, an unequivocal and most appropriate response to the untruthful declaration of the assassin Suharto that the people of East Timor 'wish' to integrate! Here in our Homeland, many of your *companheiros*, young like you, children of our people and of the same Homeland, brothers of the same blood that runs in your veins, have given their lives to the Homeland, massacred by the enemy, tortured and enduring the difficult situation that our people are going through, dying of starvation and illness.

Beloved Youth and Maubere Patriots! Your intellectual formation, your development of technical skills, is one of the many fronts of the struggle of our people. Your dedication to study is a dedication to our Homeland, to our people. Continue forward and we will show the world and those incredulous people that we are capable of raising the walls of our Homeland ourselves and that we will be able to manage ourselves and our own destiny. The adversities you find are the difficulties that face us all in the world-wide struggle of our heroic people; the victories that you achieve with your endeavours are successes for all of us involved in the difficult processes of the liberation of our people. Your young *companheiros* in the mountains of our Homeland asked me to express to you their total confidence that you will continue firm in the defence of the rights of our people and their certainty that you will continue to repudiate, as you have been doing, all forms of disunity in our Homeland.

III. End of the Conflict

1. Portugal's position

An 'honourable peace' for the East Timor conflict that is being spoken about makes it obvious that this peace can only eventuate with the integration of the territory, with or without autonomy. This 'honourable peace', which can only come about by the absence of war, means still subjecting our people to the aggressive expansionist policies and the genocide imposed by Jakarta. So who deserves such an 'honourable peace'?

According to reliable sources, we can assume that Portugal is trying to extricate itself from the problem with its honour intact and, as the facts have demonstrated, Portugal is more interested in selling off the sovereignty of East Timor to Indonesia than in resolving the case properly. We can see the Portuguese touch in this arrangement! Beyond this realisation we have witnessed the lack of interest of Portugal in doing anything to help the Maubere People, and have also noticed its interest in recognising the annexation of East Timor, in return for those Timorese holding Portuguese passports. This does not deceive us. These exchanges have the same value as the exchanges that our people used to make of kid goats with pigs and horses with buffalo. It is extremely shocking that having condemned us to the condition of slaughtered animals, they search throughout the penned flock for those who carry the brand of their masters on their hindquarters. Our blood boils with repulsion and our repudiation increases with the realisation that all this only serves to deceive the world that these are 'important Indonesian concessions' on 'humanitarian questions'.[10]

The invisible threads, linking the autonomy option, are starting to become visible and we note that they link Portugal and Australia, the countries of the EEC and the USA and, you never can tell, maybe even the Muslim representatives in the UN.[11] This is a giant conspiracy to kill the Maubere People! Portugal would be satisfied with the promise that in 'the far away Southern Indian Ocean there would be a certain number of people "dedicated" to preserving the presence of Portuguese culture'. What a great honour—to speak Portuguese—after the Maubere People have witnessed the genocide of more than 200,000 of its children! The Maubere People suffer: are tortured in prison, die of hunger and disease, are exiled and massacred for the great hon-

[10] Xanana uses inverted commas around the phases used during the UN talks. Jose Ramos-Horta describes the first UN-sponsored meeting between Portuguese and Indonesian foreign ministers: '... the two parties again discussed only side issues of a humanitarian nature, such as the repatriation of Portuguese nationals and Timorese civil servants who refuse to abandon Portuguese nationality. The fact that there is even talk about "repatriation of Portuguese nationals" implies Portugal's recognition that East Timor is no longer a Portuguese territory. A government does not repatriate its nationals from its own territory!' (Ramos-Horta, 1989, p. 171).

[11] Most Islamic nations voted with Indonesia in UN resolutions over East Timor. Dunn outlines the factions: 'During the eighties Indonesia made some gains in the diplomatic maneuvering behind the diplomatic debate. Its hardcore support came, predictably from ASEAN states, Latin American nations under right-wing regimes with poor records in the field of human rights, most Islamic states, Japan, India and to a lesser extent Australia and the United States' (Dunn, 1996, p. 329).

This may also refer to the Under Secretary General of the United Nations, Rafeeuddin Ahmed, a Pakistani diplomat. He was assistant to the Secretary General of the UN, Perez de Cuellar, and assigned the problem of East Timor. His performance and that of his Assistant, Hedi Annabi of Tunisia, in mediating on the problem of East Timor from 1982 to 1991, were considered to be very partial, in favour of Indonesia. Horta thinks they had developed 'strong ties' with Indonesia in previous dealings with them over the Cambodian conflict (Ramos-Horta, 1989, p. 167).

our of speaking Portuguese! The poor Maubere People do not know that they are fighting and struggling and dying just so that they will be 'guaranteed' of speaking Portuguese in an integrated East Timor. The poor Maubere People do not know that they are fighting and dying just to save Portuguese honour.

Australia would also emerge from this agreement with their share of honour—of this we should have no doubt. Australia will say that it was the effort made by *Senhor* Bill Morrison that achieved these 'great and important Indonesian concessions' as suggested in August last year, by *Senhor* Bob Hawke, when he stated that Indonesia should arrange an opportunity to legitimise the annexation by the 'will of the population'.[12] This was a clear indication of the policy of *Senhor* Bob Hawke trying to save the honour of Australia while at the same time our people were being killed. As we have said, Australia is attempting to try to tidy away the problem of East Timor with honour, not only as *Senhor* Bob Hawke has the honour of participating, in effect, in the plot practised by Jakarta, but also because he will secure the honour of guaranteeing the exploration of oil and natural gas that are ours. There is no justice, and rights and laws are just empty words; principle as well as honour is two-faced. Who says that Hitler did not have his own sense of honour? P. W. Botha, Pinochet, Duvalier—all of them had a definition of honour! Marcos of the Philippines also assured himself of an honourableness respected by *Senhor* Bob Hawke and *Senhor* Bill Hayden, the same gentlemen who then had the boldness to be critical of his corruption and violations of human rights—but that is honour! *Senhor* Bob Hawke maintains this pragmatic concept of honour when he gives his support to Jakarta against our people! How the bloody hell can this be honour? Is it honourable to participate in the slaughter of a defenceless population? Is it honourable to recognise as fair the repression that Jakarta exercises over the Maubere People? I think that for *Senhor* Hawke this is the lowest sense of hon-

[12] Bill Morrison had served as Minister for Defence under then Prime Minister Gough Whitlam in 1975 and was therefore familiar with the conspiracy that surrounded the Indonesian invasion. In July 1983, he led an Australian Parliamentary Delegation to Timor 'whose report remains a scathing indictment of the mission's insensitivity to the human rights dimensions of the problem' (Dunn). The Morrison Report was used by the Prime Minister, Bob Hawke, and his Minister for Foreign Affairs, Bill Hayden, to frustrate attempts to condemn Indonesia and support East Timorese self-determination. (See footnote 18 on Australian Labor Party National Conference in July 1984.) Dunn comments, 'Perhaps his [Hayden's] most cynical act was to appoint Bill Morrison as Ambassador to Indonesia' (Dunn, 1996, pp. 347-8).

Bob Hawke and Bill Hayden oversaw a reversal in Labor Party policy on East Timor after they came to office in 1983, although Hayden had been strongly critical, while in Opposition, of the Fraser government's policy on East Timor. On 18 August 1985, Prime Minister Bob Hawke recognised Indonesian sovereignty over East Timor on behalf of his Labor Government, then began discussions about joint explorations of the Timor Gap with Indonesia in October.

our because the solution that satisfies Jakarta's generals and preserves Australia's good relations also guarantees the exploration of the Timor Gap. This is the way Australia contributes to an 'honourable peace'!

For the EEC, an 'honourable solution' (and the subjugation of the people of East Timor) is one that avoids any friction with Indonesia. Honour also exists for them in this solution which avoids any embarrassment in their solid relations with Jakarta and this honour safeguards these relations which involve permitting Indonesia to do anything—use force, crime and even commit genocide! As far as the countries of the EEC are concerned, the people of East Timor could disappear from the face of the earth, because the human race would not even miss them. Anyway, Indonesia, the friendly country, the good ally, the sound economic partner, member of OPEC, member of the Islamic League, member of NAM, of ASEAN, etc, has a surplus of people that it sends to Timor, compensating for the extermination of the Maubere People. No one can deny this honour, least of all the Maubere People, who are condemned to disappear to save everyone else's honour! And what of the USA, of whom we are afraid to say anything at all for fear of being branded communists? In considering us communists, the USA has been able to supply the most varied assortment of armaments to Jakarta to enable them to continue to kill us. Because the USA has been doing this for ten years, even though we have stated we are not communists, they will continue to support Indonesia, because they want the people of East Timor to effectively disappear—the continued massacres, the obligatory birth control and *transmigrassi* prove their real intentions! The Maubere People have to accept extermination because in their extermination so much honour will be saved!

I am not even going to mention the Eastern Bloc, because from all sides, fingers of satisfaction would be pointed saying, 'See, they really are communists!' The silence and indifference of countries is the general position but even this does not scare the Maubere People. The excursion of the assassin Suharto to the countries of Eastern Europe, the recent economic agreement between Jakarta and Moscow and the support given by Yugoslavia to Indonesia in Luanda[13] are all part of the world condemnation that smothers the people of East Timor! The Maubere People are surrounded by a vast ocean of interests that must be protected, of honour that must be saved: from the backwardness of Portuguese colonialism imposed on us, up to the actual Indonesian block-

13 Xanana refers to a ministerial meeting of the Non-Aligned Movement in September 1983 in Luanda, in which a delegation from Yugoslavia actively opposed any mention of East Timor in the final declaration. They may have been reluctant to oppose Indonesia as a founding member of NAM.

ade; from the age-old Portuguese domination to the Indonesian military occupation; from Portuguese lack of interest to the immorality of the Australian government; from the indifference of governments who could help our people to the conspiracy that today beckons frustrated and susceptible East Timorese. *East Timor is a true struggle!* We have only the consolation that we will die standing, without tears, because we have already buried them alongside the victims of the Indonesian repression, without one single moan because our moans only outrage the honour of all those who persistently desire our extermination! But, at least, *we will die standing!*

2. Beloved Youth and Maubere Patriots, how can we conceive of 'an honourable solution' or 'an honourable peace'?

In the first place, we should try to understand the concept of an honourable solution. It must be understood as a solution in which none of the parties would be humiliated through having been defeated; an honourable solution would mean putting aside the armed conflict and in this way beginning along a new path that would guarantee respect for the interests of all parties. An honourable solution implies a predisposition towards a non-military solution and a will to end the conflict between all interested parties. This attitude would be regulated by a sense of justice and a respect for principles and the international community.

Thus we understand an honourable solution to be born from dialogue, a solution that is the fruit of all agreements, a solution that establishes peace, a solution that records the rights and duties of each party; finally, a solution that complements cooperation and the spirit of good neighbourliness. We, the other party in the armed conflict, have already demonstrated:

— a will to put an end to the war;
— a disposition to talk with Indonesia;
— an interest in contributing to peace and stability in the region;
— the wish to respect the interests of the USA, as well as of Australia and Indonesia.

Only Jakarta continues to be intransigent, with its obsession to totally annihilate the Maubere People using its entire military and human might. This intransigence reveals one objective: to exterminate the people of East Timor, for which it has the support of many countries, like Australia! We cannot forget that Australia, Portugal, the countries of the EEC, the USA and Japan see favourably, that which a good son of East Timor defined as the 'continued invasion' of transmigrants! The inflexible attitude of Jakarta, apparent in its barking of orders, its intolerance, its imposition of obligations upon others, is only half the problem.

The other half is the promotion by all these other countries of Jakarta's inflexible attitude because they want to avoid a confrontation with irritable Mochtar or with the insolence of Beni Murdani. It is because of this they support Jakarta in the extermination of our people! This political subservience to the murderous generals of Jakarta by countries which desire the death of our people retards an honourable solution, and prevents any efforts for this or for an honourable peace!

3. Beloved Youth and Maubere Patriots! Are we all to assume that an honourable solution (so we can create a true and long-lasting peace in the territory) includes the whole world bowing their heads to the will of Jakarta?

Does the world have to say yes to whatever Jakarta wants and if Jakarta refuses be obliged to agree with them? I think that you, Beloved Youth and Maubere Patriots, are also supporters of an honourable solution and an honourable peace that should result in a dialogue in which arrangements guarantee peace for us all. Thus, to think of an 'autonomy' for East Timor that will bring an honourable peace is pure subjectivity, purely an unrealistic dream. Let us analyse why this attitude is superficial:

— the nationalist conscience of our people is strong and their patriotic spirit is fervent;
— the Timorese inside the enemy army participate in battles and at decisive moments change sides to the armed resistance;
— many of those in Battalions 744 and 745[14] were targets of persecution by the occupiers, some savagely massacred and others arrested or exiled;
— the repudiation of integration rose in direct proportion to the intensity of the increasing repression and crime and the contempt by the occupier. These will only die with the death of our people.

A 'special autonomy' in which 'everything' will be put in the hands of the children of a people who want their independence, yet who would not be permitted a national insurrection is ridiculous. Would it not simply create a certain and inevitable insurrection that would in turn provoke a new invasion, new destruction, new massacres, new genocide? I can affirm with both my hands on the Bible that no-one will be able to restrain the popular will to continue to pursue the sacred objective of national independence.

Will the honourable solution of 'autonomy' really bring a true and long lasting peace to East Timor? We are all certain that it will not; we are all conscious that solutions like these, besides being dishonourable, will not contribute to a true peace in our Homeland. And all who think the contrary are

[14] Xanana refers to the East Timorese soldiers who were recruited to become part of the Indonesian occupation forces, Battalions 744 and 745.

only giving more trump cards to Jakarta to pursue the genocide that they have been committing for the last ten years. In 1980, we travelled through the central region of the country and the cunning and murderous Iswanto proposed to us a strategy ordained by Jakarta that consisted of:

— laying down of arms and stoppage of resistance in other forms;
— a contribution to the emancipation firstly of Sumatra, next Kalimantan, followed by Sulawesi and Irian Jaya;
— finally, that conditions would then be ripe for Timor to 'also' gain independence.

This official Indonesian assassin took us to be naïve, but today many children of East Timor are seduced by the same propaganda, dressed up more enticingly as special autonomy for East Timor!

Any honourable solution that has the aim of putting an end to the suffering of our people and guaranteeing a true 'honourable peace' should recognise the right of our people to independence. This will only result from a shift in Jakarta's attitudes. Fretilin has already initiated a demonstration of goodwill in the effort to find an honourable peace for both sides. Jakarta must also make some concessions; firstly, they should change their absurd and immoral attitude of pursuing the extermination of our people. Jakarta will never do this if Australia, the USA and the countries of the EEC continue to ignore the integrity of our compromises and the responsibility that Fretilin has assumed to respect the interests of the USA, Australia and ASEAN. Jakarta will never do it if these other countries continue to ignore the people of East Timor's desire for independence and the fact that they prefer to be exterminated rather than accept foreign domination. Jakarta will continue to be inflexible if these other countries do not listen to our affirmation that the political independence of East Timor rejects all and any form of foreign domination and that Falintil will not permit the imposition any regime or political party by force in East Timor! Jakarta will continue to pursue the extermination of our people if Australia, the EEC and the USA continue to believe that we have some connection with the Soviet Union. They should understand that for ten years the people of East Timor have been fighting alone without asking for help from anyone while in the same ten years, millions of dollars of military aid have been given to Indonesia from Australia, the USA and some European countries.[15] Just as the UN and the Soviet Union could, according to universal principles, together

[15] During the Reagan administration, the USA became less willing to address human rights in Indonesia and increased military assistance. During 1982-84, military sales exceeded $US 1000 million. This was seen as part of Reagan's strategy to make Indonesia a 'bulwark' in the Pacific against a perceived 'Soviet threat' (Dunn, 1996, p. 320).

condemn terrorism in the Security Council after the kidnap of Soviet citizens in Lebanon, then they should also be able to join together in support of the condemnation of Indonesia over East Timor. It is obvious that the people of East Timor have little influence and that they need the support of all countries for their just cause and need all countries to press Jakarta to change its attitude and respect universal principles.

We, the national struggle for the liberation of the people of East Timor, reject the view that our struggle should be seen in the context of the strategic interests of the super powers. The tension between East and West is overwhelming the sacred objective of independence and freedom of our people. The CRRN [National Council of Revolutionary Resistance] is willing to compromise if dialogue includes an East Timorese representative and has the objective of finding a just solution guaranteeing what we all desire: peace and stability in the region. The people of East Timor have already presented assurances that the interests of the USA, Australia and Indonesia will be respected. The people of East Timor do not want to cause problems for neighbouring countries and do not covet even one millimetre of the land of its powerful neighbour, the so-called Great Indonesian Nation. The people of East Timor wish to maintain good relations with Australia and relations of cooperation and good neighbourliness with Indonesia. The people of East Timor only wish to live freely and independently, to simply be their own masters and the owners of our poor but beloved land. We will open our doors to all those who want to help it in its development. The people of East Timor desire only the use of their land, the benefits that they build for themselves and the produce of their own labour. We want only to live in peace, to defend liberties, respect justice and build a democracy for all.

If the Maubere People assure the world that the independence for which it struggles (and will always struggle) will not create any threat, not to Indonesia or the region, not even to the interests of the USA and Australia, then we think that Australia, the countries of the EEC and the USA should pressure Jakarta to change its attitude, to reflect on the genocide that it has committed in East Timor and be open to making concessions, especially this one concession: the recognition of the inalienable rights of the people to independence! From then onwards, the dialogue, based on universal principles and the norms of international law, will be an effective instrument for understanding and harmony; a dialogue can thus re-establish and offer a solution which would guarantee a true and lasting peace in the territory and such a peace would then contribute to the peace and security in the region.

In this way, Beloved Youth and Maubere Patriots, using all that we know about the struggle of our people, we should do everything in our power to influence those who think that the 'autonomy solution' is an 'honourable solution', to abandon this idea. Solutions of this kind will never bring an 'honourable peace'. On the contrary, they will mean a new step in the final descent toward the genocide that everyone seems to hope for.

4. But if it is our people who are engaged in the prolonged struggle for their independence, how can conversations between Portugal and Indonesia bring about the end of the struggle?

Beloved Youth and Maubere Patriots, we should not delude ourselves with the rhetoric of Portugal which has not communicated to us whether or not it is really serious about 'promoting and defending the right of the people of East Timor to self-determination and independence' (according to its constitution).[16] Ambiguous Portuguese policy is motive enough for us to be distrustful of their platonic declarations of 'goodwill'. The first phase of the UN talks has already demonstrated that clearly. The Secretary General of the UN, in presenting his report in the last General Assembly, referred to the first phase of the talks in which 'humanitarian questions' were dealt with specifically.[17] What were the palpable, real results of these talks in which 'humanitarian questions' were highlighted as being 'important Indonesian concessions'? None. We cannot consider that 'humanitarian questions' have been addressed simply because 377 Timorese were repatriated. They made a choice to leave, not because they had a will to abandon their Homeland, but simply because they wanted to escape the repression of a foreign occupier. We should also not forget that it was an exchange of people between the two countries; therefore it was not an Indonesian concession, but a Portuguese concession that implicitly or explicitly recognised that there were Portuguese citizens in Indonesia. Secondly, this demonstrates that the 'humanitarian questions' were not directed at the populace in general who were never given the opportunity to choose (maybe because they could not speak Portuguese) and who have remained the victims of the repression of the occupiers. Thirdly, we notice that the said humanitarian questions mentioned in the report of the Secretary General of the United Nations acted as a curtain of silence drawn over the atrocities continually committed by the Indonesian assassins.

---

[16] Article 307 of the Portuguese Constitution states: 'Portugal shall remain bound by its responsibility, in accordance with international law, to promote and safeguard the right to independence of *Timor Leste*. The President of the Republic, assisted by the Council of the Revolution, and the Government shall be competent to perform all acts necessary to the achievement of the aims set forth in the foregoing paragraph' (Dunn, 1996 p. 335).

[17] Xanana is again referring to the September 1985 meeting between Indonesia and Portugal. The report he mentions concerning these discussions is *Question of East Timor, Progress Report by the Secretary General* (UN Dc.A/40/622, 11 September 1985).

Beloved Youth and Maubere Patriots, I am going to introduce just two cases to demonstrate that it is an insult to our people and all humanity to try to affirm that 'important concessions' were achieved from Indonesia in the first phase of the talks with Portugal under UN mediation, that was supposed to be reserved for the specific treatment of humanitarian questions:

a) On 3 March of this year, the forces of the Battalion *Marinir Satu* arrested *Kepala* [Chief] Vaxtu Tani (recently baptised as Martinho Ximenes), fifty years of age, a native of Horolata, from the *suco* of Lore on his land in the area of Maluro/Lore. The murderous Indonesian soldiers were picking the few cassava from his little patch under the pretext that these plants could conceal the guerrillas. The old chief (old in the sense that he was a chief in the Portuguese colonial period) asked them not to do this. Displaying displeasure he told them that his relatives went hungry because of this type of illicit action from which the population suffers (the old man thought that his status as *Kepala* would permit him to voice an opinion). The irritated Indonesian officer ordered his soldiers to tie him up and take him to the camp and in front of the local population the assassins thrashed him so savagely that they broke his skull and ribs. This was related to *Kodim*, the district military command, in Los Palos and Dili and a helicopter went to Maluro to transport him to Los Palos and other macabre scenes followed. The population was summoned to assist, but without landing the helicopter they let old Vaxtu Tani fall out and he died instantly. To terrorise the population even more the Indonesian assassins cut his testicles off as another trophy of the genocide that Australia and the countries of the EEC, the USA and Portugal seek in support of their honour!

b) Beginning 21 February, the populace in the town of Ossu lived through a wave of terror over several days this year as the enemy tried to repress the activities of the guerrillas of Company A, 2nd Unit.

Fretilin guerrillas had made their way through the houses, infiltrating to the centre of the town to the medical post from where they took all the medical supplies. Because not even a broken needle was taken from the people the Indonesian occupier immediately concluded that the people had assisted in the operation. Fretilin has been accused of committing brutalities against the populace. We have stated on several occasions that certain actions, such as this one conducted by the guerrillas, are conducted essentially to prevent enemy retaliation over the population. This is one more opportunity to demonstrate the truth of that statement.

Early on the morning of 22 February, a *pemuda*, a youth, by the name of Manu-Russo, from the *suco* of Uabubo, was apprehended by the *nangalas*, the Indonesian commandos, of the 4th Group. Taken to the Post (an ex-girls' school), the boy was brutally beaten and tortured with electric shocks and lit cigarettes applied to his face and genitals as well as being beaten by the local *Hansips,* the civil guard, under orders of the assassins. In spite of all this the boy denied the accusation of having 'welcomed the guerrillas in his house on the night of the operation'—as if a whole company could fit into one house! The boy was punished by being made to stand for two days inside a water tank that reached his waist and without eating. The unfortunate boy remains under arrest in Ossu. The assassins massacred those they considered untrustworthy and accused them of witchcraft. The aunt of Joaquim Monteiro (a *Hansip* commander shot by the guerrillas), in a state of delirium caused by the death of her nephew, had pronounced Manu-Russo's name and the assassins had then blamed the boy.

On 23 February, all strong men, around 300, from the *suco* of Uabubo, Uaguia and Ossu de Cima, were summoned by the murderous *nangalas* and were beaten and tortured for three days. Because of those atrocities, an individual called Francisco, of Karau Balu/Vikeke, who was already at the prison in Ossu, took advantage of that flood of prisoners and escaped to the bush. The *nangalas* did not think twice and arrested all the relatives of the escapee and imprisoned them in Ossu.

Following the same example, Armando, a man from the hamlet of Borala in the *suco* of Ossu de Cima, who also tried to escape because he could no longer bear the torture, was shot by the *nangala,* breaking his leg. This unfortunate man was taken back to the executioners and after having him beaten nearly to death, a *nangala* officer, aided by the section commander named Uai Loi, assassinated him by stabbing him in front of the other prisoners. Afterwards he ordered the *Hansips* to cut open his chest and remove his heart as another trophy of the genocide that Australia, EEC countries, the USA and Portugal desire and support.

The 'parliamentarian' Ricardo (and *Luirai* of Uabubo) was also imprisoned for days, beaten up and brutally tortured. Previously, he had been considered a good collaborationist but now he is being accused of supplying information to Fretilin and having collaborated on the attack just because he has a nephew in the resistance (Antonio Nascimento, Second Commander of the Company B, 2nd Unit). The 'parliamentarian' was only released after questioning in Dili when he declared that Fretilin had taken all his gold, *mitssalas* [valuable necklaces] and money. It was the only way to satisfy the insistent *nangalas* who wanted an explanation as to why Fretilin had not killed or hurt him, being a 'parliamentarian' (his house being situated only thirty metres from the medical centre). Also, the shop-assistant of Kong Fu, a shop a short distance from the medical centre, had to declare that Fretilin had taken 'all of his *jutas*' [millions of rupiahs] and even so, the poor Chinese remains in prison!

Beloved Youth and Maubere Patriots! Portugal and Indonesia under the auspices of the UN will move on to the second phase of talks to 'discuss' political questions. Western democracies and the UN itself have declared with much sonority, 'important Indonesian concession' on 'humanitarian grounds'. Indonesia has called upon itself impunity for its crimes because it knows that western countries support them and will not even criticise them over those crimes. Furthermore, it seems that *Senhor* Bob Hawke would like to supply Jakarta with the means to continue to massacre our people in exchange for the exploration of oil in our southern sea. *Senhor* Bob Hawke's hands are stained. Since his declarations in August last year, the East Timorese people have felt an increase in the murderous repression of the occupiers, whose vandalism is such that they will even castrate and rip out the hearts of the dead. We are certain that *Senhor* Bob Hawke will argue at the next Australian Labor Party Conference that all this is a lie, and that Mochtar has assured him that human rights in East Timor are more respected than in Australia itself. For this reason Bob Hawke will not be sorry, even for a moment, for being responsible for this extremely important step in foreign policy and will argue that the ALP should continue to pursue a pragmatic policy to maintain the already 'solid' relations with Jakarta, never forgetting to emphasise the extremely important fact of the current negotiations concerning the oil explorations of the Timor Gap.[18] On some issues, Mario Carrascalao, hawker of the Maubere Homeland and little Portuguese, is right: 'dirty policy, filthy policy, cynical policy'. On this we agree with him, but above all this cynicism and filthy policy we will continue to affirm loudly and strongly: *we can all die but we will die standing!*

5. The discussion of the 'political questions' on the agenda during the second phase of the UN talks between Portugal and Indonesia is easy to predict: the talks will simply be a facade with which to present to the world the recognition of the Indonesian military annexation of East Timor.

The annexation will be painted with the colours of a *fait accompli* (since the irregular forces will be defeated anyway), of 'legitimacy' (because Indonesia's regular forces have maintained an occupation that has lasted for ten years), of 'legality' (made possible by international complicity) and of a 'popular will' (because purely and simply, the intolerable and barbaric repression of our people will be forgotten). If the Secretary General of the United Nations

18 Hawke and Hayden frustrated attempts by the Australian Labor Party National Conference in July 1984 to insist on the observance of the 1982 resolution condemning Indonesia and supporting East Timorese self-determination. Hayden argued that to pass the resolution would be to offend Indonesia, (Ramos-Horta, 1986, p. 80).

also abandons universal principles it will only be because it is the desire of the countries of the EEC, Australia, the USA and others, that the talks between Portugal and Indonesia about 'political questions' become a path to legitimise the genocide practised by Jakarta.

Beloved Youth and Maubere Patriots, why is it said that 'the East Timorese case is a lost cause'? I believe that all of you, all of us, have discovered the truth behind this statement: it is the failure of countries to lift a finger to help our people, in defence of universal principles according to international norms. What is behind this statement is precisely the self-interest of these governments; this interest lends support to Indonesia in their 'heroic' effort to exterminate the Maubere People. This genocide is a *sine qua non* for maintaining good relations with Jakarta. Nazism is spoken about in hushed tones and terrorism is loudly condemned, while the genocide carried out by Indonesia and the terrorism against the people of East Timor by Jakarta are supported at every level by those countries in some kind of new political phenomenon. In the parliaments of those countries this type of politics is called *realpolitik* or 'pragmatism'! It is positively realist: if the Indonesians kill, what can be done? If they have not yet killed everyone, it is only because there are still a few left for them to kill. These killings are linked to those countries because for the Indonesians to continue with their murderous undertaking, those countries must supply aid. The justification they give is that in reality, the Indonesians have already begun killing and because it is in the interests of the Indonesians to continue, then the help rendered is only realistic. We remember well how these countries removed themselves from any blame for selling arms, planes, etc. by recommending to Jakarta that it should not use this material in the war in East Timor, in spite of knowing that this material was certainly going to be used there—this is *realpolitik*! Another aspect of this reality is that the people of East Timor are dying, so let them die—this is the reality. These governments say that in reality they are unable to prevent it because the important reality is that if the Indonesians need support to finish off the people of East Timor, it is necessary, logical and realistic that they should be given that support. So, if the people of East Timor continue to die, it is only because they are yet to be exterminated, and in supporting Indonesia to kill the Maubere People through the selling of arms, much is profited and much more can be profited while there are still Maubere People left to die! And this is realistic, above all, because the good relations with Indonesia must be preserved even if the price has to be the extermination of our people!

The case of our people is considered a 'lost case' by these immoral governments, essentially because making millions of dollars in profits is dependent on the criminal repression and extermination of our people! Australia provides Indonesia with ten million dollars worth of military assistance annually—it is a lost case because Australia has absolutely no interest in taking a principled stance, impartial and independent, in place of the profit that it collects. It is a lost case because the countries of the EEC and the Eastern Bloc who maintain economic ties with Jakarta do not want to lose the benefits derived from trade agreements with Indonesia. It is a lost case, an impossible independence, in this current climate. The current state of affairs can be understood on two levels. Firstly, the established regimes of ASEAN do not want a democratic state in the region and ASEAN is defended tooth and nail by Australia and the West. I believe that the presumption that such a state would damage the stability of the region has been disproven by the overthrow of Marcos. This showed that the restitution of democratic freedoms to Filipinos did not at all harm the stability in the region (unless western countries are secretly preparing for the overthrow of Mrs Cori Aquino to guarantee even better stability in the region—anything is possible!). On a higher level, and more importantly for our analysis, the current climate is an expression, no more and no less, of the indifference, uninterest and complicity in genocide on the part of western democracies!

Faced with a case considered lost by those countries that created a climate of tacit approval surrounding the struggle of our people, we should, and principally you, Beloved Youth and Maubere Patriots, should maintain your perseverance and tenacity in combat, in the firmness of your convictions, in the determination to pursue our ideals of liberation and in fuelling faith and confidence so that even after we are dead we will burrow out of our graves and continue to defend our sacred Homeland!

Beloved Youth and Maubere Patriots! It is obvious that without the participation of the representatives of the people of East Timor in the talks held under UN auspices, no solution can be reached and no peace is possible in East Timor! Why do we state this? Because the interests of our people will not be debated in these discussions. Portugal will only worry about purifying its image before the world. Indonesia will say, crystal clear, that the people of Timor have already chosen integration and the representatives of the UN who are religious and political allies of Indonesia, will ask Allah in all his graces for a perfect integration. If the representatives of the Maubere People do not take part in this process (a situation that betrays the sea of blood consented to by our people) the voice of our people will remain unheard; their interests and their rights will be trampled on by the honour of those countries who only have the honour of having contributed to the most horrible crime in our recent history.

The Secretary General of the UN does not consider the appeals made by a wide range of countries and organisations. By not including the representatives of the people of East Timor in the talks, a matter that touches them more closely than the other participants, the UN demonstrates its inability to solve the case, according to the guiding principles of this world-wide organisation. The UN places itself on the side of the strong, on the side of aggressors, denying its reason for existing. If the Secretary General of the UN continues to be in accord with his representative on the exclusion of the people of East Timor from the talks, we think that he has abandoned the principles that he should defend more than anyone else in the world. We have reason to worry as the UN has never given any evidence, not the smallest sign, that it will ensure a true interpretation to the term 'interested parties', and because of the dubious position of the UN, we are led to assume that an 'acceptable solution' to the international community is to develop integration under the facade of autonomy and that, after all, everything revolves around Jakarta. But, with sincerity, we do not want to believe that! We state once again that we have confidence that the Secretary General of the UN will not permit universal principles and international law to be trampled upon just to respect the capriciousness of Jakarta.

We state once again that without listening to the sovereign will of our people, no just solution can be found, since Portugal as well as Indonesia is not interested in recognising the right of the people of East Timor to self-determination and national independence. And we declare as many times as it is necessary that solutions that do not respect the true aspirations of our people, solutions that question the universal principles, solutions that disparage rights and justice, will only have as a result the continuation of the armed struggle! We prefer to be exterminated than to revile the immeasurable sacrifices suffered by our people. We prefer to be exterminated than to revile the principles that millions of human beings the world over have stood up for and given their lives for!

For that reason, Beloved Youth and Maubere Patriots, the path is still arduous and difficult, in spite of our having overcome ten long years of resistance, as is the sacred duty that belongs to us of pursuing, by all means possible, the defence of the inalienable rights of our people to independence. For that reason, we should all be capable of defending the principles already formulated. We should continue to be firm in our claims. Even if the UN itself consents to the extermination of our people so that Indonesia may continue to be a permanent member, we will not stop in face of this difficulty. The objective we pursue is simple; the objective for which we fight and give our lives is simple, but sacred: independence for our Homeland and freedom for our people! And for this objective we will pay any price necessary: our independence or our total extermination! Because nothing else will be left to us, to die for this ideal will constitute a duty for every child of East Timor. We count on you, Beloved Youth and Maubere Patriots, to continue to fight for the supreme and legitimate aspirations of our people, of our thousand-times heroic and beloved Maubere People!

IV. The Position of the Church in East Timor

1. First of all, I want to reaffirm our admiration for two sons of East Timor, the leaders of the church of East Timor, the venerable and beloved Monsignor Martinho Lopes and his worthy successor, Monsignor Filipe Belo.

The church in East Timor, during the long captivity of our people, has been a safe haven during the waves of crimes and violations. It has been the moral support in the struggle of our people, a precious helping hand that has eased the pains of our people during their heroic resistance to the vile and cowardly Indonesian aggression and its criminal military occupation of our Homeland. Yes, our Homeland, our beloved Homeland! Our consciousness that we have a Homeland that is being occupied; that we have a Homeland to liberate; that our Homeland requests the sacrifice of our lives; that the ancestors bestowed it upon us, this Homeland they were unable to save—this consciousness was made explicit in the pastoral letter of 7 April by Monsignor Filipe Belo.[19] We can see in the following passage the appeal, the call to the nationalist consciousness made by the current leader of the church of East Timor:

Raise Up East Timor
What humanity has built up throughout history has not been born suddenly. It has not been made by only one person. The states that have appeared in the world are also like this. One day a great crowd of men and women sat down to think about the matter of living together (national consciousness). Everyone has always had this one thought and with all their will raised up ideas that today we call the Nation, Homeland, Our Land. Sometimes they do it in times of war and other times in peace. We live in land called Timor. We have to love Timor: to love our land together with its people, their customs and their history. We have to defend and support the culture and all that it has to offer. To work with zeal for its progress and to press on, and thus elevate its name. All this is patriotism and it signifies our love of our land. Patriotism means all that people feel inside of them …'

This is the consciousness of our people; this is the sentiment of our people! It is for this patriotic consciousness that all of us should be determined to fight on and to offer our lives. It is for this that all children of East Timor, inside or

---

[19] Salesian father, Carlos Ximenes Belo, trained in Portugal and Rome, was appointed Apostolic Administrator by the Vatican to replace Monsignor Lopes in 1983. In 1987 the Pope nominated him as Bishop and he hosted the Pope's visit to Timor in 1989. His long years of work for peace and justice gained him the Nobel Peace Prize in 1996. On his return to Dili from collecting the award tens of thousands of Timorese welcomed him home (Bishop Hilton Deakin, 'East Timor and the Catholic Church', 1998, Jim Aubrey (ed).)

outside the country, should not let ourselves be subjugated by the trauma that would suffocate this patriotic sentiment, this consciousness of people and Homeland! And it is for this that we join our voices to the church of East Timor and, with your voice, with that of the decisive patriotic youth, who are involved in the intransigent defence of the rights of our people!

The document of the Presbyterial Council of Dili, dated 1 January 1985, touched on various aspects of a global identity that we would define as the Maubere People. Our people not only want to preserve this identity, but also to continue to create it with their own hands, look after it with devotion, form it and enrich it with the strength and all the energy that they possess, with creativity and imagination, without pressure from outsiders, without the intolerant paternalism of the dominators, without the oppression of the occupier.

If Timor becomes master of its own destiny and the Maubere People free themselves from the eternal chains of colonial slavery, then an ethnic-historical identity, a cultural and religious identity and essentially a political identity, will develop irresistibly like the torrential streams of the rivers of our nation; this identity will flower freely, at ease, affected neither by fear nor by restraint, like the flora of our land. None of this is possible if the people of East Timor continue to be gagged by foreign oppressors, whoever they may be! We trust that the church of East Timor, assuming the Christian demands of a political nature with which it is entrusted, will continue to defend the inalienable right of the people of East Timor for independence, as the only path for a real and effective preservation of the identities that distinguish our people.

A church that lives with the people, a church that suffers with the people, a church that cries with the people, a church that receives the same humiliations as the people, is a church that can never ever abandon the people! The church serves the people and because it serves the people it can interpret the wishes and the sentiments of the people. A church like this has the complete trust of the people; a church like this is a church of and for the people! The liberation preached by Christ is not based on the enjoyment of the material world; Cardinal Sin placed himself on the side of the Filipino people, because Christian liberty proclaims justice and defends freedom. The Chilean Bishops stand beside the oppressed people of Chile, in the struggle for the attainment of their freedom! We see in those places that the church has not let itself succumb by the very fact that their countries are already independent, destroying the theory (with which Australian leaders want to justify their 'pragmatism') that in developing countries, economic rights have primacy over political rights! Peace in East Timor cannot be conceived in a fanciful cessation of hostilities to attain autonomy, because the people of East Timor would still continue to suffer. A true peace in East Timor should afford at a material level the conditions for the liberation of the spirit! These conditions are that the Maubere People need to express themselves freely, think freely and act freely and that will only happen if East Timor becomes independent. In the opposite case of autonomy, the people of East Timor will be a people without life, without soul, a people without blood, a people without anything, in which some pretend Catholics will not even go to Mass, will not even contribute to the construction of a poor chapel (such work and dedication are always of the poor, of the oppressed, of the violated, of those that suffer and know that the church suffers with them). The church of East Timor must prevent that happening; prevent the people of East Timor from being shattered by misfortune.

We are certain that the church of East Timor will continue with determination to face up to all the psychological and political pressures in order to serve the Maubere People, to serve the sheep of its flock, in order for the church to identify with the suffering of the people of East Timor. The clergy of East Timor, as they have demonstrated, are profoundly knowledgeable about the suffering of the people and have a profound knowledge of the aspirations of our people and of their determination. This has occurred because the church has stood beside the people and because the church lives amongst the people.

The church of East Timor knows that the Maubere People despise the barbarian occupier. The church of East Timor knows that the Maubere People reject with all their soul the presence of the murderous occupier. The church of East Timor knows that the people of East Timor would prefer to die a thousand times than to continue to be slaves of colonialism. And we are certain that Monsignor Filipe Belo, as well as the respected Prelate of East Timor [Lopes] will continue on in the courageous battle for the rights of the people of East Timor. We take this opportunity to appeal to Monsignor Filipe Belo and to the Prelate of the Diocese of Dili, in the spirit of a liberating church, that they continue to relay the suffering of our people to all the churches in the world and that they continue to appeal to other churches for a stronger position against the extermination of our people.

The people of East Timor are alongside their church and receive as their own the humiliation that the criminal Indonesian occupiers have directed against the spiritual fathers. They suffer as their own the persecutions, the forced moves and expulsions that have already taken place and which have enlisted some faithful and dedicated priests to the cause of our people. And I should affirm that we are with the church of East Timor in its no less courageous battle. A church like this deserves and will always deserve our total respect and solidarity, without bounds.

2. It is with gratitude that we know that His Holiness Pope John Paul II continues to pray for East Timor and prays for us in that, as a last resort, we had to take up arms to free ourselves from the foreign oppressor.

The Christian norms of peace, justice, freedom and democracy give to the struggle of our people moral and political fortitude that will accompany them until they reach their objective. We appeal to His Holiness to intercede with western governments, namely Australia, to constrain their attitude in light of the martyrdom of the people of East Timor. We express our confidence that His Holiness will continue to bless the heroic struggle of the Maubere People for their liberation!

Conclusion

Beloved Youth and Maubere Patriots! Your identification as true children of East Timor signals a religious commitment that is at the same time political! This manifestation of patriotism and faith renounces the false propaganda that the Maubere resistance is a resistance essentially 'communist'. Fretilin is a Movement of Liberation in which a militancy of Christians, as well as non-Christians, co-exists. The systematic waves of Indonesian repression have not only affected 'supposed communists' as its victims; the criminal occupier persecutes, arrests and tortures, banishes, and murders indiscriminately. The essence of the Maubere resistance is the unshakable will of our people to free themselves from the foreign yoke.

We appeal to all those that make theirs the cause of our people to continue to exert pressure for the inclusion of the representatives of the East Timor people in the talks between Indonesia and Portugal under the auspices of the Secretary General of the UN.

We appeal to our friends: the people of Australia, the American people, and to the peoples of Europe, to press their respective governments to change their attitudes in relation to the genocide practised by Jakarta.

Homeland or death!
The struggle continues on all fronts!
To resist is to win!

A LEADER CONSOLIDATES

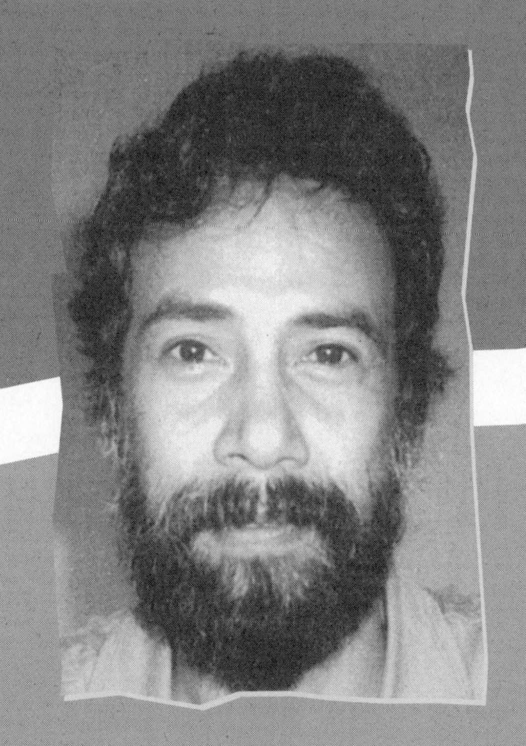

1987–1992

Ideological Turnaround

This message outlines the ideological turnaround of the Timorese resistance. Fretilin at its inception in 1974 was a broad-based national front advocating socialist democracy and independence. It became more radical after the return to East Timor and addition to Fretilin in 1975 of some Timorese students influenced by Maoism and Marxism in Portugal. Indonesia invaded under the pretext that Fretilin was a communist threat. The marxist ideology that the Fretilin Central Committee later came to assume was also the rationale behind the 'counter-revolutionary' arrests and executions that Xanana describes in the autobiography during the early years of the resistance to Indonesian occupation. Xanana says that he continued with the marxist ideology in the early years of his leadership out of a sense of loyalty to his martyred comrades but came to believe that political ideology should be secondary to the cause of national independence and political freedom of choice. Here Xanana calls for a reanalysis of political thinking and ideology. At this time he also declared Falintil a politically neutral and nationalist army and resigned from Fretilin. This has been described by some Timorese as their Perestroika. It was another year before these changes were made officially in the RER, Readjustamento Estrutural do Resistencia, *the Reorganisation of the Structure of the Resistance in December 1988. This document established CNRM, the National Council of Maubere Resistance (the precursor to CNRT, the current national body of the East Timorese resistance).*

Patriots and nationalists! People of East Timor!

We are commemorating the 12th anniversary of the shameful and cowardly invasion of our homeland by the criminal forces of the Indonesian occupation. We should all know by now how to consider the profound causes of a war that has been imposed on the Maubere People!

So much suffering, so much death, so much pain have passed that we must now agree to finally rid ourselves of any obstacles that still contribute to prolonging this painful situation.

The 7th of December 1975 did not just happen. One closely related cause was Fretilin's counter-attack undertaken to take control of the situation; nevertheless the motives did include their own politically motivated self-interest. This has been a major issue during the last 12 years of our war. When Fretilin assumed a leftist ideology it 'turned' unmistakably into a potential threat to the strategic interests of the powerful.

Today, more than ever, a variety of problems appear as extremely dark shadows on the horizon of our struggle's hopes. Twelve hard years of suffering have opened up deep wounds in our body and in the patriotic conscience of the East Timorese people. Many questions beg for answers; many points of view demand resolution. Their emergence reflects all our restlessness and anxiety. Meanwhile, time flies and we, caught up in the particular violence of war, hurtle on to an ever more difficult future.

Some accept death as a condition of struggle, as the sacrifice demanded by their country. For these people abnegation renews itself in their daily sweat, and in the certainty that they are defending a just cause. Others, with only the minimum pressure from the occupier, have become instantly alarmed. These people, ever since they were consoled with rupiahs, prefer to fatten up on *supermi* noodles. In exchange, they promote a pseudo-defence of any old identity and preach that the war is the only reason the people are suffering. These people continue to hide behind their white vests of cowardice, setting themselves apart from the sea of sweat and tears that drowns our people! The rest question the future (the nearer is seems, the further away it gets), speculating on easy victories or the horror of some terrible end! Meanwhile there are those facing an enemy which continues to do whatever it wants and whatever it can. These people experience the actual situation. They try to retain whatever political and moral force they can, so that at least they can think that even if they all die, totally abandoned, at least they *died standing*, as the very dear Monsignor Martinho Lopes has put it so clearly.

Finally, Patriots of East Timor! Twelve years of horrendous and continuous activity by the occupying forces against the glorious Falintil and 12 years of brutal repression of the heroic and defenceless Maubere People, have had a profound effect on our consciousness and our thought. These years have accentuated how fragile and small we are, but have given us back our strength.

The people of East Timor have given abundant proof of their great patriotism, and of the firm principles and determination which have always led our struggle. These courageous choices have guided their tenacious resistance to the Indonesian military occupation. But this long and difficult path has worn many out; not because they have lost their desire to see a liberated homeland but because the moral force they need to hold their heads up high has been diminished. This is nothing more than a consequence of the prolonging of war, nothing more than a sign of weakened morale in the face of the enormous difficulties that were, and continue to be, an irremovable constant in our resistance against the foreign occupation of our Homeland. Nevertheless, after 12 years, the East Timorese people have not been diverted from their Maubere consciousness, nor, crushed by their weakened morale. They continue, beneath the silence of enemy repression, to conserve intact the supreme and legitimate aspirations for which they struggle.

Patriots and nationalists! People of East Timor!

Today's date deserves dedicated reflection, deserves better clarification of thought, and a re-analysis of the political orientation assumed up till now. Today we must mark this bold 12-year resistance with a new and significant change of position. Even if change is seen as an expression of our very weakness, we simply want to clarify that these changes can or must, above all, reveal what our present perception of the situation is: that is, the changes must affirm that we are becoming, finally, more realistic!

This reality that we now perceive is no longer the crushing capacity of the occupying forces; no longer does the reality we encounter limit itself to the constant negation of our rights; nor is it circumscribed by our incapacity, at all levels, to act in the face of an international conspiracy!

The reality that we talk about, has never been put aside, not even for a moment—the fact of the incontestable patriotism of the Maubere People. The people, small and defenceless, forgotten and oppressed, have not sold out to the 'development program' that Jakarta forces on them in order to buy the acquiescence of the international community regarding the forceful and criminal annexation of East Timor. This reality is just one component of singular importance in the struggle of the East Timorese people and is part of an ideological plan.

It is essentially this point that I will go into later on, and which constitutes the main statement of this message regarding the struggle!

A. During 12 long, hard years of war—condemned to never end so that the international community will become uninterested and forget—we have committed enormous and excessive political errors. But we cannot simply ignore these errors, or worse still, put aside considering their consequences.

Right from the very beginning, the Fretilin Directorate displayed a notable political infantilism that tried to defy the world, obsessed with our non-existent 'capacities'. At no time were interconnecting relations considered, whether in the local area or with the rest of the world. From the very beginning, we presumed ourselves to be 'heroes' of a bloody revolution, of a popular revolution that would destroy all the opposing forces like an avalanche.

Our predecessors saw Marxism as the 'immediate solution' to the problems of an incredibly underdeveloped people. They saw in Maoism a shining path to a revolutionary process conducted behind 'closed doors' that would amaze the world with the 'undeniable creative capacities' of a people still relying on artisan methods of production. We were, in truth, lulled by a fanciful revolutionary processed dubbed 'Mauberism'. This political infantilism and thoughtless adventurism has driven the movement since 1974. This political infantilism has, since 1974, allowed no margin of disagreement, but rather, [has exhibited] all the political extremism which would be, from that time on, our very death sentence.

This senseless radicalism paid no attention to our concrete conditions and limitations. It made us intolerably overbearing and led us to put many compatriots on the same footing as the criminal aggressor. We have committed crimes against our own brothers and, during this difficult war, we have spent more time in arresting and assassinating compatriots than thinking effectively about capable defence of the Homeland, the results of which were evident in the events of 1978.

B. We, who only learnt Marxism in the mountains of East Timor, were influenced by a revolutionary frenzy that should have led us to realise our predecessors' dream: to create a Marxist-Leninist party in the Democratic Republic of East Timor.

As the actual situation developed came the gradual understanding that, deep down, the true problem was the internal political problem which remained in our thinking and action. (As late as 1982 the airing of these diminishing revolutionary opinions was permitted, created as much as by the East as by the West.) But, we have tried, gradually, to embrace the entire situation in all its complexity.

Meanwhile, the new 'Direction of the Struggle' was politically obligated to proceed with a change in behaviour while still continuing with the same radical ideology. In 1984, however, the 'Direction of the Struggle' had to re-consider that the creation of a Marxist party only expressed in practice the great endurance of previously adopted positions. The 'Marxist-Leninist Fretilin party' was no longer acting like any kind of living political party organisation, conceding the capacity to guide the process of liberation of the Homeland towards a Fretilin nationalist movement that was not necessarily communist!

We had already thought of dumping from the Struggle any cargo that was too heavy for us to carry on our shoulders! Last year in a message sent to the political Committee of UDT in Lisbon we tried to make everyone see the glorious Falintil will be outside the party political game. We were affirming that, in future, the National Liberation Armed Forces of East Timor [Falintil] will not permit any political party to subvert the established order and restore a regime responsible for the suppression of others. We also wanted it understood that Falintil will only have one noble mission to follow: defence of the Homeland of everyone and the maintenance of internal order, restored by one constitution that guarantees the defence of individual and collective freedoms and the respect for the interests of all the citizens and social classes in East Timor. So that glorious Falintil can fully carry out its mission within a government structure, regardless of the political tendencies of the executive, it is necessary that they affirm now their neutrality as the National Liberation Armed Forces of East Timor.

We were not the true mentors who created the 'Marxist-Leninist Fretilin party', but we were only following what we received from our predecessors. We must say, though, that at that time we were still dazzled by a vision of a miracle process of human redemption, and that humanity had closed its eyes to the extermination of the Maubere people, a genocide carried out by the assassinating forces of the Indonesian occupation.

We became aware of this fact far too late. This was obviously due to our political inexperience; today we still do not consider ourselves fully capable in this area; however, what we can affirm is that we now see more objectively and with different eyes. And this [new] reality can and must only reflect:

1) First of all, recognition of the huge errors committed by our predecessors in carrying out the process of liberating the homeland;
2) Next, a *mea culpa* for our own analytical errors which kept us back on the same politically infantile level as our predecessors;
3) Then, a process of gradual correction of previously adopted political procedures;
4) Finally, eradication of any and every tendency which keeps us tied to a rigid conceptual system regarding our people's struggle.

Patriots and nationalists. During the last nine years of war, evidence verifies that the patriotism of the people of East Timor is not simply a by-product of the 25th of April in Portugal. We understand, more profoundly, that this notion, this sentiment, is something alive that has been transmitted from generation to generation, annually invoked by the traditional celebrations which the Portuguese colonialists classified as 'rituals' and for which our people were forced to a pay a licence fee and which today they can not even practise.

If the world still imagines that, under the direction of Fretilin, the people of East Timor have resisted with incomparable bravery and undeniable commitment, simply because they were all inspired by communist ideology, then I have to declare that this is not true. However, I do not negate the beneficial character of liberty and the enjoyment of free expression and democracy. It allowed everyone to recognise how profound the changes actually were, even more so when compared with the political ditch that existed during the Portuguese colonial period and beneath the yoke of the Indonesian military occupation. We do not deny that, during a difficult situation that followed the loss of the support bases in the mountains, it was the principles and methods of organisation assumed by Fretilin that permitted the necessary political conditions for us to revive the resistance flame so close to disappearing under the enemy's strategy.

No other people, up to now, has fought without a direction and without minimal organisation. Given the conditions under which the Maubere resistance has proceeded, and continues to proceed, Fretilin, under a political obligation that determined the emergence of ASDT, as it should have, placed itself firmly at the forefront of the East Timor people in the defence of the Homeland.

Like many up until a certain time, and even more so as a member of the Central Committee of Fretilin, I participated in the struggle under the ideal of national independence. We were still trying to implement this in the last elusive message of the 20th of May this year! Since the beginning of 1976 the purging waves of massacres of nationalists [by Fretilin]—purgings that have continued since 1978—have placed many in a dilemma. They could either challenge the situation and be arrested and assassinated as reactionaries and traitors of the Homeland. The other option was to assume the politics of *seguidismo*, following, given that a combative spirit in defence of the Homeland was political and moral motivation for rejecting such a horrible death.

The suppression of any other political choice has created in our bosom a fatal divisiveness and a notorious resentment at all levels of the organisational structure. We have been unable to express freely opinions about the mistaken points of view of members of the Central Committee who rely on long-winded clarifications of Marxist precepts. Meanwhile, the practicalities of conducting the war were handed over to the initiative—more or less uncontrollable and inconsistent—of local military commanders. This was a drawback during the period of the support bases (1976–78). Being condemned to make a revolution, during a war we could not sustain, is a clear demonstration of political blindness.

The West placed itself alongside Indonesia, while the Eastern countries did not lift a finger, calling us, loudly and clearly, excessive adventurers!

Twelve years later we have to recognise with bitterness the effects of this poorly drafted political strategy on the Maubere People. It has resulted in a disastrous situation that until now no one has been able to end.

We have come to recognise through these long years that what inspires the people of East Timor to struggle is not the making of a revolution, either in large or small proportions. The objective of the Maubere People is to liberate the Homeland from its foreign occupation and to be able to live freely and independently. The Maubere People aspire to liberty and independence as the basic condition for the exercise of their rights, so they may live as they wish to live, think as they wish to think, act as they wish to act. For this I say:

1. I publicly declare my total and wholehearted rejection of those doctrines that promote suppression of democratic freedoms in East Timor.
2. I publicly declare that the Falintil *aswain*[3] will not permit the installation of a leftist regime that not only intends to provoke internal disintegration, but also to destabilise the whole area in which East Timor is situated.

We have always fought under the Fretilin flag and we will fight under it to the end! What I intend to highlight here is that, as a member of the Fretilin Central Committee, I am exempt from the requirements of the movement itself, which indiscriminately pulls together diverse political options. However, the constitution prescribes the total neutrality of the armed forces.

It is senseless suicide, today, to try to make a revolution. Today we delude ourselves if we think that communism will sweep through like a grassfire. In being so deluded we will make the Chinese mistake of ostracism or of bending over backwards so that Eastern bloc countries will equip us. We have already seen how, in the agony of our own death-rattle, we continued blindly making more enemies, while our so-called 'natural allies' have devoted themselves in silence to their own revolutions.

The ultimate objective we should pursue is the liberation of our Homeland and the independence of our people! We wanted nothing else when we accepted all these sacrifices that the war placed before us. We have no ambition for glory or power, because we are fully conscious of our extreme limitations—the only ambition that we have is to guarantee to the Maubere People the liberation of their Homeland, and the exercise of their fundamental rights as a people and as human beings within the community of the free world!

Patriots and nationalists! The war continues to be extremely hard, extremely difficult! To increase our resistance difficulties even more, the occupying barbarian has placed, in each district, more than one battalion of native armed forces, known as 'SAKA'.

I know that, in the face of enemy threats and repression, no one can refuse to be mobilised because accepting or refusing to carry arms against their own brother guerrillas has become a matter of life or death.

Many SAKA have already died, and many more are going to die, leaving widows and orphans who will be immediately taken advantage of by the occupying forces. The occupier of our Homeland has no misgivings about utilising all those who can bear arms in support of their twenty battalions who serve in East Timor! The occupying barbarian is gambling on exterminating the glorious Falintil!

---

[3] *Aswain* is a Timorese word meaning warrior. Its use ties the modern struggle to the ancestral warriors.

Today, 7 December 1987, Beni Murdani still cannot affirm to have once and for all finished off the armed resistance, but we are constantly aware that Jakarta will continue to pursue its objectives!

The courageous guerrillas of the Maubere People continue to stand tall, accepting their own extermination. They will not surrender! We accept this with our heads held high in defiance of Jakarta—and we know that we will continue to die but *we will die standing*.

We demand that Portugal assume, once and for all, the right political stance needed to promote a new framework for dialogue with Indonesia under the mediation of the United Nations, a process in which representatives of the Maubere People must participate. These obligations are conferred within the framework of the Portuguese Constitution and are within the ambit of United Nations' resolutions regarding the case of East Timor.

We call on the governments of Australia and New Zealand to reconsider their positions and give the people of East Timor the benefit of a more just and understanding attitude, as happened in the case of New Caledonia, which won the special attention of these two countries.

We call on the United States of America to follow the governments of Western Europe and no longer consider East Timor a potential threat to stability, because for many years we have been committed to preventing this. We ask that you favour the Maubere People with an attitude that will bring them peace and independence.

We call on the countries of the Non-Aligned Movement (NAM) to consider that, in supporting the just struggle of the Maubere People, they are guaranteeing their own Movement's fitness and political strength, thus safeguarding the principles adopted in Bandung.

We call on the people of the whole world to understand the sufferings of the people of East Timor, during these long and hard 12 years of genocidal war, promoted by the occupying assassins of our Homeland! Pressure your governments to review their attitudes.

Homeland or death!

To resist is to win!

The struggle continues on all fronts!

CRRN Headquarters in East Timor
7 December 1987
President of CRRN
Kay Rala Xanana Gusmão
Falintil Commander-in-Chief

Letter to Pope John Paul II

This letter was written in the week before the Pope visited Dili on 12 October 1989. He consecrated the cathedral and celebrated Mass in the open air before a congregation of 10,000. At the end of the Mass a demonstration for independence took place. Demonstrators beaten by police were filmed and photographed by foreign journalists. In the following days many people were arrested. This signalled the beginning of a series of demonstrations organised by the emerging urban youth resistance.

Your Holiness, Pope John Paul II

As faithful members of the flock of Christ, we kneel at your feet, disconsolate that we are unable to be present with our people to greet the Pilgrim Pope of faith and messenger of love, justice and peace.

As your Holiness steps on to the dearly beloved soil of East Timor we, the *guerilheiros* of the Armed Forces of the National Liberation of East Timor, Falintil, weep with emotion and sadness. Emotion, because the gesture of your visit indicates your wish to bless East Timor and its people. Sadness, because this land, this nation and this soil which we are defending with our lives would want to welcome your Holiness with the genuine joy and Christian spontaneity which are present today. Thousands of our people will go to Dili to welcome the Father of Faith, carrying with them the hopes of hundreds of thousands who at this moment are locked up in concentration camps under rigorous control. We are sad and deeply sorrowful because East Timor and its people, in their Christian simplicity and poverty, could honour the visit of your Holiness better than the garlands covered with the blood of our people and the festive streamers which disguise the pain and mourning of our people which the occupying forces of our Maubere Nation easily forget.

The Maubere People have always trusted the selfless clergy of East Timor who have never on any occasion deserted their people. On the contrary they have always encouraged deep respect for the Holy See. The Maubere People, if they had the freedom to do so, would like to express their confidence in your Holiness that they will not be abandoned by you and that they are looking forward to hearing a message of peace for East Timor!

The Maubere People greet your Holiness with jubilation, but at the same time they cannot fail to show their anguish! In another situation, in a situation of real peace in East Timor, we would be totally certain that the Maubere People would come in haste in greater numbers and in great strength, and would come in haste in a genuine explosion of joy ... the Timorese way, in accordance with our traditional hospitality.

The Maubere People are so hospitable that centuries ago they knew how to welcome with open arms the first missionary to open up East Timor to the Christian faith, the Portuguese priest Antonio Taveira.

For 14 years the people of East Timor have been dispossessed of their real joy. Spontaneity has been replaced by calculated and cautious attitudes ... for fear of brutal reprisals by the occupying military!

Your Holiness, Pope John Paul II, we, the *guerilheiros* of Falintil, kneel before you to beg the protection of your blessing and the help of your prayers to enable us to continue to fulfil our duties to liberate our nation by giving the people of East Timor the complete freedom they aspire to and the full exercise of the rights they long for.

With all humility we ask your Holiness to grant us the favour of receiving this document in which we expose our feelings, pain, apprehension and hope! These are feelings poorly expressed—sorrow and anguish barely contained, and apprehension (perhaps) unjustified in the great hope that we will die fighting for the Maubere Nation, so that one day, by finding peace, the people of East Timor may live in freedom and happiness.

Your Holiness, bless us and bless our fight!

The Resistance Command,
Kay Rala Xanana Gusmão
Commander of Falintil
CNRM General Headquarters, East Timor

Peace Plan for East Timor

This peace plan is excerpted and summarised from a 20-page document. It makes concrete proposals for a settlement through dialogue and a referendum. A rigorous campaign was mounted around this peace plan and elements of it prompted the 1999 UN-sponsored ballot.

A solution to the problem of East Timor should identify with peace … True and lasting peace will only be possible if the wishes of the Maubere People are heard.

As head of the Catholic Church in East Timor, Monsignor Ximenes Belo has already spoken on the subject of a referendum, through which the will of the Maubere People would be heard.

Holding a referendum presupposes:

— before all else, an end to hostilities;

— the adoption of international judicial mechanisms to check and control the process and make it viable;

— respect for the supreme wishes of the people of East Timor, as freely and democratically expressed.

… In order to eradicate any still lingering doubts, we add that should the Maubere People 'reaffirm' their desire for integration with Indonesia, then we, the guerrillas of the Falintil, would unhesitatingly lay down our arms without delay … Just as the UN Secretary General proposed a referendum for Western Sahara to Morocco and the Polisario Front, we believe that the same formula should be considered neither unheard of nor impossible for East Timor.

… If a fair solution should identify with peace, true and lasting peace, it should be a corollary to frank and serious dialogue. We are not demanding any absurd solutions from the world; neither are we seeking any solution which might compromise the UN Charter. We are only demanding adherence to the rules laid down by the community of nations, and respect for the universal principles which gave rise to the UN.

1. *The premise for the talks*, directed by the UN Secretary General, to be as follows:

- the illegality of the Indonesian invasion;
- the Maubere People's inalienable right to a true act of self-determination;
- the urgent need for restoration of international legality by way of Portugal's presence.

2. *The following points must be discussed with the participation of the Maubere People's representatives:*

a) The guarantees undertaken by Portugal with a view to *ensuring regional stability.*

- East Timor's commitments with regard to the interests of its neighbouring countries and its role in maintaining peace and stability in the region.
- A basic agreement of principles on the means of sharing out Timor's seabed wealth.

b) The constitution of a peace force, or an international force, or (should the latter be too costly for the UN) even a UN Commission to verify and render viable:

i) *Military reorganisation*
 - In the 1st phase — the withdrawal of Indonesia's Armed Forces over a period of between three to six months, and the return of the Indonesian civilians over a period as yet to be determined;
 - In the 2nd phase — simultaneous disarming of natives armed by the occupier and Falintil guerrillas; the latter would stay in the mountains until this moment;
 - In the 3rd phase — the reorganisation of the Army, under Portuguese responsibility, as the decolonising power;

ii) The setting up of a *transitional administration* headed by a High Commissioner, representing Portugal, for a maximum period of five years. It would be during this time that Portugal and East Timor would set a date for general elections and the handing over of sovereignty to the representatives of the Maubere People.

iii) During this transition period, under Portugal's responsibility, *agreement on cooperation* with Indonesia, Australia, the EEC and other countries will be established with a view to *ensuring quick and harmonious development* of East Timor's potential;

iv) *Formation of a National Unity Government* for a period of between five and 15 years to be set between Portugal and the representatives of East Timor.

It is frank and serious dialogue that can lead to the commitments necessary to safeguard the interests of each and of all in general, because the people of East Timor know they are not without obligations towards the surrounding area and they will not abdicate from making their contribution towards harmony, cooperation and understanding with their neighbours.

The National Council of Maubere Resistance has always been ready for dialogue with Indonesia; we continue to hope for dialogue in anticipation of the aforementioned concessions which would stabilise South East Asia. However, it is time for all to acknowledge that Indonesia's inflexibility towards East Timor is inappropriate for a government which aspires to take the leadership role in the peace process of Cambodia.

... Peace for East Timor can only be achieved by a realistic shift of position by Jakarta. For this to happen the Holy See could be a positive influence.

The Maubere People remain confident in their victory. The Maubere People will never cease to resist while there is life to carry on with the struggle, hoping that one day we will achieve peace for East Timor.

Peace is possible for East Timor!
Dialogue is a way towards peace!
A referendum will open up perspectives for a resolution and a just solution!

Chief of the Resistance
Kay Rala Xanana Gusmão
Commander of Falintil
Headquarters, CNRM, in East Timor, 5 October 1989

Report from the Mountains

In September 1990 Australian journalist and unionist Robert Domm made the dangerous and clandestine trek into the mountains of East Timor for the Australian Broadcasting Corporation to conduct the first ever direct interview with Xanana. Hundreds of people, from Bali to the mountains of East Timor, were involved in the operation to smuggle Domm up to Xanana' s secret guerrilla camp. After publication the Indonesian military attempted to round up those involved. This is only a small excerpt from the interview, containing Xanana's thoughts about indigenous spirituality and culture.

Domm: Xanana Gusmão seemed strangely out of place in the mountains, living a deprived life and hunted daily by a relentless enemy. You'd expect to find him drinking coffee and discussing politics in a sidewalk cafe in Lisbon. He was gentle and humorous, but also very hard and strict. He seemed to be cut in the mould of the classic guerrilla leader—an intellectual but also a soldier.

Meeting him, I could understand the reverence in which ordinary Timorese hold him. He's a living symbol of their resistance. Xanana is there in the mountains, and the Indonesians haven't been able to capture him in fifteen years.

Despite all their best efforts, their sophisticated American technology and thousands of troops, he survives to mount attacks against them.

The people in the towns believe there's hope in the hills; it's not all bleak. They haven't been totally subjugated because their leader is in the mountains. They see him as a beacon, keeping the flame of freedom alive, holding aloft the banner of what they call 'Maubere' nationalism.

Domm: Can you explain how important to you are the Timorese students? Can you describe how they are organised, and demonstrations which they've organised?

Gusmão: These students are of great significance, but it's not very convenient for us to talk about the way they're organised. However, they're completely mobilised to take practical actions in the struggle. This is based on their patriotic consciousness, which is in the blood of the Maubere People.

Because it's in our blood, it's not lost, and I think the whole world can understand the phenomenon of Maubere nationalism. It's not our propaganda; it's not an ephemeral, temporary phenomenon, but it's in the soul of the people, transmitted from parents to children.

The children at the time of the invasion directly suffered the horrors of war. They saw their parents being massacred; they saw their mothers being maltreated, their relatives and friends. Many of them lived in the mountains for many, many years. Others were under enemy control from the very beginning.

It's inevitable that a youngster who sees his father massacred should feel hatred towards the assassin. It's obvious that a youth who witnessed these atrocities can't distance himself from the whole situation in which we all live.

Today's students participate in clandestine organisations from Years 3, 4 and 5 of high school. For those born during this criminal occupation, the situation might be a bit different in that they didn't witness the horrors of the war—the bombardments, the battles, the long marches made in the forests and mountains. But the war didn't end with the loss of our bases in the mountains.

The difficult situation in which the people live under enemy control creates in the children a perception of the injustice of this criminal situation, which affects their own relatives, their neighbours and friends. And they're listening and understanding that in the final analysis it affects the entire Maubere People.

Domm: What have been the main changes in the traditional way of life?

Gusmão: There've not been a lot of changes. I would say there've been a lot of difficulties for the people to continue their customs and traditions. The Indonesian occupier has been exploiting what they see as Maubere identity, presenting folklore to tourists and foreign delegations. They think that the Maubere identity only resides in cultural manifestations.

This is a failed policy, because the traditional way of life of our people has changed radically in the sense that it was radically prevented. Our people are essentially rooted to their culture and traditions; they have their own concepts of life, of existence and live to realise them. They're impregnated spiritually and existentially with these concepts.

They conceive their passage through Mother Earth as a temporary time, ephemeral, in which they have to realise their traditional concepts. Our people are profoundly attached to Mother Earth. All their acts, cultural manifestations, and even life, are destined to consecrate, to honour, to worship Mother Earth as life.

Letter to José Ramos-Horta

About the Leadership of the Resistance

This letter to Nobel laureate Dr José Ramos-Horta was written while Xanana was in hiding in a small house in the west central part of East Timor. He had recently escaped a near-capture by Indonesian forces on a mountain-side near Ainaro subsequent to the Domm interview. The military commander Tri Sutrisno had flown in and was calling for him to surrender himself from where he had been encircled. Xanana has said he was only able to escape to a nearby village with the help of the luliks, *the local spirits of the land.*

Companheiro and brother Ramos-Horta, warm personal esteem and fraternal embraces.

I received the copy of your letter; the original remained with Hodu and you may have already received a letter from him. Your small gift made me extremely happy, especially since I have just escaped a very difficult situation. We are witnessing the largest military offensive of the last two years, which resulted in the surrounding of the CNRM Headquarters, located in the area of Bunaria, between Same and Ainaro, in the vicinity of the place where we met with Robert Domm. For the purpose, they used five battalions, personally led by the *Panglima*.[1] As a result of the offensive, all the documents and other materials, as well as munitions, were captured and it also resulted in the deaths of many of our guerrilla fighters.

It is within this new political context that I now address the issues raised in your letter. I also address them, not only in the spirit of Prof. Barbedo Magalhae's memorandum, but as oriented by the resolutions passed at the Aitana meeting.

1. The RER[2] [Structural Readjustment of the Resistance] had the practical and concrete aim of coordinating a joint and vigorous approach which would provide an image of combat solidarity to the whole Timorese resistance. This would avoid, amongst other things, the disregard of discipline and would help unify the diverse streams of information reaching the outside world. This was felt by us to be a seri-

[1] The Panglima is the Chief of the Indonesian Armed Forces, who at the time was General Tri Sutrisno.

[2] The RER or *Reajustamento Estrutural da Resistencia* was the restructuring of the resistance that formed CNRM, the National Council for Maubere Resistance.

ous problem because it weakened the whole movement in that it fragmented efforts. What was so hard for us to solve from the mountains, would have its appropriate response in the proper action of structurally disciplining internal/external relations. At the same time it would cater for the international capacity of the front outside which must face its own activities as a unified front—an action never taken by Fretilin or the UDT—thus overcoming the stage where there was convergence of principles but dispersal and disorder in their realisation.

It was not possible to make a structure prevail that followed the proposed forms, and today I must tell you that I am morally and politically inhibited from exercising [my] 'leadership over the process'. Not that I resented in any way the discordance about the RER, but it hurt me that my actions did not deserve your complete trust. This also automatically removed from me the moral and political capacity to decide about any other matters. On the other hand, I must say that I am not a cynic. Yes, I do like to see the irony in situations, and at times, I am perhaps offensively ironic. But I have tried to act with honesty, utilising however some subterfuges which only intend to cover up 'what I want to say but cannot'. I must confess, with all honesty, that it displeased me tremendously having to take on alone certain responsibilities in this process. Because, here, war has taught us here to speak clearly and to honestly assume responsibility for our own actions, I will never forget the moment in which I saw myself forced by circumstances to write with anger the 'mea culpa open letter' ... only to express my repudiation!

2. The SIR[3] appeared to me to be a complementary necessity in the face of the dispersed efforts of all of us and I was willing to contribute personally and in the most efficient way possible to its projects. Let us say, in passing, as captivating as the need for innovation and creativity was to overcome a certain morbidity, it was still was disheartening!

Furthermore, the SIR went against what I was preparing for 'afterwards'—a civic organisation of political character, non-partisan, independent and of weight, that was to be the answer to the crucial question of national life. Since 1988 I had already comprehensively sought to gain supporters for this political project within the different bodies of the armed resistance. Nevertheless, today, I must respect the accord which I assumed on 17 and 19 of September.

3. As to the Presidency of Fretilin and Falintil, the resolutions of the Aitana meeting have already answered in advance your proposals and suggestions.

---

3 *Secretariado Intercional da Resistencia:* International Secretariat of the Resistance.

4. About 'profiles'. My brother, we are humans and no matter how cynical and false one can be, one cannot avoid being defeated in moments of sincerity. I speak to you as a brother, in a relationship that only the struggle can build. I was touched by your demonstration of consideration and esteem, and, I must say, of an inappropriate and unmerited veneration.

After pondering the demands of the situation after the [1978-79] campaigns, I assumed without hesitation the command of the resistance, without the slightest feeling of vainglory, but bathed by my own tears. It was a very personal decision, transmitted afterwards to everyone. I knew and was conscious without the slightest drop of pride, that I was the most appropriate, because I felt ready to assume responsibility for the process. I knew and was conscious that my inexperience in commanding such an extensive and complex whole could crush me. I knew and was conscious that even if I excused myself, I would be the vilest coward because I would betray my own ideal of the struggle. I knew and was conscious that I must fulfil my duty to my country and to my people.

On the one hand it was a difficult period, crucial in the destiny of our Homeland. On the other, it was an easy and opportune period, for gathering and housing the seeds of ambition for power, for incorporating the realisation of a personal goal into the duties which particular roles assigned. My brother, I won a difficult struggle, constantly on the alert, repudiating the slightest weakness in the sense of a weakness which would have betrayed my own principles of serving, totally and solely, the Homeland! Today, I am in a position to tell you that the hardship of war and the passage of time have made me immune, morally and politically, in this matter.

I accepted, and keep accepting [my role], fully aware that I am only doing my duty, that they accept me and consider me 'leader of the resistance'. It is in this spirit of combat that I assumed, with neither presumption nor pride, leadership of the resistance within the RER.

I believe that, for reasons that you must understand, the May decisions of the extraordinary meeting of the CNRM did not manage to change the schedule of responsibilities prior to that meeting and hence the schedule that the resolutions of that meeting tried to modify had only theoretical or symbolic consequences outside.

Internally, the structures provided by the RER are the ones that continue to direct the thinking and political activities of the resistance and, I believe, even have implications for the exterior. The 'confusion and discontent' regarding my departure from Fretilin only existed out there. It was not because I wished or wish to maintain and consolidate my personal leadership or, even less, that I wanted to directly or indirectly influence the internal status quo. It would have been totally confusing and truly disappointing if I had abandoned my position in the common trench [alongside the soldiers]. I accepted and continue accepting this role [as resistance commander] and I shall not be side-tracked from the duty that the Homeland demands and the people entrusted to me. To escape from these responsibilities would truly be treason. However, I knew and assumed that this mission would end when the war ended, and the country was liberated … if ever I had the happiness to contemplate that in the absolute tranquillity of a peace we are constructing. However brave and courageous a soldier might be, and whatever the circumstances, he can never merit promotion to general. To do so would be to ridicule the entire army.

As my eyes glanced over the 'profile of a Timorese statesman', I merely smiled to myself in commiseration. I understand the extent of your emotion; I understand the intensity of your esteem; and I also understand the depth of your gesture of admiration. But the imaginings of time and distance have constructed an idealised conception of me. Brother, I will accept that the leadership of the resistance must again be theoretically and structurally formulated, in so far as it guarantees that the armed resistance can be identified and included as a necessary part of any proposed new solution.

I will never accept, however, a comparison with, or appointment to, statesman. My only ambition, which I continue fulfilling with all my strength, is to contribute to the liberation of the Homeland. After that, and if I live until then, I only wish that I will have time to walk the trail again trying to recognise the footprints left by the Falintil in the forests of East Timor, remembering everything they have done and all their sacrifices. Any pretension to a personal career would be an affront to the suffering of my men and I shall not be so vile as to commit such an act!

Furthermore, my dear brother, I know myself all too well and though it may seem improbable, it is much easier to wage war than to fulfil ambitions! Many years ago, on receiving a letter of this kind, I would be afraid of myself; today, fortunately, I no longer need to run away from my own thoughts. Finally, my brother, I thank you for respecting the vow that I made to my men: to fight solely for the liberation of the Maubere Homeland!

In conclusion, I emphasise the trust and esteem in which I have always held you, together with Bukar and Hodu and of all the guerrillas. We are certain that, relaunched into the fray, you will pursue the struggle with us—a struggle which you began before me.

From all the Resistance, embraces
Kai Rala Xanana Gusmão

O Publico Interview

by Adelino Gomes

This interview was recorded on video on 2 and 3 June 1991 in the mountains in the eastern part of the island and was published in O Publico *on 6 September. On 18 February 1988, the Indonesian Government had invited members of the Portuguese Parliament to send a delegation to East Timor on an 'observation' mission which Xanana is expecting, here, to come at the end of the year. The negotiations they speak of are the talks under UN auspices between Indonesia and Portugal (see Introduction to the Message to Catholic Youth of 20 May 1986, p. 86).*

Gomes: Should the Timorese be called to participate in the negotiations? When? Who should represent them?

Gusmão: The process has become a ball game and perhaps it is too premature to identify the exact opportunity for Timorese participation. It is our point of view that should the negotiations break down (if Indonesia continues with negative attitudes), the most coherent response should be to let the representatives of East Timor be called in.

Gomes: When?

Gusmão: After the visit there will be a sequence of actions that will come about from the report of the Portuguese Parliamentary Delegation. Thus we believe that this will be the exact opportunity for the participation of the Timorese.

Gomes: Who will represent them?

Gusmão: In principle, the CNRM [National Council of Maubere Resistance] from inside or simply the National Convergence [coalition between Fretilin and UDT]. However, I will admit in some circumstances that I would not mind, for example, meeting face-to-face with Mario Carrascalao just so as to facilitate the negotiations.

Gomes: What actions do you think Portugal should have taken that it has not already taken in favour of the Timorese people?

Gusmão: I prefer not to be the judge of Portugal's actions. I can only try to understand Portugal's great limitations. To demand more than what has already been asked by Portugal can only lessen our right to demand all that we want to achieve, that is, our own liberation. And what more can I say about what Portugal could have done or not done when I read that the 'Eventual Commission'[1] complains of logistics and that the Ministry of Foreign Affairs (MNE) keeps everything so secret?

Gomes: Two years have passed since the Pope's visit to Timor. How do you evaluate the Pope's attitude?

Gusmão: I have followed for some years the polemic of the theology of liberation. A few times, the clergy of Latin America have referred to the Pope as a 'Pole living in Rome'. The Kurds are more children of God and their suffering is lived more intensively by the Pope.

Father Tucci [the cardinal who was in Jakarta preparing the Pope's visit to Timor] affirmed that it would be simply inconceivable that the Holy See would sacrifice its high interests for a handful of Catholics being pressured by the *Pancasila* [constitutional ideology of Indonesia].

In the end, it is the politics of those who do not play politics. St Peter must be listening to us [smiles]. Rumours in East Timor say that the old apostle will not open the heavenly gates for the Indonesians. Hopefully, he will do the same for the pro-Indonesians.

Gomes: At the moment what is the relationship between the resistance and the Timorese church? What do you think of the recent stand of Dili's bishop, Monsignor Ximenes Belo?

Gusmão: Within the Timorese clergy, the spirit of unity is excellent, apart from three or four local priests not wanting to intrude in other institutions' matters. I'm led to believe that his open letter [May 1990] reflects a complex internal situation in which the explanation lies in the restricted field of work of the church itself, work which is led or simply executed by Dom Ximenes Belo.

Gomes: You abandoned Fretilin in December 1988 and later you asked to be reinstated. What is your present relationship with this party?

Gusmão: I left Fretilin in December 1987. Today the relationship is less tense but there are political suspicions, which are not created nor wished by me.

Gomes: And the rest of the guerrilla commanders: do they belong to Fretilin or not?

---

1 *Commissao Eventual para o Acompanhamento de Timor-Leste*, the Portuguese Commission for the Future, was formed by the Portuguese parliament to follow developments in East Timor.

Gusmão: They all accept the non-partisan concept.

Gomes: Is there any commander or resistance official affiliated with or representing any other Timorese party?

Gusmão: No.

Gomes: What is the present role of the students in the anti-Indonesian resistance?

Gusmão: I would define it essentially as a role of continuity. The new generation feels they must keep the flame of the resistance alive.

This call, promptly answered by the students, has aspects which are greatly reflected in the popular and overall resistance. The old generation, which has lived through two wars, sees in that a palpable result of their sacrifice and the answer to their expectations, hopes and faith.

It is, on the other hand, a confirmation that people can die, but not ideas. Lastly, I believe that what is most important is an incessant search for innovation, a desire to explain the present and a careful preparation for the future, which belongs to them.

Gomes: Is the civil resistance non-partisan or are its actions subordinated to the command of the armed resistance?

Gusmão: The resistance is not totally non-partisan when we acknowledge Fretilin's great political influence. But it is non-partisan or made non-partisan because its actions are subordinated to the command of the armed resistance.

Those scared of this situation, of, let's say, political or party disunity (which is not totally true), are those who have limited contact with the war.

The people, as well as Fretilin officials, conceive the present struggle in terms of liberation of the Homeland and not in terms of, for example, Fretilin being the only representative, being the forefront, having control, having majority support or even of Fretilin leading the struggle and not UDT.

They don't deny the relevant role assumed by Fretilin but acknowledge that UDT could win general elections in case Fretilin (eventually in power) did not live up to its electoral promises. They understand that if this happens in the future, the people cannot be slaves to the politics of the *katuas* (veterans). This perception of the future does not withdraw any value or glory from Fretilin in the present.

Gomes: In what areas of the territory do the guerrillas act?

Gusmão: I think a map was published by the enemy around 1984-85 where you can see the locations of the guerrilla groups. Today, with successive changes produced by the establishment of strategic villages deep in our areas in the interior, I can say or should say that the definitions of the zones in general terms remain the same.

Gomes: How many armed fighters are there?

Gusmão: I prefer to say that since 1979, we have remained the same 50 fugitives from the eastern point. [This is an ironic reference to the Indonesian authorities who since then always spoke of the same few dozen fugitives.]

Gomes: Do you believe in a solution for the coming years? From your point of view, which solution will prevail? The diplomatic [through the UN], political [through change in Indonesia] or military?

Gusmão: For 16 years we fought for that to happen. I believe the solution will be a diplomatic solution, where Portugal as well as we ourselves can act more broadly and with more promising results. Depending on eventual circumstances, the change of regime in Indonesia could be favourable. However, I think that won't happen so soon. I can only put these changes into perspective if the democratic opposition proves capable of moving the masses.

The regime is still very strong and the Indonesians seem to be embarrassed about *Pembangunan* [the Indonesian Government development program] ...This is only a very personal opinion without much knowledge of the movements.

Gomes: How is your daily life?

Gusmão: Entirely dedicated to the struggle, with all its internal difficulties and the need to obtain global perspective.

Gomes: Do you sleep in houses or in the bush?

Gusmão: More than 90 per cent of the time I sleep in the bush with my companions.

Gomes: What do the fighters eat?

Gusmão: Anything that can be digested, from what can be picked or collected from the land's natural resources or collected from the rice fields and vegetable gardens.

Gomes: What do they drink?

Gusmão: Normally coffee, because we have in our control many small coffee plantations. Depending on the place and length of stay, some groups extract palm tree wine. It's only used for occasions like weddings, festive days or to celebrate a meeting between groups.

Gomes: Do you feel constantly pursued and are there moments of high tension? What do you do in those moments?

Gusmão: Pursued? Not at all. I've stayed in some places for 12 to 15 months. I shift base when signs of our presence are likely to attract the enemy's attention. I would call moments of tension the periods I stay with forces of one or more groups. There I deal in solving problems, to learn what they feel in the great difficulties of this war. There we establish new ideas, formulate new action plans; we reaffirm our convictions, our principles, our determination, our ideals.

On those occasions, I treat the wounded and the sick, play with the children and help my fellow fighters. We also work in the kitchen, produce *sagu* [flour extracted from palm trees] or pick *caleics* [nuts] or I even mend my clothes.

Gomes: What do you miss the most from the daily life of a free man? Going out? Going to the cinema? Lunch in a restaurant?

Gusmão: The question is irrelevant. It is the struggle to which I am committed and it is above all those things. As you may have heard, I have been in Dili and returned with a stronger will to fight. This is the only time I had contact with ways of life that could bring back memories. What I really miss is peace and I will continue to fight to regain it.

Gomes: Did you ever panic during the struggle? In what moments?

Gusmão: Not for a moment. I did have moments of anguish because I felt incapable of avoiding some disasters, such as the surrounding of Aitana in September 1981, only six months after reorganising, or when I passed to the central regions in 1980. The emptiness I found really scared me. Not Ma'Huno, nor Txay, nor even myself, the three surviving members of FCC, had the minimal subjective conditions to conduct the resistance in that state.

Later, the war hardened my feelings. Any difficulties were always felt within context and always with the firm intent to bear them or at least avoid them.

Letter to Boutros Boutros Ghali

Secretary General of the United Nations

This letter to the newly elected Secretary General of the United Nations, Boutros Boutros Ghali, takes the opportunity to outline the history of the invasion and occupation of East Timor, and remind him of the UN resolutions concerning East Timor. It documents the then recent Santa Cruz massacre of November 1991 and the need for Timorese participation in the UN-auspiced talks on East Timor.

Your Excellency,

With respectful compliments and on behalf of the people of East Timor, I have the honour to greet Your Excellency as the highest-ranking officer of the United Nations.

Your election constituted yet another victory for the Third World, symbol of North-South disparities. Your brilliant career and rich diplomatic experience, as well as the fact that you have a first-hand knowledge of the plight of the Palestinian and Saharawi people, give us confidence that Your Excellency will not forget the existence of a people, in Oceania, a people fighting for the universal rights enshrined in the United Nations Charter.

The signing of the Salvadorean peace agreement, right at the beginning of your mandate, filled the people of East Timor with joy and hope for their aspirations. We are conscious that greater problems will require your attention; East Timor, however, is not a new case; it was entrusted to the Secretary-General by General Assembly resolution 37/30.

East Timor was the object of eight General Assembly and two Security Council resolutions; the latter urged Jakarta immediately to withdraw all its forces from East Timor.

Cases such as Kuwait showed how the international community vigorously repudiates acts of expansionism, perpetrated in total violation of international law and norms. Cases such as Cambodia, on the other hand, reveal the good will of the international community to settle differences and conflicts through the most appropriate means, that is, the path of dialogue.

Resolution 37/30 mandated the Secretary General of the UN to initiate consultations with the parties involved. The wrong interpretation given to the spirit and the letter of this resolution derives from the lack of definition of the substantive question. If we talk about international law, then the East Timorese people should have that right [of consultation]—if we spell out those universal rights, such principles should be applied to the Maubere People as well.

In East Timor, an armed conflict has persisted for 16 years; in East Timor, a generalised political resistance by our people persists against Indonesian military occupation. From September 1975, Indonesia had been violating our borders and these acts of aggression culminated in the murder of five Australian journalists who had witnessed the violations. On 7 December 1975 it invaded. As a result of the vandalism that followed the invasion, more than 80 per cent of the population abandoned their homes and their possessions and moved up to the mountains, in a natural and spontaneous demonstration of their repudiation of foreign aggression and a determination to defend the sovereignty of their Homeland.

Until August 1977, the aggressors only controlled the main roads and a few villages. In the following months, the Jakarta generals launched major search and destroy operations against several resistance bases. This offensive only ended in November 1978. Using scorched earth tactics, with daily air, sea and artillery heavy bombings, the invading army forced the people into constant displacement. Many died as a result of the shelling and from starvation and disease. The physical exhaustion these people endured under such a large-scale offensive weighed considerably in their decision to give themselves up to the enemy. Numerous massacres were perpetrated as the people surrendered—horrible crimes that only occupation forces could commit. The people, confined to areas surrounding the villages, totally controlled and under all kinds of restrictions, succumbed to starvation and disease. During the years of 1978 and 1980 burials were a daily event.

Besides the starvation and disease, 1979 and 1980 were also the years when the occupying forces emptied the prisons—it must be mentioned that there were prisons in all of the administrative councils and in the majority of the outposts—where the surrendering cadres and community members who were active in organising and mobilising the masses during the difficult period of the resistance were sent. Individual and collective killings systematically occurred on a daily basis. If people were missing, that meant only that the place where those victims were killed was unknown, because there was no doubt that they were being taken to 'Jakarta'. It was during that period of hunger and strict surveillance that the Indonesian forces killed many villagers who were compelled to walk to surrounding bush areas to gather leaves, wild roots or fruit in order to survive. They spared no one, not the elderly, not women, not children.

In the first half of 1981, a new wave of imprisonments and killings shook the territory, especially Dili. Ataúro opened up its doors to accommodate tens of thousands of deported people. Torture, as a generalised practice, increased. Violence, persecution, massacres and extortion of the victims were all elements of the climate of terror. A person walking on a road to another village would be killed for not carrying a *surat jalan* [travel document]; a person would be killed for staying longer at the farm and returning to the *apel* [compulsory assembly] at late hours. Killings would happen also inside the farms, through which the Indonesian troops would return from their raids against the guerrillas. Women were raped by entire platoons; women were shot to death when they tried to resist; parents were tortured and killed in the presence of their children and husbands in the presence of their wives.

This prolonged situation was worsened by incessant hunger, because no crops could be produced. It became very hard for anything or anyone just to survive.

At the end of 1983 and throughout 1984, another wave of imprisonments, killings and missing people left all of East Timor in pain and bereavement. It should be pointed out that from March to July 1983, a cease-fire agreement between the warring parties was in effect. In contradiction to the intentions that led to the establishment of a dialogue, Jakarta threatened to decimate us if we would not surrender, taking a provocative attitude in a clear violation of the cease-fire agreements.

From 1985 to the present, the threats and particularly the persecution carried out by the vast secret police organisation, as well as the imprisonments, have continued unabated—unequivocal evidence that Jakarta continued these intolerable practices because it felt it was being backed by many western countries which frequently use double standards in similar situations of total disrespect for fundamental human rights.

The brutal repression that unfolded in the wake of the illegal occupation of East Timor culminated in the Santa Cruz killings of 12 November 1991 and the cases of arrest and torture that followed the incident.

Mr Secretary General. We can state, with all conviction, that more than 200,000 Timorese lost their lives as a consequence of the bloody invasion and illegal occupation of East Timor.

The events of 12 November are a sufficient indication of that. While the estimated death toll was 150 to 180, Jakarta's official version referred only to 19 (later changed to 50, due to international pressure). Therefore one could raise the question that the official death toll [for the period of occupation] of 60,000 to 80,000 should in all fairness invite the reservations of the international community, namely the United Nations. The Indonesian Government has adopted the policy of playing down its practices of torture and denying the killings. Before the US Commission on Human Rights and its Sub-Commission, the Indonesian delegates tried to subvert the ethical, moral and political values of human rights, bringing up the absurd justification that any statements denouncing violations of human rights in East Timor are 'false accusations by people who don't like Indonesia'.

Jakarta has always opposed the access to East Timor of any international, independent inquiry missions, alleging that it is an Indonesian internal affair. Not even the presence of the UN Special Rapporteur, Mr Peter Koojmans, could curb the policy of genocide in which the Jakarta leadership have been engaged. President Suharto managed to win the sympathy of friendly countries like the USA, Australia, the Netherlands, Japan and Canada, because they were satisfied with the 'evidence' that the number of people killed in the Santa Cruz incident was 50, not 19. His efforts, however, did not change in the least Indonesian policy toward East Timor.

After the two high-ranking officers who were made responsible for the incident were transferred, there was an official statement that revealed the true intentions of the new Military Commander. Control measures were stepped up, with *kopassus* [elite troops] posted across all Dili neighbourhoods and other places in the interior, in addition to ABRI [the Indonesian Army] platoons, also called *masuk desa,* supposedly deployed to 'mingle' with the local population. These troops subject the people, on a daily basis, to a program that has as one of its goals an almost absolute control of the youth, by monitoring their movements and activities.

Young men from all *desas* [villages] summoned to go to the Dili *Kodim* [District Command], were themselves suddenly taken on trucks to Taibesse, the barracks for Battalion 744, to receive military training. Daily sports activities are mandatory in some *desas,* and that became a sure way of controlling the youth. The authorities continue to make persecutions and to expand and strengthen the secret police apparatus. The Indonesians themselves say that the 'the rule of *manis* [sweetness] is over—from now on there will be a *senjata* [armed] rule'.

And it will continue that way, as long as the occupation forces remain in the territory. The repression exerted by Indonesia is a consequence of this situation and, as long as there is imposition by the force of arms by one side, there will always be a rejection of a foreign presence by the other side.

Jakarta claims that the situation is an internal affair and supports its claim with the 'Declaration of Balibo' as the document that gave origin to the '7th

July Integration'. Many East Timorese, including the UDT Vice-President, Joao Carrascalao, have denounced the farce of the 'Provisional Assembly'. The key argument in support of the 'internal affair' allegation is that, through the so-called 'Provisional Assembly', the people of East Timor 'chose integration by their own free will'.

The late Bishop Dom Martinho Lopes, who witnessed all the tragic events in East Timor from the beginning of the invasion, up until his own expulsion from the territory eight years later, always spoke out loud and clear, protesting the fact that no one ever asked the Maubere People whether they wanted integration or not. I must add that such an act, presented as 'an act of self-determination', was implemented at a time when the vast majority of the East Timorese people were under heavy pressure from the invading forces with constant air, sea and land attacks.

I must point out, Mr Secretary General, that besides the facts of the tragic situation of the people who resisted in the mountains, there are testimonies by those who witnessed and/or participated against their own will, who declared that those 'elected' to the so-called 'People's Assembly' were recruited by the Indonesian military.

Recently, Bishop Ximenes Belo portrayed the prevailing situation in a letter addressed to the [outgoing] UN Secretary General, asking for a referendum to be held, because the people of East Timor had never been given the opportunity to express their will freely. He said, 'We are dying out as a people and as a nation'. In fact, many governments—I would even say all of the governments who may recognise the 'sovereignty of Indonesia over East Timor'—do not agree with the way in which the 'integration into Indonesia' was carried out. Under international law, this act can only be considered as the illegal annexation of East Timor, carried out with the use of force.

The United Nations and its appropriate bodies have condemned the acts of aggression and military occupation perpetrated on East Timor. International organisations, namely the European Community, European Parliament, Council of Europe and others, prominent individual entities, and parliaments and governments from various countries have also condemned Indonesia and urge all parties involved, including the East Timorese, to search for a negotiated solution to the conflict.

Mr Secretary General. Humankind can breathe the winds of democratic change. Recent and current developments in some regions of the globe seem to have revived the phenomenon of people's nationalism. It has been proven beyond doubt that the use of force can put down rebellions, but it cannot destroy people's minds, and that repression can subjugate a people—an entire people—but it will not destroy that people's aspirations, no matter in which latitude on the globe or at which point in history.

Self-determination as a principle and as a right is a most cherished aspiration for any people in the world. Self-determination is a legal process, in which a people determines its identity and decides on its destiny and therefore any act of self-determination must be exercised in freedom.

A New World Order is being shaped out of the Cold War and the collapse (surprisingly sudden) of the Iron Curtain. The process of democratic renewal, whose effects are being felt the world over, reflects the awareness of the peoples that materialistic deals are not satisfactory when one's spirit is being oppressed and when one's body is being subjected to violence, when justice is ignored and freedom and reason and truth are suppressed.

All the peoples in the world want to walk hand-in-hand towards a future of peace and freedom on our planet. The settlement of many conflicts underscores the validity and fairness of dialogue as the basic principle for good relations among human beings and among peoples and nations.

The signing of the peace accords in El Salvador augurs a promising mandate for Your Excellency. May we convey to you our best wishes for success in attaining the goals of peace and the strengthening of democracy, freedom and human rights and the narrowing of the gap between the North and the South. Dialogue is the only appropriate path to eliminate differences, the fairest means to bring together warring factions and the most appropriate way to seek solutions and build up peace.

What we need is political will on the part of everyone concerned, particularly the leadership, so that through dialogue we can continue to build, piece by piece, a world of enduring peace. The present international political situation makes it easier for dialogue to prevail as the most appropriate way towards the strengthening of the New Order. We can no longer rely just on idealism. The changes dictate otherwise—for the rock-solid defence of the human and fundamental rights of the peoples. We can no longer rely on idealism—the future compels us to do otherwise, to defend universal principles. We can no longer rely on idealism—human conscience compels us to do otherwise, to defend justice and liberty!

Life in the future cannot continue to be dictated by the interests of the strong and powerful. Life in the future must be more humane and more faithful to the foundations of freedom and democracy. Only a more humane and less egocentric vision, only a more collaborative and less self-interested vision, only a fairer and more balanced and less dishonest vision—on the part of the rich and economically-strong countries—will help find the right direction to alleviate the sacrifices endured by Third World peoples. While everything revolves around economic interests, while everything is defined by regional strategies, while everything is measured on a scale of advantages and disadvantages, poverty and disparity will prevail, political incoherence will prevail and the New World Order will, after all, be marked by the submission of the poor and weak to the callousness of the rich and the strong.

But we believe in the good will of human beings. We believe that things will be re-established in a positive way and that the Middle East talks now under way will result in substantive agreements which will help foster new Arab-Israeli relations and enable the Palestinians to have a future with rights to which they are entitled. We believe that the profound differences that became an obstacle to the Western Saharan referendum being held within the established schedule will be overcome, for the benefit of all parties involved, and that, within the framework of the United Nations, a peaceful, just and lasting settlement can be achieved.

We also believe that the irreversible process of the dismantling of apartheid will continue its course without further delay, towards the establishment of a democratic and multi-racial system where all individuals are equal, with the same rights and obligations.

We believe that the processes of national reconciliation under way in Africa, in Asia and in Latin America will bring peace and concord among people.

We believe that peace is not the privilege of just a few peoples, because peace is essentially an aspiration of humankind.

Only justice can ensure peace, because injustice means total disregard for the universal values of freedom and the rule of law. East Timor is a case that falls under international law. The prevailing situation in East Timor constitutes a violation of international norms and a rejection of universal principles.

We also believe that the time has come for the government of Indonesia—a great, thriving Third World nation—to reflect upon the need to take the right step, in the right direction.

Unfortunately, having exhausted all the arguments to justify before the western world the act of aggression against East Timor and its military occupation of the territory, recently Mr Ali Alatas, referring to the massacre of 12 November, brought up again the original argument of the 'existence of a Communist threat'. A minimum of common sense should have made the Indonesian Foreign Affairs Ministry stop and think before saying something of this nature. We believe, even so, that new thinking fostered by these changes will prompt the Indonesian leadership to reconsider their attitude of inflexibility before the international community, even if only for the sake of affirming the principles that served as the basis for the foundation of the NAM.

Mr Secretary General. Your Excellency has a mandate, under resolution 37/30, to deal with the question of East Timor.

Portugal, as the Administering Power for the territory, which is recognised by the international community, has stated the need for participation by the East Timorese, in tripartite talks. On our side, I would like to reiterate our total willingness to participate in a dialogue. Our proposal of a dialogue without pre-conditions, which was extensively endorsed by various international organisations and various countries' parliaments, politicians and individual entities, as well as by several governments and human rights organisations, has the objective of enabling all parties involved to be on an equal footing, so a discussion can be initiated on ways and means more consistent and satisfactory to all involved, for a just, lasting and internationally acceptable solution.

However, we appeal to Your Excellency, Mr Secretary General, to replace the mediator in this process. It has been demonstrated in several instances that the role of mediation is crucial to advancing or thwarting efforts. And when those efforts are made within the framework of the United Nations, the impartiality and the fairness of the UN representatives are moral imperatives.

Lastly, Mr Secretary General, I have the honour to inform Your Excellency that there will soon be general elections in Indonesia. Jakarta has in the past used the elections to affirm that the people of East Timor have already demonstrated twice the validity of the act of integration.

We believe that it would be enough to mention the massacre of 12 November for people to grasp the true meaning of the 'popular will' expressed in the past two elections. With this rationale, it will not be surprising to hear about a massive participation of the people who voted for the all-mighty Golkar [the official government political party]. As a matter of fact, instructions were already issued to the effect that everyone should vote for Mr Golkar, in order to avert retaliation.

The ship *Lusitania Expresso*, which was on a peaceful mission, has been the objective of repeated threats of destruction [see Introduction to the Letter of 18 May 1992 p. 167]; its mere presence provoked unprecedented restrictive measures against East Timorese youths; more than 100 college students were arrested and taken to the Battalion 744 barracks in Taibesse. In addition to that, dozens of other students were drafted to receive mandatory military instruction, a preventive measure to keep the young people under control upon the arrival of the ship.

Situations such as these, which reveal the kind of repression exerted under military occupation, remove all credibility from the elections which are expected to take place in the next months. It is simply inconceivable that anyone would try and make believe that there is a possibility to contest the situation, through a so-called abstention by a people victimised by repression and control.

Please accept, Your Excellency, the assurances of my highest consideration.

Kay Rala Xanana Gusmão
Member of the CNRM
Commander of Falintil
Command Headquarters of the Maubere Resistance, East Timor
31 January 1992

15 MAY 1992

Letter to President Mandela

This was written during the three-year period when both Nelson Mandela and Xanana Gusmão were at liberty. After 10,000 days of imprisonment, Nelson Mandela was released in February 1990 into a new South Africa, while Xanana, who had become a seasoned guerrilla leader, was honing his skills in the ways of international diplomacy, as this letter shows. Not long after his release, Mandela had spoken out at the United Nations General Assembly about the case of East Timor after contacts with Jose Ramos-Horta. This letter is one of thanks and a request for continued support. Again in 1996 the two exchanged messages and Nelson Mandela sent Xanana his autobiography with a message of encouragement. On Nelson Mandela's state visit to Indonesia in July 1997 he requested to meet with Xanana. President Suharto arranged for Xanana to be brought to the Indonesian presidential guesthouse for a formal dinner. Mandela reassured him that he supported a just solution for East Timor. They agreed that the embrace of all parties was essential in the process of national reconciliation.

To the President of the ANC,

Your Excellency, Mr President of the ANC,

My deepest regards to your Excellency.

First of all, it is a great honour to address your Excellency and to express our highest admiration for the example set in your struggle for freedom, justice and democracy.

In our own on-going 17-year resistance, we have always had the struggles of SWAPO and ANC as sources of inspiration for the perseverance that guided the two movements through long decades.

Just causes, Mr President, have never been settled easily. Just causes have always been maintained by the strong will of the combatants, by the heroism of those who fight for the ideals they proclaim. Your Excellency is indeed a symbol of the struggle for justice, a symbol for the struggle of the oppressed. Unfortunately, the struggle of the oppressed continues to be, to this day, a question for the conscience of humanity.

The West, defender of freedom, has made its support for such struggles conditional on a safeguarding of its own interests, so that oppressed peoples are left with no options other than violent confrontation. If this were not so, we would not have witnessed in the last decade of the 20th century the aberration of apartheid.

With great pleasure, today, as a result of the ANC's long struggle, we are witnessing an enormous shift in attitudes and a great opening of the spirit. Of undoubted importance was the government's political disposition to initiate dialogue and this great victory of De Klerk now marks the beginning of a new South Africa.

It was also an important victory for the black majority, denied their rights by a system that was a stain on humanity. It was a victory for the ANC and a victory for all oppressed people.

It was also, equally, a victory for the people of East Timor! With great pleasure, we note the better prospects presented to the black majority in South Africa. We congratulate the ANC and we congratulate your Excellency. We also take the opportunity to congratulate his Excellency, the President, Mr Frederick De Klerk!

Your Excellency, Mr President, we were much moved by your remembrance of the tragedy of the East Timorese people. Hearing your pronouncement at the UN General Assembly defending the Timorese cause, we were encouraged to continue our struggle!

I believe it unnecessary to recount the history of the difficult struggle of the Maubere People, since only full knowledge of the cause could have motivated your Excellency to raise your voice in defence of justice and peace in East Timor. We feel strengthened, although we are small and weak, that in your Excellency we have a strong advocate for the sacred aspirations of our people.

At stake, your Excellency, are the international law and the universal principles; at stake are the fundamental rights of all people and justice! Just as in Kuwait! It is the politics of double standards that has relegated the issue of East Timor to the 'dossiers' of the United Nations while priority is given to the Middle East, Afghanistan, Cambodia and Yugoslavia, conflicts which are of the same nature as ours.

The people of East Timor, like the people of Western Sahara, continue to be victims of the complicity and indifference of governments which continue to focus on economic ties with Jakarta. A flagrant case of complicity is Australia's policy of 'cooperation and partnership'. In that country their own indigenous people, the Aborigines, are victims of an unspoken but nonetheless real and painful racial segregation.

We believe that dialogue, for both big and small conflicts, is the best means of achieving a solution. Recent history proves this to be uncontestable fact.

Dialogue without pre-conditions, with the participation of the Timorese, is our firm proposal. Through frank and constructive dialogue, we can evaluate the interests of all parties involved. There will be no losers or winners. It will be like two brothers and neighbours finding a way to a long-lasting peace.

It is this message of dialogue that we ask your Excellency to deliver to Jakarta and please never stop mentioning the need for a solution for East Timor or alerting the international community to the suffering of the Maubere People.

Your Excellency, Mr President, your noble political stance, and your historical international stature represent to the martyred people of East Timor a gift in their own struggle for the liberation of their Homeland.

Help us, your Excellency, to achieve peace! Help this weak, small and defenceless people free itself from the ties of oppressive colonialism, ties which have characterised its history. Help us remove the bars from this big prison that is East Timor so our people can be free, by appealing to the western governments to consider the East Timorese people's right to self-determination and by exerting pressure on Jakarta to accept dialogue, thus supporting Portugal's efforts in discharging its responsibilities towards East Timor.

Your Excellency, Mr President, we are certain that you will not disregard the appeal of our people who have suffered violently for almost 17 years!

Thus, as we believe in a new South Africa, where peace, justice, social harmony and equal rights will prevail, we also strongly believe that your Excellency's interventions on behalf of the East Timorese people will provide East Timor with respect for the fundamental rights of the Maubere People!

Viva the ANC! Viva the solidarity between the oppressed peoples! Viva the people of East Timor!

With the highest regards,

Kay Rala Xanana Gusmão
Falintil Commander
Headquarters, in the mountains of East Timor, 15 May 1992

Letter to Father Jaime Coelho

Jaime Coelho is a Portuguese priest. He was involved in the 'Peace Mission to East Timor' of 1992. In March of that year, the Portuguese vessel Lusitania Express *sailed from Darwin to Dili intending to lay flowers on the graves of those who had died during the Santa Cruz massacre. It carried people from Portugal, the United States, Australia, Canada, China, Europe, Indonesia, Korea and many other countries. The East Timorese resistance had prepared banners and coffins and hoped to accompany the visitors to the cemetery, and many Timorese believed that despite the the failed Portuguese Parliamentary Delegation and the Santa Cruz massacre this mission would truly restart the process of peace through dialogue. However, Indonesian military security had been stepped up in the month prior to the visit and Indonesian immigrants had deserted Dili. The* Lusitania *had already sighted land when it was prevented from proceeding by the Indonesian navy which had seven ships patrolling Dili harbour. The flowers intended for the graves were instead strewn over the sea.*

Reverend Father Jaime Coelho

I received your letter very late, but your great love for the Timorese cause touched me and your contagious optimism greatly impressed me.

Warm greetings from the Falintil guerrillas in the East Timor mountains. I will try to make my people aware of your letter, so they will know another friend and companion of our cause. The Committee members and I embrace you with profound recognition of your friendship.

It is difficult, right now, for me to explain the possible situations that might compromise Falintil's code of honour. As a Commander leading an armed struggle, I overstep the boundaries of ethics and morals when I encourage my men to face death and when I reprimand them for being unable to kill the occupying soldier. I do not believe in the moral principle of 'hara-kiri' but for me honour complements duty.

For years now I have witnessed the continual depletion in numbers of my fighters, and I have felt bitterly our increasing limitations in securing an armed resistance as active as before—one capable of smashing small enemy fronts, defying Indonesian battalions, of dying laughing on the battlefields with a sense of duty fulfilled. Realising all this, I knew the great difficulties I would have to simply ensure the basic survival of Falintil, and one question stuck in my mind: Is all this collective suicide?

I felt this during the years Portugal was kidding itself that it had behaved honorably on the Timor issue, during the early years when Falintil was feared, when it was capturing small sophisticated guns from the occupant. As a Commander, I should have foreseen the future of the armed struggle so I could create more even conditions, seek new methods of fighting and develop new resistance strategies.

Thirteen years have passed in the new phase of our country's liberation in which Falintil took upon itself the responsibility of maintaining the struggle.[1] Nine years after the failure of negotiations with the occupying authorities, we continue to fight—continue to die—in difficult conditions! Each death, each capture, each surrender of armed fighters, is a deep wound in the flesh of our armed fighters, in a body exhausted by the scars of war and covered in splinters from combats, but always with sufficient courage to defy time itself.

In 1979, I went from house to house, village to village, town to town, and asked my people if they were willing to continue the fight and they demanded that I never ever surrender! My people wish, rather demand and prefer, that I die on the battlefields! *Such is the high sense of honour of the people of East Timor!* And I am this country's soldier, and servant to those one thousand-time heroic people!

Today, the struggle offers me a difficult predicament, more difficult than the initial years of reorganisation. Today the struggle demands a decision. Today I have to assess the future continuously!

The people of East Timor have already chosen their own destiny, and it is difficult to explain that to you, as after all we do not control our own destiny! We might have, if God's hand had slipped and he had pushed East Timor, only East Timor, just a little bit outside Suharto's archipelago. But as things are, just guaranteeing the present state of resistance is already beyond our actual capabilities.

The action of solidarity groups is now fundamental, even decisive. Your Excellency asks me how you can help us to 'remove the Military from Timor'! And 'other things'! I can only advise, dearest Father, grasp hands with the various solidarity groups, this front that is becoming broader, stronger and more united regarding the principles to be adopted. Continue pressuring the political and governmental circles of each country, namely those in Japan, Australia, the USA and the members of EEC.

Note for example, Reverend Father, that when Holland cut economic aid to Indonesia, Japan immediately stepped in to fill the gap. In such cases, only the

---

[1] Xanana is counting from the late seventies when he restructured the resistance after its near demise..

solidarity groups can intervene, and we trust in the capability of those mobilising in Japan. I deeply appreciated the prompt response from the Japanese solidarity group when I appealed to them directly. I am now hoping that these groups will become even more active in sensitising their own government.

Only through such international solidarity actions can we sensitise governments and counsel Jakarta to modify its attitude. A very difficult task!

I do not have specific knowledge of the various Timorese solidarity groups around the world. However, I notice, for example, a reasonable profusion of groups in Japan; a more favourable Australian public opinion, and practical protest actions in England during Ali Alatas' visit there, etc.

We all wish, Reverend Father that peace might come quickly to East Timor! And that the Mission for Peace in East Timor could have achieved its proposed objective! But it was an action that reminded the international community how fragile the operation [of the *Lusitania Express*] was. Indifference was aggravated by the political manoeuvering of Jakarta and the governments which act as its accomplices. It was an operation that made news and captured the world's attention for a moment! Yet an action as fragile as the cause of East Timor itself!

Meanwhile, we admired your courage as you defied this hypocritical world, your tenacity in defying obstacles. But, like us, you had to halt the fight when stronger and more powerful forces defined the battle line. The Peace Mission in Timor accomplished what a gesture of peaceful solidarity could. It is for that reason that the Mission has to continue, so that the flowers of peace [you dropped from the ship] can be valued as marking the start of a crusade throughout the world! It is difficult, it will be difficult, but we believe in the power of will, demonstrated by the *Lusitania Express*!

Reverend Father, I reaffirm to the international solidarity groups, our utmost confidence that you will not abandon my people in the crucial moment of its struggle. And consequently I simply ask the groups to intensify their actions in making the public in their respective countries even more aware by clarifying in greater depth the essence of the problem and unmasking the webs of political deceit spun by Indonesian diplomacy.

We share one obvious wish: peace! Peace through dialogue. And this objective must be reached: *dialogue*! Dialogue to achieve peace, dialogue to find the way to peace. That peace which the *Lusitania Express* cultivated when, in sight of land, you strewed your flowers over the sea, in commemoration of the death and suffering of a people! I hope that your Excellency's involvement in that mission to this unfortunate half-island [is not in vain]; that, dear Father, your optimism heralds the longed-for peace.

Only international pressure can lead Jakarta to dialogue. Only the international solidarity groups can ensure the effectiveness of this pressure! Through open letters and protests, through the distribution of historic documents about East Timor and the film of the massacre, through schools, universities, churches, political groups and every other way possible, a concentrated action with a common strategy: *seek peace through dialogue!*

And what the solidarity groups have done! We all understand that such actions, only when done consistently, can help the people of East Timor! We know that we ask *everything* from the solidarity front! And we are aware of how difficult such a mission is, but that is what we are asking, and we must ask it!

Our case will be decided by the Americans, the Japanese, the Europeans and the Australians. Not Jakarta! Nor the third world countries, indebted and dependent, though their opinions do influence the 'majority' we seek in the United Nations' General Assembly. The power of veto, however, is in the hands of the above-mentioned powers!

The people of East Timor are not so completely isolated, as I sometimes like to claim, almost denying, so to speak, the sacrifices, the vigils, the long hours of hard work and dedication, the determination and combative courage of all those who embrace with true love, the struggle of our people. Unfortunately, even united in strength, united by ideas and principles, everyone together, we are as we are, alone and frail!

But we trust in you, and the extensive array of East Timor solidarity groups! And I do believe, even more united and together, we may take another step that Portugal has forgotten to take. Regrettably, it seems Deus Pinheiro [the Portuguese Foreign Minister] also stands alone amongst his party members from the community of common interests [aligned against East Timor].

Your Excellency asks of me: 'Don't kill even one more Indonesian soldiers!' I must clarify that since 7 December 1975, Falintil has only responded in legitimate defence. Never have we fought the occupying soldiers with hatred or the *putsch* spirit.

We proved it during the first three years of invasion, in 1983, and afterwards on various other occasions, releasing the soldiers who surrendered during battles. Quite to the contrary, the Indonesian soldiers are the inhumane ones and it is not worth recording here all that has been done in this war.

When we seek the initiative in battle, it is only because our arsenal is in the Indonesian soldiers' hands and we must obtain it. We do not manufacture ammunition; we do not own gun factories. If we do not replace our arsenal then we either die stupidly unarmed, or we must raise our hands in surrender.

The ideal that you propose is beautiful in its aspirations, but difficult to practise, at least in our war, because opposing us are brutal forces, assassins without compassion. While they kill and destroy for duty, everything for duty, we kill only to survive. We defend our country not by intervention as the multi-nationals did in Kuwait; our defence is a resistance which seeks manifestation by challenging the times themselves.

In this spirit, we have always been open to dialogue and are prepared to accept, at any time, the cessation of all hostilities! We would sit at the same table, share the same food, and smoke together! We have already noticed that Indonesian soldiers are very sensitive and feel they have been and are still being forced into this war.

The letter from the Australian friend did not arrive, so I could not do what your Excellency asked.

I thank you, dearest Father for what you have offered [to the process of peace].

A hug of friendship,

Commander of Falintil
Kay Rala Xanana Gusmão
General Headquarters, 18 May 1992

9 JUNE 1992

A letter to Xana Bernades

and all young Timorese youth in the diaspora

This letter to Xana Bernades, a young East Timorese woman living in Australia, was in response to a letter from her along with funds raised from a solidarity cricket match and festival in Melbourne. It was the first direct link between Xanana and the greater diaspora beyond the political parties. It signalled the beginning of broadening support amongst diasporan communities.

Dear Xana,

I received your letter, a special letter that is unique and full of commitment. I was moved by your feelings, by the simple way you expressed your thoughts, by your courage and self-confidence, and by your great sense of political responsibility.

Dear East Timorese young ones. Our sacrifices are real: they reach you and link us to you, the brave and proud Maubere youth. We, the armed combat fighters, put all our trust and hope in you, because only you can build a happy future for our sacrificed nation. You are the trustees of the great Maubere spirit. You are the descendants of the great-grandfather crocodile.

I do not thank you for what you have sent me because that would insult your sense of patriotism. But we were moved by your token of solidarity. And we are amazed by the depth of your understanding of the difficulties we face in our resistance. I know that you are 'independent' [of the political parties] but nevertheless, you are united to us. You are part of us. And we, as the older fighters of the nation, are proud of you. *Juventude aswain-loriqu lorosa'e.*

Dear Xana, please pass on to the secretary of the Victorian Timorese Association our appreciation for your work. Your organisational capacity, your broad view of the problems we face and your own participation in our struggle are incentives for us to consolidate our own strengths and to persist in our military resistance.

In truth, all true children of East Timor, all those of you aware of our dear people, cannot stand aside from this tragedy we have suffered over the last 16 years. The struggle continues to be difficult: we could even say as difficult as it has ever been. And the solution, in my opinion, is still very far away. But we will never abdicate the fundamental right of our people. However, we may have to find ways to minimise their suffering and diminish their sacrifices.

I repeat, dear Xana, that I have sworn a thousand times to our heroic people, I have sworn on the bones of our heroes, that I will fight to the end, for the liberation of our dear nation. All the politics that I may have to participate in will not negate this sacred oath, but will allow me to honour it.

I hope that you and the other young people who put their political trust in me will always stand by me in your thoughts during this struggle.

The unique circumstances of our war demand from us great flexibility of spirit and ability for mental gymnastics. Everything I have is dedicated to the single objective of winning this war. My dear young ones, we will win one day! We will liberate our nation! And then, we will embrace you.

I trust, simply, that you will always be by my side supporting our glorious Falintil. Your guerrilla brothers send to all of you our hugs of deep esteem. And for you, Xana, an affectionate hug.

Xanana, Commandant of Falintil

I Am Not a Myth

Interview with Rui Araujo

On the video footage of this interview (20 July), Xanana responds to questions sent by Portuguese journalist Rui Araujo, against a backdrop of mountains and a foreground of the flags of Falintil, Fretilin, UDT and Portugal. The video was broadcast on Portuguese television (Channel RTP) and published in O Publico *on 26 September 1992. This is the final section of the interview.*

Araujo: What is day-to-day life in Dili like?

Gusmão: Dili is like a combination of different worlds. On the first level, that which pertains to the Indonesians and the integrationists of the first social plane, it is one where life is lived serenely and in total tranquillity, and may be seen to be so. Below this, one finds a lower minority of Timorese who, one way or another, succeed apparently in living a life without setbacks.

On the third level one finds the presence of the Indonesian troops and the Intel (Indonesian Political Police) agents, who are both Indonesian and Timorese, who populate the city. Mixed in with this layer are the transmigrants, Indonesians, who are either hawkers peddling their wares throughout the length and breadth of the streets of the city or the owners of kiosks which have sprung up all over the place, all of these having the mission of observing and informing. Downtrodden by the layer above, conditions are grim for the majority of the population who visibly live in a state of permanent insecurity and struggle for their subsistence.

Lastly, there are all of those who are black-listed and who, therefore, have a sombre existence. Their houses are watched by Intel agents, who make no attempt to hide their presence and spend the whole day making notes on who enters and leaves. Every step they make is watched, as well as their contacts with others, whether indoors or in public places. Any strange face immediately raises suspicion and the house-owners are questioned as to what the person is doing, who they are related to, where they live.

If there is little movement, then the Intel agents make a series of visits, questioning about supposed links with the Armed Resistance, with the clandestine organisation, and so on. Whenever they are in any doubt about a gathering, even family get-togethers, they get in touch with the nearest military post and the house is immediately surrounded by troops. And, in certain cases, the *nangalas* themselves break into the house.

After 12 November, all of these [settlements] have troops assigned to them. They watch over the population by patrolling the villages, and also take advantage of the patrols to sexually abuse the womenfolk. Young people are obliged to take part in daily sporting activities, absences being recorded. On public transport or in the streets, drawing their insolence from the uniform they wear and the arms they carry, they brazenly harass the girls, before the impotent gaze of our patriots. They appear in private houses, enter farms everywhere, by day or by night, and oblige the people to provide parties on an almost weekly basis—and hurl abuse when people do not turn up.

Araujo: Who is Xanana?

Gusmão: He is not the myth which some people have helped construct; even less so the legendary figure on the lips of others. He is a man confronting many many difficulties. A man who fights down a struggle within himself. A man with many defects but who, at the cost of the blood of his companions, has been forced to learn from his own mistakes. A combatant for the Homeland, one among many, who acts on a basic principle, a very important principle: I always believed in my people, and today, I have to add that I believe in the force of international solidarity.

I will take the opportunity once more, to appeal to everybody, women and men, children and young people, politicians, journalists, students, workers, members of the church, artists, ordinary citizens, to all of you who are part of the international solidarity with East Timor. I want to make an appeal for a concerted action on the objective you have outlined: that 1992 be the year of dialogue with Timorese participation. The respect, affection and esteem of our people go out to you, friends of East Timor, who have been defenders of the cause of the Maubere People. Together always, in the name of the ideals of liberty and peace. Always, along this difficult path to peace.

CAPTURE AND IMPRISONMENT

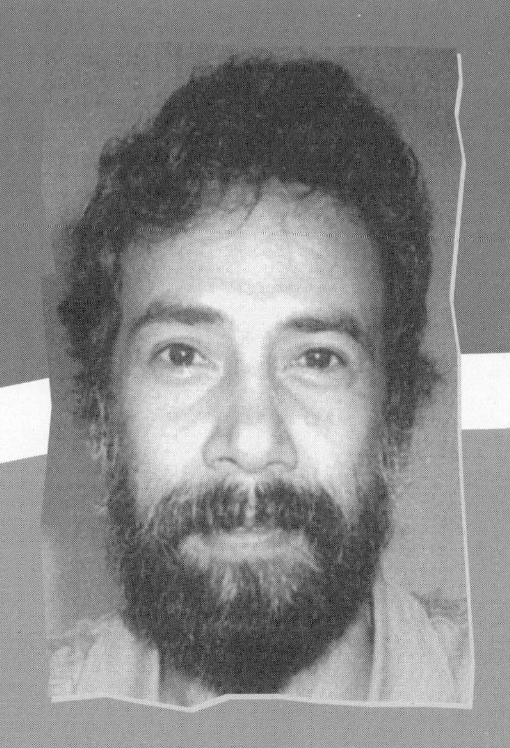

1992–1997

Capture

The cool dawn
of a dusty Dili morning
of mist and smoke
of the day in a life.
Ushering in another
a destiny
which began in the dark
confusion of spirit,
somewhere between belief and disbelief
that everything or something
had happened
uncontrollably like this…
A terrible day
in the sensation of
brutalised weakness
condemning the laughter which
wanted to be hatred…
Bitterness of fate
which ended a march
in the struggle,
the long march of
the best years of life…
A destiny…
The turning of a yellowed page
of a difficult time
never to be forgotten.

Xanana sent this poem in a letter to a friend on 20 November 1995 to commemorate the third anniversary of his capture.

12 DECEMBER 1992

Xanana Is Unrepentant

O Publico interview with Joao Gabriel

Portuguese journalist Joao Gabriel was given permission by Indonesian authorities to interview Xanana a month after his capture. The interview took place in an amphitheatre normally used for teaching at the police barracks in Jakarta, where Xanana was being held prisoner. The interview was recorded by an army film crew and observed by about three dozen people, among them many high-ranking military and five Indonesian censors. Gabriel said, 'The entire interview refutes the idea of repentance suggested by the video recording of Xanana's interview with Abilio Soares.' (On 25 November 1992 a video was played on Indonesian television of an interview with Xanana by Soares, the Governor of East Timor, in which Xanana recanted the struggle and claimed he was an Indonesian citizen.) 'I think that Xanana was extremely skilful throughout the interview, attempting not to repeat what he had said in the interview with the Governor while at the same time avoiding later reprisals', Joao Gabriel insists. 'Frequently he said, "I am outside … I have nothing to do with that". Also, he regulated very well his pauses and some long silences, giving us to understand that he did not feel what he was about to say.' Of introducing himself to Xanana, Joao Gabriel said, 'I gave him a hug from Portugal. Xanana responded with a strong handshake. I apologized for my role here—trying to "extract" information from a man in such an extremely complicated and critical situation. He smiled and said: "There's no problem".'

The 'authorised' interview

Gabriel: *Have you been well treated by the authorities since your arrest?*

Gusmão: I have always been well treated.

Gabriel: *Isn't there anything you can mention?*

Gusmão: Nothing to mention [silence] … In fact I found it excessive in comparison with my other companions.

Gabriel: *Have you been treated too well compared to your companions? What you said in the interview with Abilio [Soares], did you say of your own free will?*

Gusmão: Yes.

Gabriel: *When you were captured, it is said that a list of priests was found in your house, and that they would have collaborated with the resistance. Do you confirm this?*

Gusmão: Yes, I confirm it.

Gabriel: *Did the Timorese church always help the resistance?*

Gusmão: I confirm it.

Gabriel: *Monsignor Ximenes?*

Gusmão: In one way or another.

Gabriel: *Xanana, why were you captured? Was there betrayal, or was there some imprudence on your part?*

Gusmão: I excuse myself from answering that.

Gabriel: *Did you used to go often to Dili?*

Gusmão: Yes.

Gabriel: *One of the problems in your respect which has been posed (and which has been spoken about lately) is that of your nationality: now, are you Portuguese, Indonesian or Timorese?*

Gusmão: According to the statements I made [hesitation] … that I signed as an Indonesian citizen … [I take upon myself] all … all the consequences for my acts.

Gabriel: *Do you want to stay here?*

Gusmão: In Timor, if it were possible.

Gabriel: *If the Vatican could, eventually, intervene and manage to get you out of Indonesia, would you accept?*

Gusmão: No.

Gabriel: *You want to stay?*

Gusmão: Yes.

Gabriel: *Throughout the resistance in Timor, did you ever receive money from Portugal?*

Gusmão: From solidarity groups … yes, I received money.

Gabriel: *Is it Xanana who, at this stage, has a legitimate right to speak for the Timorese?*

Gusmão: I cannot state and I am [now] outside that reality.

Gabriel: *There was recently a fund-raising campaign in Portugal. It is your wife who is in possession of that money. What would you like her to do with it?*

Gusmão: No [silence] … I repeat that I am not [hesitation] I am entirely out of that question now.

Gabriel: *Xanana, when one day you get out again, are free again, what would you like to do?*

Gusmão: I also said this to the Indonesian authorities that [hesitation] … I have no ambition … other than to help that people to … to build itself up.

Gabriel: *To help the Timorese people, through integration with Indonesia?*

Gusmão: Yes, I think so.

Gabriel: *You led the resistance, and one of the questions on which accusations against you could eventually be based is whether you killed anyone directly, during those 17 years …*

Gusmão: Whether I killed anyone directly? To myself [hesitation] … I do not pose that question … I do not pose that question … What I pose is my responsibility over all the acts … which took place in East Timor throughout these years … Of course, whether I killed or not is something secondary … All the acts, under Indonesian law, are subversive so I take responsibility for all that happened.

Gabriel: *Would you like to be extradited by Portugal?*

Gusmão: No.

Gabriel: *Are you, therefore, rejecting a past, almost half of your life? The principles which you defended all these 17 years?*

Gusmão: I am not a conformist, but [hesitation] … I think that [hesitation] … I think that [hesitation] … I should agree with the facts.

Gabriel: *Do you agree that, at this stage, integration is best for Timor?*

Gusmão: Yes, individually [hesitation] … I think so, because I have nothing to do with more [silence] … with other contexts.

Gabriel: *With regards to Portugal, do you think it was and continues to be the guilty party in relation to the situation in Timor?*

Gusmão: I excuse myself from answering that because it is a question that concerns Portugal itself [hesitation] … At this time I [hesitation] … do not hold the same position … as when … as some time ago. I have nothing to do with that. I think that Portugal … should also reconsider its own position [silence].

Gabriel: *Do you support integration?*

Gusmão: Well, it depends on Portugal … I have nothing to do with Portugal.

Gabriel: *Xanana, these statements, the last ones that you have made, will they eventually lessen your sentence? Has anyone spoken of that?*

Gusmão: I am not interested [hesitation] … in knowing about a reduced sentence, since I accept responsibility for all of that. I accept that [hesitation] … I accept that I suffer the consequences of all this rather than my companions, and I have spoken with the authorities about this once. I am prepared to receive [hesitation] … in the others' place, as the one responsible for the situation provoked in East Timor.

Gabriel: *Has the resistance in Timor finished?*

Gusmão: I cannot say, can I? I cannot say.

Gabriel: *But about the appeal you made for the members of the Falintil to surrender, do you think that the Indonesian authorities are sincere about the amnesty that has been promised?*

Gusmão: I cannot make any statement on that subject [hesitation] ... I made the appeal, now all depends on them. They were not fighting for me, they were not fighting for me.

Gabriel: *Do you have any particular message, at this stage, for anyone?*

Gusmão: It is not the right time for messages. No, it is not the time for messages for anyone.

Gabriel: *Are you being well treated?*

Gusmão: Yes ... without reservations.

Gabriel: *The resistance (namely Fretilin) is accused of killing innocent people.*

Gusmão: I believe that belongs to a past, about which Fretilin itself has already [hesitation] ... already stated to the effect that it recognised this error.

Gabriel: *Do you admit that there have been some excesses?*

Gusmão: In the early days ... of the invasion.

Gabriel: *I again ask you, do you have any message for anyone in particular, for Portugal, for example?*

Gusmão: No, I have not [silence].

Gabriel: *Do you think that the negotiations between Portugal and Indonesia still make sense?*

Gusmão: That is up to them [to Portugal and to Indonesia], not up to me.

Gabriel: *Wouldn't you like to send a message to the Portuguese minister who will be meeting the Indonesian minister, Ali Alatas, on the 17th?*

Gusmão: I have nothing to say [silence].

Gabriel: *Xanana, by taking up this position—which I do not believe you do of your own free will—are you not afraid that, one day, you will be branded in history as a traitor?*

Gusmão: One man alone does not make history [silence].

Gabriel: *But isn't that strange, coming from the mouth of the man who ...*

Gusmão: I am aware of that.

Gabriel: *... of the man who, until just a few months ago, was part ... and now ...*

Gusmão: I am aware of that [silence].

Gabriel: *And you say that of your own free will?*

Gusmão: I am aware of that [silence]. If you don't believe it [silence]. You can believe it.

The five Indonesian censors kept the cassettes of the interview for 11 hours, while they cut out eight minutes of the approximately 20-minute interview. Gabriel reported that the main cuts were:
Two sentences were cut from Xanana's reply on whether he defends integration with Indonesia: 'I am replying in a way in which, if I were free, I would not' and 'I think I ought to agree'. With regards to the spokesman of the Maubere Resistance National Council, Jose Ramos-Horta: everything was cut, as Xanana only said 'I am out now. I don't want to say anything.' without repeating the criticism of the first video. Concerning Ma'huno, the new armed resistance leader: 'If he wishes, he has the conditions in which to carry on the fight'. Regarding the forthcoming New York talks: a long reply was completely erased, in which Xanana spoke of 'an international and global solution for East Timor'.

Mountains

Mountains
    that stir up the minds
    of voices that go unheard

mountains
    of shedding sweats
    that smear the rains green

mountains
    that silence in their heights
    unheard battles

mountains
    of suns burnt blue
    by spilt tears

mountains …
Mountains of East Timor

mountains
    pregnant with blood
    giving birth to pain

mountains
    mournfully dressed with bones
    bemoaning the struggle

Mountains of the clouds
Mountains of the winds
Mountains of the cold
The cold of the homeland …
Mountains — the sanctuary
    of the warrior
    who has not fallen!

Xanana
Written in six minutes, thinking of you all …
(Smuggled out by tape and transcribed late 1992)

Defence Plea of Xanana Gusmão

These are excerpts from the 28-page defence plea, hand-written in Portuguese, that was presented in the Dili district court on 17 May 1993 by the defendant, Xanana Gusmão. After he had read the first two pages, the court ordered him to stop. The document was confiscated.

These translated excerpts were made available to the press and others on 21 May 1993 by TAPOL, the London-based Indonesian human rights group (the name means political prisoner in Indonesian).

This defence plea was written while Xanana was being held in Dili prior to his trial. His Kopassus guards were instructed to keep him awake or occupied but over several nights he managed to stay awake into the early hours after they had fallen asleep. After he finished writing, with pens and paper stolen from military intelligence, he made a second copy. This was smuggled out and released (although Xanana says parts are missing and out of order.)

First of all, I would like to thank you for the opportunity you have afforded me to express myself freely, without coercion of any kind.

I have always insisted in all my conversations with everyone, including my conversation with the Indonesian ambassador to the United Nations, Mr Nugroho, that considering the circumstances under which my earlier statements in Jakarta were made, they cannot be construed as being credible.

This is the appropriate moment for me to explain everything. I hope that Indonesian intellectuals will understand my frame of mind at this moment when I am making use of my freedom of expression as a result of my rights.

I hope that the new Indonesian generation or, to be more precise, the Indonesian youth, will appreciate the importance of the law of freedom both as a fundamental aspect of human life today and of the modern society in which we live.

I hope finally that the international community will appreciate the worth of all my declarations, considering the time and place in which they were made.

I thank you once again, honourable judge, for allowing me to speak in my own defence.

★ ★ ★

I am resistance commander Xanana Gusmão, leader of the Maubere resistance against the cowardly and shameful invasion of 7 December 1975 and the criminal and illegal occupation of East Timor for the last 17 years.

On 22 November last year, in Denpasar, I signed a document in which I affirmed that according to international law, I continue to be, like all Timorese, a Portuguese citizen and, before my own conscience, I am a citizen of East Timor.

It is in these terms that I reject the competence of any Indonesian court to try me, and particularly the jurisdiction of this court which has been imposed by force of arms and crimes against my Homeland, East Timor.

I believe that the international press has not failed to notice the massive political stage-managing that has occurred. But in case this has gone unnoticed, I now want to draw the attention of everyone to the fact that I feel like a foreigner in my own land. In prison at *Polwil* [the regional police command] I am completely surrounded by Indonesians; officers from BAIS [the Strategic Intelligence Agency] and men from *Kopassus* [the Indonesian elite troops] are my warders. I asked for a visit from the Bishop and they sent me an Indian priest who is a defender of integration.

Here in this so-called court, I see only Indonesians and, above all, Indonesian military from *Kopassus* and BAIS. According to Indonesian law, trials of this nature should take place in public. Every time I enter this courtroom, the public that I see are these same military authorities, some of whom have been the main actors in my case, throughout my imprisonment. The Timorese, my compatriots, are out in the street under strict surveillance. This is the blatant rule of the occupier. This is the display of foreign oppression, foreign domination, which flaunts the arrogant contempt of the colonisers.

The question of East Timor is the responsibility of the international community, a question of international law. It is a case in which universal principles are at stake, a case where the decolonisation norms of the UN have been manipulated, a case where Indonesia has disregarded the resolutions of the UN—a case therefore of the flagrant violation of the principles of the Non-Aligned Movement, and of the universal pattern of law, peace and justice.

Every Indonesian is bound to the policy of their own nation, and their understanding of East Timor is the product of how their government sees it, unless they listen to their own consciences and commit themselves to the universal principles of justice, freedom and the rule of law.

For 17 years, East Timor, the other side of the coin, has been the story of the great Indonesian farce. For almost four months I have been used as part of this shameful farce. Whether cleverly or unfortunately is not for me to judge. This court claims that it is trying me for crimes committed against the Indonesian state and for the illegal possession of firearms. I know that everything has been arranged for me to be acquitted [if I acquiesce to their terms].

The ones who should be standing before an international court are, in the first place:

— the Indonesian Government for crimes committed in the past 17 years in East Timor;
— the US administration which gave the green light to the invasion on 7 December 1975 and has since given military aid and political support for Indonesia's genocide in East Timor;
— the governments of Australia and Western Europe for their policy of complicity towards Indonesia;
— and, finally, the Portuguese Government for its grave irresponsibility in the decolonisation of East Timor.

The UN recognises as legitimate all means of opposition to the colonial presence in any part of the world where people are fighting for liberation. My struggle and the resistance of my people and of Falintil should be placed in this context, standing above Indonesian law.

Mr Sudjono [Xanana's Indonesian-appointed legal counsel], in his demurrer, tried to adopt a more liberal position when he questioned the 'Balibo Declaration', but he did not deal with the fundamental problem—the illegality of the annexation of East Timor by means of force. The key question in this court is the so-called 'process of the integration of East Timor'.

I remind you here that in Denpasar I was compelled to make statements apologising to the Indonesian army for the massacre of Santa Cruz, a massacre which was perpetrated by the Indonesian army and not by me. I remind you as well that in Jakarta, I declared, on the specific instructions of the puppet governor, Abilio Soares, that I was prepared to surrender.

★ ★ ★

This court must surely agree with me that it went too far in saying that Fretilin 'dared to impose its will on the people'. And also in saying that the 'Balibo Declaration' (which compromised Timorese leaders signed and which invited Indonesia to liberate East Timor from Fretilin on 30 November 1975) expressed the genuine will of the people of East Timor. The court omitted the one political element which would have given it the juridical validity on which everyone insists: representation of the will of the majority of the people. This is the condition *sine qua non*.

Until this very moment, the UN does not recognise Indonesian sovereignty over East Timor, a sovereignty which was imposed by the means of force, by the practice of violence and the systematic violation of the most fundamental human rights.

This court mentioned 17 December 1975 as the day of the formation of a provisional government and a local assembly. And since all the Indonesians have forgotten, it is my duty to recall here the tragic day, 7 December 1975, which witnessed the cowardly and shameful Indonesian invasion, the day on which Indonesian troops indiscriminately massacred the defenceless population of Dili, causing thousands of deaths among the elderly, women and children, including an Australian journalist.

While the Balibo statement was signed with the blood of five Australian journalists who were murdered by Indonesian troops during the attack on the village of Balibo, the so-called Indonesian provisional government was formed over the corpses of the Timorese massacred between 7 and 17 of December of that year.

★ ★ ★

This provisional government was established to the accompaniment of the sound of the sea and land shelling of the defenceless population, to the sound of advancing tanks and cannons—can such a government claim any juridical standing? In my opinion, it has the same standing as the advance of the Iraqi troops in Kuwait, the same dimension as the advance of Russian tanks into Kabul, the same character as the Vietnamese invasion of Cambodia.

★ ★ ★

The court said that Fretilin was opposed to a referendum, should the people choose integration. However, quoting the so-called petition, the court mentioned that Arnaldo de Araujo, Guilherme Gonçalves, and the President, General Suharto, convinced parliament to approve, in haste, integration without any referendum. So, who was it who did not really want a referendum, Fretilin or Indonesia?

On behalf of whom was that so-called petition signed? Today, the Indonesian Government can show the world its de facto control of the territory, and claims to be developing the territory which it is occupying, while at the same time condemning Portugal who was not able to do this. It is because Portugal failed to develop East Timor for 400 years, that we Timorese have had to pay for the errors of one coloniser while also paying for the crimes of the other coloniser?

★ ★ ★

The lies of the Indonesians. I have been lectured a lot about the backwardness of Portuguese colonialism, as if I had not lived under that colonialism. They want to show me the development in East Timor as if this were just a matter of statistics, to be compared with the Portuguese colonial period. I should ask whether colonialism can be quantified as good or bad.

★ ★ ★

I have been in contact with Irian Jayan officers who spoke to me about the great Indonesian family and I was disgusted with these men. I met a Sumatran, a translator from BAIS who speaks Portuguese and had nothing but praise for his Javanese brothers, and I felt repulsion. I have met officers from Sulawesi who told me about Indonesian 'standards' and I felt an emptiness inside me.

The concept of *realpolitik* has acquired a new dimension for me. Political realism is political subservience, the denial of the individual conscience, the death of the conscience of a people.

I understand very well what scares Indonesia today, as it did yesterday: the ideological anachronism/orthodoxy of ethnic groups which has motivated the war in Yugoslavia and in the republics of the former Soviet Union. The theories are not proving history to be right; it is history which is validating genuine and false theories.

★ ★ ★

The facts described by Mr Sudjono originate from the misconceptions which he has as an Indonesian citizen who is bound to the policies of his government. By the way, he was appointed by BAIS and therefore by the Indonesian Government. On 22 December, I read a letter that was addressed to me by the LBH [the Legal Aid Institute]. On 23 December I replied to that organisation, accepting a lawyer. But I was compelled to renounce it. On 30 December, I had to write a letter to the LBH refusing their offer. My initial letter, which had been intercepted, was returned to me.

★ ★ ★

BAIS is a powerful machine of the Indonesian secret police, and *Kopassus* are their sinister tentacles. The Indonesian military do not accept any policy other than the one dating from 7 December 1975. In my legal case both BAIS and the government decided to conduct it by taking the fewest possible risks and manipulating the entire proceedings. To be able to be here today and to be able to talk as I am now doing, I also chose to take risks inherent to my struggle. I have always told them: 'You are talking with Xanana and not with one of his *eanggotas* [subordinates].

My own situation, in which all my movements are rigorously controlled, reminds me of the situation of total control that followed in the wake of the cowardly massacre at Santa Cruz, over the population of Dili and in particular against the heroic youth of East Timor.

In Polwil, where they try to flatter me with exaggerated attention, the inscriptions written by the prisoners, my companions, on the prison walls, remind me constantly of the sufferings of many of my compatriots, victims of all kinds of torture, and also remind me constantly of the unforgettable 12 November 1991. What did the peaceful demonstration of 12 November want? To remind Jakarta and to remind the world of the need for dialogue; to remind

Jakarta and to remind the world that there is something profoundly wrong in East Timor.

On the day of my capture, in the meeting I had with General Tri Sutrisno, I mentioned the question of dialogue with representatives of the people of East Timor. One of the 20 generals who were present, congratulating each other for the imminence of their easy victory, asked me, furiously: '*Rakyat mana*?' [What people?] and when I answered, 'Let's have a referendum', the Indonesian generals had to swallow their own arrogance. On the next day, 21 November, when I was already in Denpasar, the wife of the local *panglima* [military commander], surprised by the extent of the support I had, said, 'After all, many people support him'. A high-ranking officer said, 'Possibly all the people of East Timor'.

During the period of interrogation by BAIS in Jakarta, I realised the following: the war in East Timor is in essence a matter for BAIS; it is not a political issue for the government in Jakarta as one might have thought.

Mr Peter Koojmans was the UN Rapporteur sent to East Timor with the agreement of Jakarta to investigate in loco violations of human rights in the territory, violations which had always been denied by Indonesia at the UN. During his visit, a massacre was perpetrated in cold blood …

The corpses have disappeared to this day or, rather, were thrown into mass graves. Where? Only the forces of occupation know. Many of the murderers are present in this room, men from *Kopassus*, *Intel* [intelligence] men, the men in whose hands the entire political life in East Timor, and also of Indonesia, rests.

★ ★ ★

What or who are the Indonesian forces of occupation afraid of? Of the defenceless population, of a population that you, gentlemen, say are satisfied with integration? Who do you want to terrorise?

In the UN, Jakarta cannot suppress the fact that Portugal is an interested party in the solution of the problem. And so Jakarta should also never forget that the Maubere People have already demonstrated that the idea, the objective for which they have fought and resisted to this day can never die. People die but ideas stay alive.

If the Indonesian Government does not know this, BAIS knows it very well. The witness, Saturnino da Costa Belo, is a clear example of the heroism of these people.[1] The farce of the hastily drafted medical certificate stating that

[1] Saturnino da Costa Belo was convicted and sentenced to nine years imprisonment in connection with the Santa Cruz demonstration in 1991. He was brought out as a witness for the

Saturnino was ill should make you blush with shame, all you gentlemen here present, because you know very well that this case rests here with you.

On the first day of my capture and on the following days, they asked me whether I considered myself to be an Indonesian and I always replied in this way: If I say yes, the *bapaks* will not believe me. First they laughed but then they gritted their teeth.

The Indonesian generals do not care about the spirit, the consciousness of the people. They are quickly satisfied when we just do what they want. I don't know if this is because of naiveté or because of the culture of their military training.

I know that BAIS made the necessary arrangements for me to be spared the death penalty and that if I were to praise integration, I would be acquitted.

I remember once while in Jakarta, in order to make a change from recording all my movements in jail, they took me, handcuffed, for a tour of the city and they showed me the gold of Monas, the national monument of Indonesia. I felt like shouting to my warders that l would never sell my soul for the crest of gold Monas, and still less would I ever sell out my own people. I cannot betray the hope of my people to one day live free and independent.

I could never recognise as legitimate the criminal occupation of East Timor simply in order to be able to live on for a few more years. My struggle is superior to my own life. The people of East Timor have sacrificed their lives and continue to suffer.

I continue to recall the need for dialogue, with the participation of the East Timorese. I have always said to all those who wanted to listen to me that the Maubere People don't like the word *pembangunan* [development]. The problem is that it is not free. Freedom is what my people value, the aim of their struggle. Dom Ximenes Belo put it very clearly when he wrote to the UN Secretary General: 'We are dying as a people and as a nation'.

The Indonesian ambassador to the UN came to ask for my cooperation. He asked me to be consistent in what I said. I noticed that the Indonesians have completely forgotten that I fought for 17 years and, in order to be consistent, I must be consistent towards my people and never towards the assassins of my people, towards the invaders of my homeland.

prosecution during Xanana's trial. He entered the courtroom, greeted Xanana, shouted '*Viva Timor-Leste!*' and was removed. The prosecution later produced a police doctor's letter stating that Saturnino was unfit to appear in court due to 'mental instability'.

Minister Ali Alatas in a speech last January said the following: 'If Jakarta will not accept a referendum, it is not because we are afraid of losing the vote but because many people have already suffered so much'.

The ambassador to the UN told me, 'The problem is that dialogue as it is conceived by us (and therefore by Jakarta) has its parameters. We will not accept a referendum'.

In 1983, during the ceasefire, the then Majors [name illegible] and Gatot told us clearly: 'We will not accept a referendum because we know that all the people belong to Fretilin!'

★ ★ ★

Many witnesses who were brought here were inhibited from saying what they wanted to say. All the defendants had to declare that they surrendered of their own free will.

★ ★ ★

This court condemned the victims who were held in Polwil, but these prisoners were treated inhumanely. It is enough just to look at those witnesses who were brought here and who are still in jail. They are so thin.

Were those responsible for the murder of East Timorese ever brought before this court to answer for their crimes? What is the worth of a law which closes its eyes to the ghastly crime of 12 November? What moral values, what system of justice, do the Indonesians uphold, that can declare criminals to be heroes and condemn the victims.

★ ★ ★

All the proceedings connected with my trial are matters for BAIS and *Kopassus*, and their officers fill this room, watching everything and everybody. Jakarta should be ashamed of its criminal behaviour in East Timor and should, for a long time, have recognised that it has lost in East Timor.

The Indonesian generals should be made to realise that they have been defeated in East Timor. Here today, as the Commander of Falintil, the glorious armed forces of national liberation of East Timor, I acknowledge military defeat on the ground. I am not ashamed to say so. On the contrary, I am proud of the fact that a small guerrilla army was able to resist a large nation like Indonesia, a regional power which in a cowardly fashion invaded us and tries to dominate us by the law of terror and crime, by the law of violence, persecution, prison, torture and murder.

The moment has come for Jakarta to recognise its political defeat on the ground. I don't know if it was to impress me that they placed armed *tentaras* [soldiers] on the route from Polwil to the court.

I have been flattered in all kinds of ways in order to convince me to behave here like a docile Indonesian. I have had to behave like one, and the witnesses brought here have also had to behave in the same way. I know that behind me, the men from BAIS and *Kopassus* are gritting their teeth with rage. Although they should be doing it for being the real murderers of the Maubere People.

Who is afraid of a referendum? Why are they afraid of the referendum? I am not afraid of a referendum. And if today, under international supervision, the Maubere were to choose integration, I would make a genuine appeal to my companions in the bush to lay down their arms and I would offer my head to be decapitated in public.

Whoever is afraid of the referendum is afraid of the truth.

Why is there all that military apparatus in front of this disgusting court? Why are there armed soldiers posted along the route with their arms held at the ready?

I appeal to the new generation of Indonesians to understand that the people of East Timor attach much more value to freedom, justice and peace than to the development which is carried out here with the assistance of Australia, the United States and other European countries who maintain close economic relations with Jakarta.

I appeal to the people of Indonesia to understand that according to universal principles and international law, East Timor is considered to be a non-autonomous territory in accordance with the norms that govern decolonisation. I appeal to the Indonesian people to understand that East Timor is not a threat to Indonesia or a factor threatening Indonesia's security. The story they tell you, that East Timor is communist, is stale. We don't want to dismember Indonesia. The fact is that East Timor was never part of Indonesia.

I appeal to the international community to understand that it is time to show that the New World Order is about to begin. This requires acts that will bring to an end the situation inherited from the past.

I appeal to the European Community to be consistent with its own resolutions and also to be consistent with all the resolutions adopted regarding East Timor.

I appeal to all the friends of East Timor, parliamentarians from Europe, America, Japan and Australia, to go on pressing their own governments to change the double standards applied to similar cases where systematic violations of UN resolutions occur, as in the case of Indonesia's behaviour regarding East Timor.

I appeal to President Bill Clinton to reconsider the problem of East Timor and to press Jakarta to accept dialogue with the Portuguese and the Timorese in the search for an internationally acceptable solution.

I appeal to the Portuguese Government never to abandon its responsibility towards East Timor.

I appeal to the Secretary General of the UN to ensure that the solution he seeks for East Timor is based on universal principles and international law.

Finally, I appeal to the Government of Indonesia to change its attitude and to realise that the moment has come to understand the essence of the struggle in East Timor.

From today, I will start a hunger strike, as a practical way to appeal to the EEC, the US Government and the Government of Australia.

No agreement can be reached between a prisoner and his warders.

To the Secretary General of the UN, I would like to say that I am ready to participate in the negotiating process at any moment or in any place. I will, however, never accept to be a part of the Indonesian side in the negotiations because I am not willing to participate in the farce of integration and in the criminal repression of my people.

As a political prisoner in the hands of the occupiers of my country, it is of no consequence at all to me if they pass a death sentence here today. They have killed more than one third of the defenceless population of East Timor. They are killing my people and I am not worth more than the heroic struggle of my people who, because they are small and weak people, have always been subjected to foreign rule.

Dili, 27 March 1993
X. Gusmão
Member of CNRM
Commander of Falintil

Letter to President Suharto

More than 20 people, including those who sheltered him and members of his family, were arrested immediately before or after Xanana's arrest. Many other Timorese also remained in prison for resistance activities, many of them associated with the Santa Cruz demonstration and massacre of November 1991. Here, Xanana asks for consideration for them. This is an official translation by the executive office of CNRM.

Mr President Suharto, your Excellency,

Allow me, first of all, to address to you, your Excellency, Mr President, my best wishes. I am Kay Rala Xanana Gusmão, the leader of the Resistance against the Indonesian presence in East Timor. The court in Dili imposed on me a life sentence. Your Excellency, Mr President, offered me, in August, a reduction in the sentence to 20 years in prison. This is an act of generosity for which I am enormously grateful.

Allow me, Mr President, to explain the reasons for this petition. Considering that until the day of my capture on 20 November 1992, I was the one directing the activities of the resistance in East Timor; considering that in the court in Dili I claimed full responsibility for all the activities practised until then; considering that competent authorities in Dili stated that no other trial would take place after mine, which lasted from January till May this year; considering that such a decision relieves any individual of guilt; considering that there are individuals who are now in prison for having executed activities of the resistance under my command; considering also that there are others who were arrested in connection with my capture and that as a consequence of the lack of a trial they are in prolonged detention; it is completely logical and legally plausible that the said individuals, a list of whom I am enclosing, be the beneficiaries of yet another act of generosity by your Excellency.

Your Excellency, Mr President, taking into account that I continue to claim for myself the right to be considered a Portuguese citizen in accordance with the United Nations' General Assembly resolutions which recognise Portugal as the Administering Power (just as France, legally and politically, exercises circumstantial physical power over New Caledonia) and also taking into account that, in the context of my own resistance, I consider myself in all liberty to be a citizen of East Timor, I do not accept and will never accept any verdict imposed by Indonesian courts. I appeal to your Excellency, Mr President, to release unconditionally all prisoners of conscience mentioned above in exchange for an even heavier sentence against myself.

Finally, I wish to appeal once more to your Excellency, Mr President, for a greater willingness to dialogue regarding the case of East Timor. Only a frank and constructive dialogue can bring peace to East Timor and stability, harmony and understanding among all parties in this conflict. Only a just solution based on the UN resolutions may enable all interested parties in the problem a peace of the spirit and complete openness towards a true peace and lasting cooperation. Finally, I wish your Excellency, Mr President, the best success in leading the Indonesian Nation and the supreme goals of the Non-Aligned Movement. I wish also all prosperity for the brotherly Indonesian people. I hope that my appeal is only one among many cries for peace, harmony and understanding among nations and peoples.

With highest respects

Kay Rala Xanana Gusmão
Jakarta/Cipinang, 31 October 1993

Message to the East Timor Talks Campaign

Excerpts from an address recorded by Xanana Gusmão in Cipinang Prison, Jakarta, for the East Timor Talks Campaign. It was written on the anniversary of the Robert Domm interview of September 1990 (see page 142).

Dear friends of East Timor.

This is the anniversary of a very important event in the history of the Maubere resistance. On behalf of the glorious Falintil guerrillas and the martyred Maubere People, I salute with emotion all present and everyone all over the world making their own the struggle of the East Timorese people.

What brings us here today is not just marking the unforgettable meeting with Robert Domm in the mountains of East Timor, a meeting which proved to the world the massive involvement of our people in the struggle against the Indonesian occupation. It is also an opportunity to present a new dimension to our struggle: our openness to dialogue. That was the olive branch that we extended to Jakarta: our readiness to dialogue without preconditions, our commitment to real peace.

Dear friends, I know you would like me to speak about our peace plan and perspectives on this process, but this is a subject that can be handled by my official CNRM representative, Jose Ramos Horta. I apologise but I prefer to speak about the internal and external factors which bear on the talks on East Timor that are under way.

There are currently contacts between Portugal and Indonesia being overseen by the UN Secretary General. We all hope this will end the problem and are unhappy that progress is so slow. But we all remember the bankrupt ten years under Javier de Cuellar when the principles of the UN were so corrupted. Today Dr Boutros Ghali is displaying initiative and concern about the East Timor problem. His efforts should be supported more and more by all of us and all of you.

Portugal is consistent in its obligations and its limitations are not its fault. I know there are factors beyond Portugal's capacity but I continue to expect a lot of Portugal. Nevertheless, it is Jakarta that is responsible for the lack of progress in the talks. Jakarta is responsible for the criminal invasion, for a war that made victims of more than 200,000 East Timorese, for the abuse of our universal rights and the resolutions of the UN Security Council, for the continuing violations of human rights in East Timor, for crimes committed in East Timor for all these 19 long years. It is Jakarta which is the obstacle to our search for a just solution acceptable to the international community. Jakarta is the only party not interested in a solution.

There is a new element in this process and that is the recognition of the necessity of the East Timorese being consulted. Timorese participation in the consultations, though still indirect, is already a fact. The Timorese must have a central role because they are indispensible to any solution.

I want to elaborate on this issue of the role of East Timorese. Sadly, I understand that some East Timorese do not have the best interests of all at heart. I urge the East Timorese people to fill their efforts and minds with common sense and political goodwill. I remind those who are playing the role of democratic opposition and exercising 'freedom of opinion' to use their intelligence to serve their country and to remember that power in an independent East Timor will never be a copy of the current regime in Jakarta.

A small group wants Portugal to return and recommence the decolonisation process. They suffer from nostalgia and cannot see any other possibility. CNRM does not oppose future relations with Portugal and is proud of the offer for East Timor to become an observer in the community of Portuguese-speaking countries. But CNRM knows that it is not through the return of Portugal that we will be decolonised.

Another group of politician-intellectuals, known as the London group, wants 'reconciliation'. Abilio Araujo and his bevy of politicians and intellectuals are a *garuda* egg hatched by Ali Alatas. They claim they have opened a diplomatic front other than that of CNRM its partners, Fretilin and UDT. They claim the difference between the two is that they advocate independence while CNRM advocates autonomy. The real difference is clear, however, from the fact that Jakarta will not talk to CNRM or its partners, UDT and Fretilin, while these others cooperate with Indonesia's diplomacy. The difference is like the gap between Lisbon and Dili! They claim their strategy will improve human rights. But all their contacts have done nothing to dissuade Johnny Lumintang [Indonesian military commander] from repressing our youth and our people in our Homeland. In my opinion AA can mean Abilio Araujo or Ali Alatas. I regret deeply that this group was formed on the basis of feudalist racism, which is unacceptable in our times.

I appeal to all of you to understand better the role you have in this process and to endorse the CNRM peace plan so that we can force Jakarta to respect our people's wishes.

If you say that I am imposing my opinion on prestigious and intellectual Timorese, I answer that I am only imposing our people's wishes. There is no alternative. While our people are suffering and they are strolling around healthy and rich, I am not in a position to play games about democracy. I want democracy and respect. We are at war fighting a powerful enemy and as Falintil Commander and head of CNRM I have to demand everything from each Timorese—everything, that is, except support for integration. I do not care if they are high-calibre politicians or intellectuals full of knowledge. I am simply demanding this for the ordinary people and children of East Timor. Once again, I appeal to everyone and your nationalist consciousness to unite behind the CNRM peace plan as proof to the world of our Maubere political maturity and capacity. We should never give the enemy even a minimal opportunity by clashing with each other unnecessarily.

In East Timor we also have the East Timorese church, led by Bishop Carlos Ximenes Belo. The principled position of the church, as articulated by its head, is that there has to be a referendum to achieve a permanent solution. In the eyes of the international community, and in our own conscience, no solution can be considered final if it is not the legal and political outcome of a referendum. Recently, Bishop Belo offered to mediate between all sides. More importantly, the Apostolic Administrator is trying to find concrete ways in which he can join efforts developed by the United Nations.

The Indonesian military likes to raise the spectre of civil war every time we speak of a referendum. This is nothing but an obsession with an alibi that would serve to cover up what they fear, a referendum. Those inside East Timor who fear a referendum are those guilty of crimes, people who participated directly or indirectly in the crimes perpetrated by the occupying forces, people who aligned themselves with the enemy in the massacre of our people, those who oppose our fighters. These are the people who have a burden on their conscience. All in all, there are no more than 500 such people in the whole country who refuse to change. It is no secret to anyone that the majority of the members of the Hansips are supporters of the resistance. It is no secret that a majority of the Intel agents are agents of the resistance. It is no secret, either, that the 744, 745, and 746 Battalions are harmless today because the occupational authorities no longer trust them. The Indonesian authorities do not even trust their puppet governor, Abilio Soares.

Civil war is therefore not even a hypothesis. I am not at all worried about the problems among the East Timorese because reconciliation among the Timorese has been our practice all these years. All our people are fully aware about the necessity to forgive those brothers and sisters of ours who have failed. All our people are aware that the leadership of the resistance will not accept that those who collaborated with the enemy should be insulted or humiliated.

It was difficult for our people to understand this but now they all have accepted it as a political principle, as something that represents the higher interests of the nation. Some people in our society, in conversations with me, asked whether at least they could make faces when they see collaborators! I advised them that they should first look in the mirror and see how ugly they look before they pull faces at others. They all then understood what I meant.

Dear friends, throughout the world efforts are being made to find solutions to conflicts. There is a widening acceptance of the following: (1) that armed conflicts are detracting from human intelligence that should be channelled to caring for our planet and the well-being of people; (2) that only a frank and open dialogue can respond to the challenge of our times; and (3) that there is a growing interest regarding the problem of East Timor.

Gareth Evans [then Australia's Minister for Foreign Affairs] asked Jakarta to give East Timor political autonomy, greater respect for its distinctive culture and to withdraw its occupation forces. This means that even the Australian Government is beginning to reconsider the East Timor question. I believe this to be only the first step in the right direction.

Pressure has been put on Indonesia to withdraw its forces and to recognise the right of its people to self-determination and national independence. Time, which was a factor working against us in the sense that the world would forget about the problem of East Timor, has become in fact a boomerang for the Indonesian generals. And Suharto has understood this and has said that he does not want to leave East Timor as a time-bomb for his successor.

Dear friends of East Timor, with East Timorese united we can find a solution. The CNRM peace plan is the only instrument for East Timor's freedom and must be the focus of our diplomatic effort. This must be supplemented by pressure against governments which put economic relations with Jakarta ahead of their obligations to respect universal principles and actions, to have Indonesian forces withdrawn and a referendum for East Timor.

Long live a free and independent East Timor!

Xanana Gusmão
Falintil Commander

Letter to President Clinton

This letter was delivered to the White House by the Portuguese Embassy in Washington on 10 November 1994 in advance of President Clinton's departure for an APEC meeting and a state visit to Indonesia which included one-to-one meetings with President Suharto.

The Honourable President of the United States of America

Dear President Clinton,

It is my honour to present to you my warmest compliments, in an era in which the international community has renewed its faith in, and is making new efforts towards, achieving a more just and equitable world in which peace and justice are the backbone of the freedom of individuals, societies and peoples; in an era in which humankind expects from its world leaders a decisive vision aspiring to a future of progress, based upon the parameters of conservation of our planet and of cooperation and friendship among the people of the world.

We recognise fully the importance of the moral authority which the USA commands and must continue to command in the interests of guaranteeing world peace and in defence of the universal standards of freedom and justice. Mr President, under your administration, the United States continues to honour the democratic traditions of a great nation whose successes in international politics speak for themselves. The process of peace in the Middle East, which has ended irreconcilable antagonisms, permitting the Arabs and the Jews to construct a climate of trust and the promise of peace and cooperation, attests to the great and unsurpassable efforts your government has made in response to the American nation's historical obligation to assure the people of the world that the end of the Cold War is truly the beginning of acceptance of democracy and of peace on our planet.

Nevertheless, in this era of rapid technological advances which are rendering the world smaller and less mysterious, human life unfortunately continues to be without value in many parts of the world where peace is threatened by interests which violate universal principles and where ideological elites are usurping political power and persisting in denying their people most fundamental rights.

We denounce the aberrant philosophical belief of authoritarian regimes, specifically those holding power in Asia, such as Indonesia, China, Iran, Iraq, Myanmar, according to which it is argued that human rights, freedom and democracy are relative in nature and must necessarily accommodate considerations of local culture. Such a philosophy is nothing more than the expression of a feudal mentality of domination and servitude on the one hand, and ideological alienation on the other.

The universality of problems affecting our planet centres upon human beings, a global sense of their existence, of their fears, of their suffering, of their will and of their struggles for survival. The universality of thought which makes human beings intelligent actors capable of seeking solutions for all humanity, prevails over the spiritual, emotional and psychological postulates characterising humanity in terms of socio-economic materialism. Such regimes justify making the distinction between those two facts by pointing to the material unpreparedness of their citizens, which in turn is defined as a specific cultural trait of these countries.

Civil and political rights are an inseparable part of the nature of humankind in its continuing struggle to understand the precise meaning of its existence, its relations with others and its role within society.

Any spurt of economic or social progress recorded by nations such as Indonesia is the fruit of the repression of the Indonesian people themselves, and is a consequence of the priority which is granted to the physical and material aspects of development so applauded by western governments but for which the people pay such a high price. There can be no justice at the socio-economic level without respect for the civil and political rights of the people, and Indonesia is a real and living example of the conceptual arbitrariness of regimes built on the strength of repression.

It is a great shame that western nations or, more precisely, the countries of the north, continue to allow the regimes of the south to advocate cultural differences in order to deny universal human rights in favour of economic development and at the expense of the lives of imprisoned and murdered workers, of the appropriation of farm lands, of the repression of youth and any form of opposition, of the abolition of freedom of the press.

Honourable President, we are profoundly grateful for the initiatives taken by your administration to remind Indonesia that cases of systematic violations of human rights in East Timor are unacceptable to the USA which, in averting a second invasion of Kuwait by Iraq, has proved more than adequately to the world that it will not tolerate flagrant violations of international law. Since last year, which marked 18 years of Indonesia's military occupation of East Timor, the USA has, under your administration, taken a much firmer stand in its refusal to allow the transfer of F-5 aircraft from Jordan to Indonesia, prohibiting the sale of small, non-lethal weapons, halting the military training of Indonesian officers under the IMET scheme, acting upon the resolution supported by your government and passed in favour of East Timor at the Geneva Human Rights Commission.

In addition, we are immensely appreciative of the pronouncements of Secretary of State, Warren Christopher, and of the Assistant Secretary for East Asia, Mr Winston Lord, both of whom have raised the problem of East Timor with Indonesian Foreign Minister, Ali Alatas, and other Indonesian officials.

We are profoundly grateful for the attention and concern you displayed in addressing the issue of East Timor with President Suharto at the 'Group of Seven' summit in July 1993 in Japan, and at the APEC summit in Seattle in November of the same year. We believe, Mr President, that justice will always be the motor for action and that freedom and democracy will continue to be the mainstay of US foreign policy, as has been amply demonstrated by your government's support of the restoration of democracy in Haiti.

Honourable President, East Timor continues to be a territory under the responsibility of the international community. The good offices of the Secretary General of the United Nations have been engaged with a view to reaching a solution to the problem.

In the sequence of peace processes which are occurring as a logical consequence of dialogue, the case of East Timor in turn faces a dialogue process and it is our desire to bring to an end the 19 years of suffering of the Maubere People. However, Jakarta, as always, is wishing to impose its own law, its own definition of values, upon the world, just as Iraq did and has attempted again in relation to Kuwait. A clear parallel exists in the basic facts between the invasion and military occupation of East Timor by Indonesian forces and Iraq's invasion of Kuwait. However, one colossal difference exists: one section of the international community supported Indonesia's policy, whilst Baghdad was taught a lesson for violating international law.

Jakarta has been difficult in its handling of the East Timor question. The economic, military and therefore political importance of Indonesia in South-East Asia and the Pacific region has allowed it to become today a member of the UN Security Council, in spite of its failure to honour the resolutions passed in relation to East Timor by this organ of the UN. It is this same importance which has allowed Indonesia to assume the role of host of the forthcoming APEC summit and which now stands in the way of a successful solution to the East Timor problem being found. Jakarta has shown itself to be intransigent in its attitude to the substance of the problem, whilst Minister Ali Alatas continues to focus his efforts upon diverting attention from the need for a plebiscite for the people of the territory.

CNRM, which I represent, has proposed a solution in the form of a three-phase Peace Plan which will permit a climate of political stability, both within the territory and in relation to Indonesia, ahead of a referendum to be conducted under international supervision.

Allow me to remind you, Mr President of the existence of another striking parallel between the Gaza and West Bank Autonomy Plan and CNRM's own plan which aims at achieving a just and internationally acceptable solution to the East Timor problem. If, with the influence and laudable efforts of your government, Israel and Palestine have come to an understanding that it is time to lay down their weapons and to make peace, bringing to an end a case defined as intractable and characterised by a wide range of complexities, we believe that the USA is capable of contributing decisively to the search for a solution to the East Timor problem, encouraging the Jakarta regime to engage in dialogue with the Resistance.

I write to you now to appeal for your support in raising with President Suharto, on the occasion of the APEC summit, the need for Jakarta to display greater political goodwill in addressing the problem, acknowledging the essence of the problem and the legal and political status of the territory of which the United Nations continues to recognise Portugal as the administering power.

With the highest consideration
On the behalf of the CNRM

Kay Rala Xanana Gusmão
Commander of Falintil
Cipinang Prison, Jakarta, 1 November 1994

The 70th Birthday of H.J.C. Princen

Xanana wrote this piece for a collection to mark the 70th birthday of H.J.C. or Haji Princen, a Dutch-born Indonesian. A well-known human rights activist, he began his illustrious career by changing sides during Indonesia's war of independence with the Dutch after World War II (for which some Dutch still regard him as a traitor). He was imprisoned under both the Sukarno old order and Suharto new order regimes and is now the Director of the Institute for the Defence of Human Rights in Jakarta. He protested to the Minister of Defence, after Xanana's capture, for calling him a criminal and common street thief. His friendship with Xanana began when he helped take care of Timorese activists seeking asylum in various embassies in Jakarta during 1994. On one of his monthly visits to political prisoners in Cipinang Prison, he met Xanana and told him on one such visit, 'Now there are more people who understand your struggle. You will never be alone'.

Over the course of history, and especially in this new age of information technology, it is necessary to make sure we record the deeds of national heroes.

Life today is obscured by a kind of development focused merely on luxurious materialism, ignoring the development of independent and critical minds. The regimes of authoritarian rulers not only dominate the minds and souls of their subjects but they also enslave them.

In doing this, dictators claim certain privileges, and immunity from wrong thoughts or actions. They behave however they want, imposing decisions on their subjects. By annihilating and insulting the independent thinking of their subjects, these dictators sow the seeds of hatred of the people toward them. Ironically, history often only records the deeds of cruel rulers such as Mao Zedong and Deng Xiaoping in China, Kim Il Sung in North Korea, Saddam Hussein in Iraq, Ferdinand Marcos in the Philippines and many others in the developing world.

These dictators rule arbitrarily, making decisions on behalf of their subjects, ignoring the consequences. Their wishes become the actual and normative realities, deified as infallible dogma for all to obey. They silence rebellious and critical voices. They claim to be the owners of truth. They use their absolute power greedily to accumulate wealth for themselves and their families.

These dictators make laws against anyone who criticises them. They, the power-holders, cannot be criticised because they represent absolute truth itself. Though people know they are corrupt, that they are liars and murderers, with absolute power in their hands they can create their own heroic history. They are self-appointed and self-proclaimed heroes who fear the truth; heroes born from bloodshed; heroes blind to the equality and human rights of all; heroes creating justice according to their own will.

These power-holders feel that they stand at the helm of the ship of history. They feel they can deny the free course of the development of humankind. But the universality of the human condition cannot be a mere cultural contingency for one person's political interest because this would contradict the nature of development and our understanding of human existence.

Feudalism in its various repressive forms, both communist and non-communist, alienates human beings. In a dictatorial communist system, coercion is based on the slogan of economic equality. In the repressive non-communist regimes of the Third World, the power-holders sacrifice their people for their own selfish interests through the formation of the 'national bourgeoisie' who become the power-wielders.

With great pretension, these repressive power-holders develop the economy and the technological sector in their countries through dependence on loans from developed countries. Such unpayable foreign debt eventually has a huge negative impact on the lives of their people, the poor.

Intellectuals and academics are persuaded to become part of the ideological superstructure of the oppressive regime. These intellectuals and academics betray their moral duty and responsibility for the sake of power, money and fame, and help shape the meaning of justice, peace and freedom in a way that serves the interests of the power-holders. The minds and spirits of the majority are dominated through systematic indoctrination and propaganda. These intellectuals and academics develop and maintain the influence of latent feudalism, in the long run creating an inert and dependent mentality.

The basis for understanding human rights is a sense of justice. Only then can a real notion and practice of justice be secured. If human rights are denied then the majority will be treated arbitrarily by the elites.

Differences are inevitable in human society. Without them freedom of choice is impossible. Thus differences, the ability to perceive these differences and the freedom to choose from many different possibilities are the essential nature of human beings and are what make us human.

In general, history speaks only of the agents of material development, perpetuating only the names of those who control the future of a nation. The praise given to power-holders and their works, in closed societies based on dogma, is made in an effort to cover up the real feelings toward those power-holders. This is nothing else but flattery or sycophancy. The spiritual contribution from those with strongly held moral principles is often ignored.

Why do I say all this? Because in my view, under certain conditions, everyone can realise their own potential in their lifetime. A personality may be strong or weak, depending on a perception of and reaction to justice and injustice in the world. It is only after death that an evaluation of a person's thought, character and deeds becomes clear and definitive. But this is not the issue. Rather, I would like to talk about Princen who is now turning 70 and is in his wheelchair.

Princen betrayed the Netherlands army and joined the Indonesian army during Indonesia's struggle for independence. This courageous act of betrayal proves that he lives according to values nobler than simple nationalism. As a citizen of the Netherlands, who was provided with armaments with which to oppress and terrorise the Indonesian people struggling for independence, he challenged the people of the Netherlands, his own people and its leaders, with the idea that human rights are universal. It is hypocritical to go to war against a people when you recognise human rights, as the Dutch did. Dutch colonial law condemned Princen as a rebel and traitor, but Princen was awarded *Bintang Gerilya*, the Guerrilla Star, by the Republic of Indonesia.

Princen's actions were based on strongly held moral principles. His actions make the idea of universal human rights more meaningful for all people, whether they are powerless or powerful, rich or poor. Those rights include, among others, the right to be independent, the right to be self-determined. The fact that Princen lived according to his moral principles shows that he is a man of moral integrity.

As a man who also took part in the struggle against colonialism, Princen understood that independence is simply a means, not an end in itself. This is because independence only finds true meaning in true freedom, only when people's rights to freedom are secured and protected, and only when government accepts the responsibility to protect those rights.

Princen has taken risks in defending those rights. For a man like Princen, independence does not simply mean replacing the colonial right to exploit a nation with the right of an elite group of national bourgeoisie to do the same thing. For a man like Princen, this would be meaningless: independence as nothing more than a national flag and anthem to be respected by others, but the President using colonial laws to abuse his power. From 1962 to 1966 Princen was imprisoned simply because he defended these views.

The constitution of Indonesia did not guarantee the rights of the citizens because the laws were those inherited from the former Dutch colony. Basic human rights were still not a prority in Indonesia. Instead, economic rights, used corruptly to shape the national bourgeoisie, were made a priority.

In 1966 Princen founded an institution for defending human rights. He faced difficulties created by the economic and political power-holders. They claimed relativism in human rights values, claims still used by the powerful in Indonesia today.

The power-holders maintain irrational views based on feudalism; this ideology is used to legitimise a repressive regime.

No regime can change when its constitution is obsolete. Defenders of such a system advocate an attitude of feudalistic subservience in order to defend national culture and to justify the maintenance of the obsolete constitution.

We often hear the phrase 'new order', as opposed to the 'old order'. The new order replaces the old order but the new one will in its turn become old, because all things are born, evolve and die. This is the fate of all living creatures; the natural law of life. People's consciousness also follows this natural law; adapts itself over time, revises itself and then dies away. It is confined and contained by time and space.

The journey of history never ceases. At every station there are passengers who get on and off; such is the law of change which is the basis of development of human society. In this conception of history the new passengers are the young. Everywhere in the world! At whatever period: past, present and forever!

Princen found himself at the most potent face of the tide of transformation: he fought with the student movement. In 1970 he helped establish LBHI, the Institution of Legal Aid of Indonesia, because he needed to fight Indonesian laws—elite laws used to oppress the weak. Since the 1965 massacre when at least 500,000 people were brutally killed, Princen has always defended the weak. He also defended the rights of the weak at the massacre at Tanjong Priok in Jakarta in 1984.

The intervention of the military is a condition *sine qua non*, for the perpetuation of the repressive status quo. This is even worse if the regime is also colonial. It is what happened on 7 December 1975, when an enormous massacre took place in Dili. The East Timorese were brutally tortured and forced to accept integration with Indonesia. (Ironically, the Indonesian Government criticises what is happening today in the former Yugoslavia, suggesting that NATO intervene and settle the conflict through dialogue.)

Twenty years have gone past since the shameful invasion of East Timor. The Jakarta regime continues to kill the East Timorese people and the war persists. The Indonesian generals have attempted to destroy the nationalist consciousness of the Maubere People with the sophisticated weapons at their disposal.

Recently, using the case of an Indonesian flag burning, the government and military aroused the spirit and sentiment of nationalism in the people of Indonesia. Those same people who fought for two years to expel the Dutch also oppose us. We apologise to you, the Indonesian people, for having injured your undeniable feelings of nationalism.

We want to make the people of Indonesia aware that for 20 years the Indonesian military has burnt our flags, stolen our property, burnt our homes and killed more than 300,000 East Timorese people.

How can we accept that the people of Indonesia ostentatiously celebrate their 50th independence anniversary while the basic right of independence for the simple people of East Timor is denied? Independence means freedom from the chains of colonialism. How can you celebrate the 50th independence anniversary in Indonesia while the history of Indonesia records the forced annexation of a territory whose right to independence has been internationally recognised?

The people of East Timor were oppressed by Portuguese colonialism for 450 years, a century longer than the Dutch colonisation of Indonesia. The people of East Timor struggled continuously against Portuguese colonisation and the largest and final uprising took place in 1912. With the support of the Australian guerrillas, the people of East Timor also fought against the Japanese occupation.

The people of Indonesia fought for just two years against the reoccupation of the Dutch but the people of East Timor have fought for 20 years against the Indonesian military occupation of East Timor.

We have a deep understanding of our sense of nationalism because this is the burning fire in our hearts, a fire whose flame is unextinguished, a fire that motivates and strengthens us to fight for our nation, our East Timor.

It is for the noble cause of our basic rights to self-determination that we dare to sacrifice our whole lives. The incident of 12 November 1991 is a case in point. On that day thousands of young people took to the streets to appeal to the international community to recognise that Indonesia was oppressing our people, that Indonesia was denying our rights to self-determination, that we needed an open and genuine dialogue to eradicate the injustice inflicted on us in our territory. The Timorese youth demanded justice. They demanded just and dignified solutions that could be accepted by the East Timorese and the international community.

Colonialism is repressive. The Indonesian generals have no other solution to conflict except guns.

The Indonesia press very often describes as 'sadistic' the criminal acts of gangsters who mutilate their victims, but no one dares to describe the brutal killing and mutilation at Santa Cruz or the individual and mass killings in East Timor before that time as 'sadistic'. And no one disagrees with the military regime when they say the people of East Timor asked for integration with Indonesia.

Princen has been always faithful to the principles of justice, people's rights, and their basic human rights. He has taken a clear and courageous moral stand.

People who have moral integrity are people who have moral courage. They are the ones who defend truth and fear nothing but lies and falsehood.

For a long time, Princen had to report every month to the military authorities. Former political prisoners of East Timor have shared the same experience. They are never 'released' unconditionally. In order to be 'released' they have to make statements accepting the integration of East Timor with Indonesia or take oaths in front of the Indonesian flag accepting integration. Then they have to report to the military intelligence for the rest of their lives.

Undoubtedly, Princen is a part of Indonesian history. Perhaps historians have forgotten to record him. But that is not important. What remains forever in the minds of those who love justice and freedom is his active participation, his dedication and commitment to the transformation of thought and his willingness to stand by that transformation.

His physical condition does not allow him to move about freely. His body, like that of any other mortal being, is weak. But his spirit is strong and will live on in our memory. His noble deeds and thoughts are unerasable.

At the age of 70, H.J.C. Princen is a candle that illuminates the spirit of those who love and strive for transformation and progress. He is a candle that warms and encourages democratic forces in Indonesia.

Princen deserves to be honoured.

The people of East Timor wish Princen, their friend, a very long life.

Cipinang Prison, 18 September 1995

Letter to the Ploughshare Women

This letter is to four British women from a group called Ploughshares for Peace, who were arrested in January 1996 at British Aerospace after damaging an Indonesia-bound Hawk warplane with household hammers. Singing peace songs, the women had videoed themselves with the banner-garlanded jet and called police to come and arrest them. They were charged with burglary and criminal damage estimated at £31 million and refused bail. British Hawk sales began in 1978 and reports from Timor suggest the planes were used in bombing raids against civilians since 1983. The women had been calling for the cancellation of the Hawk deal for three years during which time Britain had become Indonesia's second biggest arms supplier. Both British Aerospace and the British government insisted that the Indonesians used the Hawks for training only. The trial began in Liverpool on 22 July; among supporters was José Ramos-Horta who gave evidence. The women were aquitted by a jury.

Very dear friends,
Lotta Kronlid, Andrea Needham, Joanna Wilson, Angie Zelter

I write to you from Cipinang Prison with special personal esteem and with the profound affection of the East Timorese people.

Dear friends, we were greatly touched by the courageous protest action that you undertook against the sale of more weapons by the British Government to the colonial regime in Jakarta. However, dear friends, we are immensely saddened to hear that you have been in prison since then. You have had to pay a high price for serving the Timorese cause.

Dear friends, believe me, your action has warmed our hearts, and the hardships you have to bear are a very precious source of inspiration to us; not only to me and to all Timorese prisoners in particular, but also to the entire Maubere People. They ask me to send you, not just their sympathy, but their love; and to remember, in moments of pain or disheartenment, the warmth that your own loving example has provided.

You are in our thoughts and in our hearts. I promise to send you, at the earliest opportunity, some mementos of the Maubere Homeland.

Many warm hugs of solidarity in the struggle and thousands of kisses from us all.

CNRM
Kay Rala Xanana Gusmão
Commander of Falintil

LEADER OF CNRT

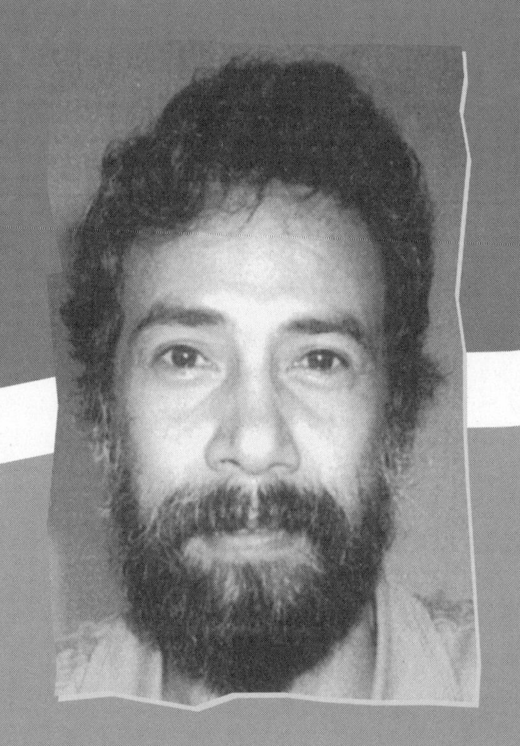

1998–

Message to the National Timorese Convention

This message was to the National Timorese Convention held in Peniche, Portugal, which established the National Council of Timorese Resistance, CNRT, the internationally-recognised representative of the East Timorese people. The convention also unanimously voted Xanana Gusmão as CNRT President. The creation of CNRT was the culmination of a tortuous political journey for the East Timorese. It and its antecedents (CRRN and CNRM) have been the cornerstones of East Timorese resistance to Indonesian occupation for 24 years. Since the August 1999 ballot, when 78.5 per cent of East Timorese voted for independence by indicating the CNRT flag on the ballot paper, Xanana has passionately asserted the place of CNRT and the national army Falintil in shaping the future of the new independent nation, Timor Loro'sae.

Mr President, Prime Minister, UN Representative, Ladies and Gentlemen, Dear Friends of East Timor,

In the name of the heroic people of East Timor, I wish to thank you all for gathering here today. Your comradely presence has given this historic event a profoundly human dimension.

I know that, from today, we East Timorese will have to live up to great expectations. There is no doubt that this event has raised many questions. Although it was greeted with scepticism, it has helped to bring many issues to light.

The aim of this convention is to clarify these issues, to design a political project that can bring all East Timorese together in such a way as to be able to coordinate their actions.

The National Convention of the East Timorese in the Diaspora is above all a challenge. It challenges our minds, our habits, our behaviour and our allegiances.

We do not promise to produce anything extraordinary but we promise to act responsibly and to be serious. We do not promise to be perfect but we promise to be honest and admit our mistakes.

Dear compatriots. Who would have thought that it would take the East Timorese 24 years to realise that we have wasted so much moral, psychological, intellectual and political energy since the Carnation Revolution?

It has taken us far too long to acknowledge the just principles of our struggle. It has taken us far too long to realise that we must not continue to swim against the tide of challenges that have constantly confronted us, to realise that we must unite so as to be able to face up to these challenges, to achieve more tangible and worthwhile results. It has taken us far too long to realise that we were riding in different compartments of a single train, running along the same track, harbouring the same desires, the same determination to win.

There is irony in the happy coincidence that the convention is taking place on the anniversary of the Portuguese 25th of April Revolution.

Our political wandering since April 1974 has been long and bitter. The celebrations for 25 April should encourage us to reflect seriously and deeply on the political consequences of all this, in order to remind ourselves of the historic significance of that event for the fate of East Timor.

A few moments of retrospection will show that we have never been open to the concept of unity, of working together to solve the problems of our nation. Unfortunately, our history teaches us that good intentions are not enough if we do not accept the same principles. Our history teaches us that the lack of consistency in our commitment to our people and our nation has led to confusion, preventing us from advancing towards a new stage in our struggle.

In 1974, the creation of a coalition was a significant political step in our advance towards decolonisation. The breakdown of that coalition weakened the nationalist movement; it was a fatal, historic mistake.

In 1986, the Nationalist Convergence was formed in an attempt to dispel the climate of suspicion that existed between the political parties but, once again, good intentions were not enough to create harmony between our separate objectives.

Along with the creation of the Nationalist Convergence and the desire to broaden the struggle to encompass all social and political participants in the National Resistance, an attempt was made to imbue the struggle with a new spirit. The CNRM was founded. However, this desire to unite East Timorese society was again defeated by the sectarian mentality that still prevailed in some circles.

Faced by this serious challenge, we made a pledge to our people to staunchly uphold the principle of 'Unite in order to be able resist better'! Side by side with our people, who easily understood the objectives of the CNRM, we were ready to cope with all the consequences. But there were distortions in the way the CNRM was perceived. It was seen as a party and incorrectly regarded as yet another player on the scene. It would have been better had this not been so and we had never stopped hoping that, one day, East Timorese politicians and intellectuals would listen to the people.

Sovereignty lies with our people; it is our people who deserve honour and respect. It is our people who give the orders and draft the mandates. It is not up to us—weak, imperfect individuals as we are—to decide. Our decisions, our commitments are legitimate only in so far as they comply with the will of our people.

Too often, we are more preoccupied with the reactions we provoke than with the feelings and the suffering of our people. Too often, we try to satisfy others' opinions without stopping to think that we might be offending our people, insulting the blood of our young ones, the tears of our mothers and the sacrifices made by one and all.

We ignore our responsibility to the suffering of our people every time we think more about ourselves than about the heroic greatness of our people. We act as if it was our people's duty to struggle, suffer and die to give legitimacy to our personal positions, status and ambitions.

We have fostered too many contradictions, we have nurtured too many internal conflicts, fuelling a highly polluted environment. Instead of mutual respect, we have sought power. Instead of understanding, we have created distrust. Instead of supporting each other, we have undermined each other.

And we all know that the atmosphere is still weighed down by doubt, mistrust, discontent and complaints. Bearing all this in mind, we are gathered here with the resolve to join hands, to move ahead, to begin a new chapter in the history of East Timor.

Dear companions of struggle. We are now convening the National Convention of the East Timorese in the Diaspora as it cannot be held on our own soil which is occupied by the Indonesian armed forces. This will be the first gathering of representatives of all Timorese political and social formations.

Our beloved, martyred people are watching us in the conviction that we will be able to produce something positive for our struggle. Above all else, our people believe that their interests will be the basis of our debates and that the interests of our abused nation will dictate the decisions that we make.

We shall make it crystal clear, and as forcefully as possible, to the Indonesian regime and to the world that the East Timorese people demand the right to self-determination and independence. Centuries of history and culture have given the East Timorese people an identity of their own. International law, universal principles and the UN Charter and its resolutions legitimise our right to determine our own future.

We have been fighting for this right while resisting the criminal aggression of the Indonesian military. And we shall keep on fighting as long as necessary. This does not mean that we advocate confrontation. Many people look upon us as the aggressors, but in fact we are the victims of aggression. Many people tell us that we should halt all armed activities, while they go on selling weapons to Indonesia so that the forces of occupation can go on killing us.

The East Timorese people love peace. The East Timorese were forced to take up arms to resist the brutal military invasion of 7 December 1975.

The East Timorese people long for peace. Our people will only be able to realise their full potential, to build a happy future for the coming generations when a real and lasting peace is achieved in East Timor. But a real and lasting peace can only come about as the result of a just resolution of the conflict, which enables our people to feel truly free and in control of their own future.

The illegal Indonesian military occupation has had disastrous consequences for East Timor: suffering, famine, disease, death and an intolerable physical and psychological repression have been the fate of our people. The occupation has also prevented our people from building a just, democratic and free society.

We advocate respect for basic human rights, for a pluralist democracy for East Timorese society. We are in favour of peace and disarmament. We defend the principle of dialogue to solve conflicts and we will contribute to peace and harmony between peoples and nations.

In order to reach these objectives which are fundamental to our struggle for freedom, we are compelled to resist the occupation of the Indonesian forces.

In this era of globalisation, no country can hope to prosper in isolation and ignore the complex relationships between peoples and governments. We therefore appeal to His Excellency, the Secretary General of the UN, not to lessen the frequency of his initiatives nor to undermine the significance of actions already taken to establish open and serious negotiations which include the East Timorese resistance, to find a solution that can bring an end to the suffering of the East Timorese people.

We appeal to the international community in general and to the US government and the European Union in particular, to give effective support to the efforts of the UN Secretary General in the search for a just and peaceful solution that will respect the legitimate interests of the East Timorese people as enshrined in universal principles and international law.

We appeal to Portugal in its capacity as the administering power to take any course of action necessary to defend the inalienable right of our people to self-determination and independence.

We appeal to the Indonesian Government to acknowledge that it is time for us all to correct the errors of the past and display the political will to regard each other not as enemies but as neighbours who are able to build a future of freedom, mutual respect, friendship and cooperation between the two nations.

Respected friends. I want to take this opportunity, on behalf of the East Timorese people, to express our deepest gratitude to the Portuguese state and our brothers and sisters, the Portuguese people, for the support and solidarity they have shown towards the East Timorese cause to this day.

We also extend our deepest gratitude to the governments of the PALOPs and our Lusophone brothers and sisters, to friendly governments, and to the international solidarity movement that has always supported us very effectively.

We also wish to express solidarity with the martyred peoples of Western Sahara and Palestine, as well as with the democratic movement in Myanmar.

We also want to tell the Indonesian people that we closely follow the progress of the democracy movement in Indonesia. The Indonesian and Timorese peoples are fighting for different objectives which are based on the same principles of law, justice, freedom and peace. The two peoples—brothers, sisters and neighbours—are oppressed by the same repressive regime.

Independence for East Timor will mean freedom for the Indonesian people. Justice and democracy in Indonesia will mean the liberation of the Maubere People.

Together, we will fight for peace, for justice, for freedom and for the rights of all the people of the world.

Long live East Timor!
Homeland or Death!
To resist is to win!
The struggle continues on all fronts.

Interview with Manuela Paixao

Manuela Paixao, from the Portuguese newspaper, Diario de Noticias, *was one of the first foreign journalists allowed to interview Xanana in Cipinang Prison after the fall of President Suharto in 1998. At this time international calls for his release were increasing.*

Diario de Noticias (DN): How are you?

Gusmão: I have a cold and cough but I'm not really sick and, in the main, I'm fine.

DN: What is your daily routine here in prison?

Gusmão: It's hard to be precise, as it varies from day to day. I have time and opportunity to read, write, paint, study, and for sport. There is no hard and fast rule about the schedule.

DN: The settlement proposed by Indonesia includes your release as an intrinsic part of an autonomy deal—an extensive autonomy, but nonetheless, autonomy. What do you think of it?

Gusmão: In the first place, it is not very attractive to think that, after so many years of political inflexibility, the Indonesian government is beginning to open the doors with only a half-hearted will to really resolve the problem. Linking my release to a comprehensive settlement could have negative or positive consequences.

DN: How do you mean?

Gusmão: It depends from which viewpoint the program is considered. It was very hard for the Resistance to get through these past 23 years, always clinging to the belief that Suharto's regime would one day fall, and there would be a place in Indonesia for a more democratic regime. We believed that if there were a democratic regime in Indonesia, East Timor's case could then be discussed openly in public, nationally. There are already some newspapers here that are publishing much more freely.

DN: Do you think then that it is conditional upon democratisation in Indonesia?

Gusmão: If there were democracy, no Indonesian citizen would tolerate repression, the use of force, annexation of a territory, denial of the right to speak out. However, after 30 years, we are now seeing greater openness.

DN: Does that mean that the present government has a more open attitude towards the question of East Timor?

Gusmão: Yes. Before, it was all hard-line, inflexible. Now, they are thinking of offering us autonomy. However, there have been no promises yet—it is not a democratic government yet.

DN: But do you think that the general elections in Indonesia could bring in a democratic regime?

Gusmão: It is not a matter of general elections, but rather a question of real change—and that means changes to legislation, statutes, everything. There seems to be certainty that the new options are really democratic. I believe that, overall, there is progression towards a certain degree of change in the constitution, with regard to political parties and freedom of expression. But we are not in a hurry.

DN: What do you mean?

Gusmão: If we accept autonomy now, we might find that, in the future, there is a democratic government that says to us, 'Tomorrow you are free to choose. Choose, like Portugal did; choose what you want'. We are not mature enough to see that things are going that way …

DN: Are you saying that autonomy with a democratic regime in Indonesia could one day lead to greater autonomy in East Timor?

Gusmão: Not exactly. I am saying that this period under Habibie is a period of transition only to democracy. I believe that one day it will arrive. When it does, our problem is going to be seen only from the democratic point of view. In other words, each person may express his/her own opinion, and their view is respected by others. A democratic regime is going to say to us, 'You have the right to express your views on your own destiny'.

DN: Would you agree to any other methods which would enable the people to express their choice?

Gusmão: You mean in addition to a referendum?

DN: No. Instead of a referendum.

Gusmão: I do not think there are any other ways. East Timor could take part in the general elections and the number of abstentions would be an indication of opposition to integration in Indonesia. But that would require a lot of preparation. A referendum is easier for people to understand: the choice is clearer—it's either yes or no. The other way would be confusing, as only those in favour of integration in Indonesia would take part in the elections. I think that holding a referendum is a better way.

DN: Are the negotiations between Portugal and Indonesia, with the UN Secretary General's mediation, making progress?

Gusmão: Not as far as I can see. On the parts of Portugal and the UN, a lot of effort is being made, but Indonesia is still inflexible—that is, Indonesia and the Suharto regime. Ali Alatas is stubborn, arrogant and a product of the former regime, so people do not accept him. Amid the reforms which they say they are undertaking, the key players have not changed their principles or their outlook. In my view, Ali Alatas is not the right person to be dealing with the East Timor issue. He is too linked to the former regime.

DN: What concessions are you prepared to make in order to reach a settlement for East Timor?

Gusmão: We are prepared to make a lot of concessions because we have a good idea of Indonesia's fears and its interests. For example, one aspect which is often spoken about is that parts of the Indonesian armed forces are ashamed of losing, being 'defeated' in the war in Timor. We could undertake commitments to create a situation, atmosphere, solution in which the military would not feel defeated, but rather participants in the process.

DN: On the subject of armed forces, don't you think that the announcement/promise that some troops will start to leave Timor heralds an opening of attitude?

Gusmão: There have been many promises over the past 20-odd years. Only international supervision of all the measures and points that are agreed between all the parties will convince me that troops have been withdrawn. Even yesterday visitors told me that the *ninjas*—men in camouflage, trained by the [Indonesian] army and ordered to spread terror—have re-emerged.

DN: What is the latest news about the ninjas?

Gusmão: Five of these *ninjas* were caught by a neighbourhood defence group. One was from Tambua, armed with a gun. They were handed over to the

Bishop. They say that they are preparing something. I heard that they are training 2000 armed men, and a further 4000 to take part in destabilising activities, in order to show that the government is right when it says that a referendum could spark off a civil war. When there is international supervision checking to see whether all the measures and agreements are being fulfilled—that is when I will believe in promises.

DN: In Indonesia, trouble is flaring up in various parts of the country, such as Irian Jaya, with calls for independence. Could this jeopardise negotiations for East Timor?

Gusmão: I think we should not have to pay for the problems of others. Our problem is different from theirs. We have nothing to do with the situation in Aceh or Irian Jaya because we are not, nor ever were, part of Indonesia. The Javanese say they are brothers of Irian Jaya. But the boundaries of Indonesia were drawn by Holland as a coloniser. Timor never formed part of that historic link, so we do not belong to Indonesia. Their problems are not the same as ours, and they should not link theirs to ours.

DN: Don't you think that if these conflicts continue the government might be less disposed to settle the Timor issue in case it has to do the same in other areas?

Gusmão: That is precisely why I am saying that we should not be confused with other problems. Our case is different. Our problem is unique.

DN: How do you see the role of the church, the Vatican? Would you approve of the idea of, for example, Bishop Belo officially taking part in the negotiations?

Gusmão: I do not think that is possible. I thought you were going to refer to the example of South Africa where, as in Mozambique, the problems were national, internal. Ours is an international issue. The Bishop of Dili could not completely get away from the fact that he is a citizen and native of Timor. Furthermore, the complexity of the East Timor problem now demands far more than the Bishop's level. The international community is also putting pressure on Indonesia to bring about an internationally supervised settlement.

DN: What about the Vatican—the Sant' Egidio Community, for example?

Gusmão: No, I do not think that having the Vatican as one of the mediators would be a good idea. Indonesia is mainly Moslem. I fear that, in order to save two million Catholics in Indonesia, the Vatican might hand us over as a province. It is not that I don't believe in God's justice, but the problem is an international one.

DN: Are you satisfied with Kofi Annan's mediation?

Gusmão: Up against the Suharto regime's wall of inflexibility as he is, I cannot say that he is not making an effort—a big effort.

DN: Do you see any difference between the present government and the previous one?

Gusmão: I think some differences have emerged. Suharto always used to say that there would be no independence, and that East Timor was the same as the other provinces ... Now, by agreeing to autonomy, they are opening doors so that, in a few years time, they will accept independence. I believe that this transition period will lead to democracy; otherwise there will be uncontrollable chaos. It is a progressive process towards democracy.

DN: In what way?

Gusmão: When there eventually is a truly democratic regime, we are going to propose that they practise that democracy with us. For self-determination.

DN: Independence or autonomy? What do you think about East Timor's economic survival?

Gusmão: The question makes me laugh because it is what the Indonesians always ask me. The Indonesians, who stole our oil, are always saying how much they invest in Timor and how much they pay for us to survive, and how they build this and build that. But they omit to mention how they receive funding from Australia, the EU and other countries, to build schools and for health care in Timor. They pocket over half the aid money that is sent from Australia for Timor. There are much poorer countries than ours which are independent and which survive.

DN: How was the meeting with the 'European troika' representatives?

Gusmão: Basically, what they expressed was the eagerness of the EU for a settlement that is the result of the will of the people, of all the parties involved. They appealed for non-violence. I promised them that, although our objective is a referendum, our principle is to respect the different opinions—those of the pro-integrationists and those who want autonomy. They came mainly to gather ideas and viewpoints from all sides. They did not say whether they were in favour of independence or autonomy, but expressed the view that we should try to create an atmosphere conducive to dialogue.

DN: Does that request from the EU mean not responding to provocation, and not meeting violence with violence?

Gusmão: Yes, precisely.

DN: What did you reply to their request?

Gusmão: That we would certainly try, but that they too should understand that, after these past 23 years, after an experience such as ours, after so much suffering, it is sometimes hard for people to control themselves. I said that they should realise that, with the troika's visit to East Timor, it was like opening the floodgates for the first time. I believe, however, that after a while everyone will be more in control of themselves and less emotional than the first time they were finally able to express their feelings, and shout.

DN: Marker's [Jamsheed Marker, the UN Secretary General's envoy for East Timor] visit to certain areas in East Timor could be jeopardised for fear of further demonstrations. Monsignor Basilio do Nascimento thinks that it would be enough if he were to just go to Dili. What do you think?

Gusmão: Monsignor Basilio is out there, and knows better than I do. But I am still sending out messages appealing for calm. I was told yesterday that the young people, and population in general, are responding to our appeal, but I was also alerted about the cases of provocation by *ninjas*—it will be hard to prevent reaction to such provocation by the neighbourhood defence groups. The government knows that.

DN: What do you ask from the Portuguese people—not the Portuguese Government?

Gusmão: [A long silence followed. Then, with eyes glistening with tears, and voice altered with emotion, he replied] That they continue to love us. Because the Timorese people love the Portuguese.

New Year Message for 1999

Following the May 1998 ousting of Suharto, President Habibie offered the East Timorese wide-ranging autonomy and announced major troop reductions in the territory. Jubilant demonstrations took place in East Timor. With options of autonomy and independence being negotiated throughout 1998 Xanana expressed a willingness to accept three years or more of autonomy under Indonesian rule as a transitional stage toward independence. Such a process had been spelt out by CNRM as early as 1989. The mood in Dili—which was initially euphoric following Suharto's fall—had become bleak by October 1998 as early promises of change failed to materialise. Pro-autonomy militia violence increased in Timor and the Indonesian Government began to explain the conflict in East Timor as one between pro-autonomy militias and pro-independence groups, portraying its own military as a neutral and benign force (a similar scenario to that advanced following the initial invasion).

Companheiros da Luta! Compatriotas de Timor-Leste!

We are about to enter a new year in the struggle for the liberation of our Homeland, East Timor. For 23 years our people have dedicated their energy, their indomitable courage, their determination and life itself to the sacred ideal of national independence.

It was because of this extremely long suffering and deep patriotism that our people have kept alive their resistance against the shameful Indonesian invasion and the criminal military occupation of East Timor.

We knew since the beginning of the war that we faced a powerful enemy—the dictatorial/colonialist Suharto regime. Despite being aware of the imbalance between us and the Indonesian invader, we never, not even for a single moment, hesitated to continue struggling for our inalienable right to self-determination and national independence.

Many Indonesian generals are now retired, others have been promoted at the expense of our people's blood, at the expense of the crimes perpetrated in East Timor. We spent years of extreme hardship; we faced extremely difficult times. The grief and the tears, death and pain were but the bricks that built our steadfastness in the struggle and our faith in victory.

Last year, 1998, was marked by a radical change in Indonesian socio-political life, with consequences for our own process. All of Indonesia trembled with the extraordinary social movement that shook the pillars of the repressive and corrupt *Orde Baru*.

The feeling that a moment of great hope had arrived was once again felt in East Timor. Euphoric attitudes took some people back to 24 years ago, forgetting the constraints of 1998's context. Our concerns gained their real dimension, not only because of the memories they brought back but also because of the way they reflected the vision of the future which awaits us. A mixture of fear and optimism took over all of us and warned us of all the possibilities which can lead our process to be an undesirable one. And the more we stop to analyse East Timor's social fabric, the more we are led to consider that we must avoid disastrous childish political attitudes.

For 24 years, we all demanded the right to self-determination and national independence for East Timor. A great number of strategies were designed, and numerous ideas were developed, from the simple return of Portugal to CNRM's Peace Plan to a so-called 'third way' which was never really elaborated.

The acceptance of CNRM's Peace Plan (dismissed by the 'third way' as an 'integrated autonomy') was never preceded by an in-depth study of its contents. Today, doubts arise over acceptance of an autonomy proposal. Today, more time is spent on debating time frames than on analysing and understanding our process.

We were suddenly struck by the turmoil of events in Indonesia and immediately set ourselves apart from Indonesia, forgetting the political constraints of the regime which goes on without significant alteration of the basic *Orde Baru* principles.

No effort is being made to try to understand, to try to analyse all aspects regarding the endeavours and the intention to solve the problem. Many are only thinking about a referendum; some even demand immediate independence. As if all the others did not yearn for independence, as if the others did not advocate a referendum as the most just way towards the solution. As if we had all been struggling against Suharto (who could have given us benefits through corruption) only to now yield to Habibie who faces a serious economic crisis that has thrown over 90 million Indonesians into desperate poverty and led to the sacking of over 24 million workers.

It is regrettable that 23 years after the beginning of the war for national liberation, people do not bother to spend some time thinking and analysing the process in order to understand it better. Some people do not agree that it is necessary to educate our people politically and argue that our people are politically prepared, the proof being that they resisted for 23 years. This is beside the point; these people are mistaking patriotism for political awareness.

Some are already concerned with power, worried about his or her party and wishing to ensure a favourable political juncture for it. Because they see nothing but the party, they are not able to see the interests of the Homeland, the interests of our people! Sometimes the word 'interest' is used as a synonym of 'yearning for independence'. They are unable to understand any further or discover the real dimension of the meaning of 'the nation's interests'.

Still others emerge as the champions of realism, covering up their shame for not having done anything after receiving large sums of money from Suharto in exchange for hindering the process of liberation of our Homeland. Such people are now drawing the extraordinary conclusion that we are acknowledging that they were right, when they have been proven to be totally wrong in recognising the invasion and making a full 180 degree turn in their all-revolutionary 1974 ideology!

Today, opportunism appears in the guise of an extremely poor political pragmatism. Mbak Tutut [Suharto] must be feeling ashamed for having had such money-thirsty friends willing to address great speeches in tribute to the Suharto and Habibie regimes.

Well, this stage is drawing attention to the on-going political immaturity of so many, the so-called East Timorese politicians, when we ought to be thinking more carefully about the responsibilities we bear in order to put an end to the suffering of our people—to end it and not permit it to be perpetuated. Too often we do not study the meaning of words; we do not know the semantics of some expressions. We learn sentences, slogans and mottoes by heart and then pronounce them without being fully aware of their real meaning.

Dear *Companheiros da Luta*!

One must emphasise that what happened in our Homeland can be explained. Our people are losing their patience; our people have lost faith. Our people have lost faith in the UN; our people have concluded that UN resolutions no longer have any value, that the UN is only favouring Jakarta. Our people are led into thinking that the only way to free themselves is to increase the level of confrontation in East Timor.

Our people are tired of all the Jakarta lies; our people feel that the best way is to take advantage of the social, political and economic problems Indonesia is going through.

Our people know that the Suharto/Habibie regimes refuse to recognise the crime it perpetrated with the invasion and annexation of East Timor and that it lacks political will to find a solution. Our people can no longer stand Jakarta's on-going ill-faith because they know that serious, open and positive dialogue has always been rejected by the colonialist regime.

This attitude is nothing but a legitimate reaction to Indonesia's on-going disregard for international law, universal principles and UN resolutions. Our people's attitude merely shows that Suharto's ousting meant nothing for East Timor and that, after all, 'the flies have changed but the manure (*Orde Baru*) remains'.

The attitude of our people is in itself proof of their disillusionment with the international community. The countries usually considered as the champions of democracy and human rights are apathetic about the democratic process in Indonesia and about the East Timor problem.

Many countries supported the Suharto repressive regime by fuelling the corruption that led to Indonesia's bankruptcy. Today, those countries hardly lift a finger in favour of the democratic movement and, on the contrary, are looking only at prospects for new investments in an economically vulnerable Indonesia.

The countries that helped cast the Indonesian people into poverty are now salvaging a good relationship with Habibie, scrambling for the profits Indonesia promises as a bankrupt country. The values of democracy, justice and human rights remain an internal matter for Indonesia to grapple with, despite the fact that these values are alien to a regime undergoing a process of cosmetic reforms.

This interest-driven policy of the international community also has an impact on East Timor. The international community does not feel responsible for the fate of 200 million Indonesians, be it under the Suharto or the Habibie regimes. Not to mention some 700,000 East Timorese—it is a too small a number to deserve any consideration in terms of law and justice! The Indonesian people are obsessed with putting Suharto and his clique of generals and ministers on trial and are forgetting the role the international community has played in propping up one of the most corrupt and repressive regimes in the world. While the international community is still looking at Indonesia as a market for major profits, as a multitude of consumers, the situation in Indonesia may lead to more intense political and social turmoil. We are concerned; the international community is not.

The same is happening with the East Timor problem.

We know how much Portugal has done so far in defence of our right to self-determination and national independence. We are aware of the UN's efforts, the commitment of the Secretary General and the engagement of Ambassador Jamsheed Marker and his staff.

However, we are also aware of the constraints Portugal and the UN face in seeking a solution. The UN limits are due to the total disregard Jakarta has shown for this international organisation, and to the international community's indifference towards increasing its pressure on Indonesia.

We appreciate and express our deepest gratitude to the USA Congress and Administration, both of which have recently adopted a law recognising the right of the East Timor people to self-determination. We also appreciate and express our gratitude to the European Union for adopting a resolution supporting the holding of a referendum. However, reality is showing that it is not enough, that greater pressure must be brought to bear on Jakarta, not just to demand a more transparent and serious process of political reforms but also to seek a just and long-lasting solution for East Timor.

Companheiros da Luta! A just and long-lasting solution! No solution is fully fair if it is not long-lasting, nor can a solution be long-lasting if it is not just. Just and long-lasting are two terms within the process we all seek for East Timor. We have often, maybe hundreds or even thousands of times, cried out for a just and lasting solution. We have used this expression so often that it was starting to lose its meaning.

In conformity with international law, a just solution can only be reached with the holding of a referendum. But this is not enough. So that the solution may be lasting, we must be concerned with and sensitive to a whole range of social and political issues regarding East Timor. Such issues will have a bearing on our future. Such problems, if not duly analysed and assessed, may lead to political instability, restless minds and a climate of social conflict.

We are aware that our people are beginning to show a lack of patience, that radical groups are emerging and will choose confrontation to break the current deadlock provoked by the arrogance of the Suharto/Habibie colonialist regime.

We have already stated that we will not take advantage of the current (and on-going) political and social turmoil in Indonesia. In doing so, we wish to express our respect and solidarity with the struggle for democracy and justice of the Indonesian people whose rights have been trampled on for 32 years by the *Orde Baru* regime!

Many people foresee greater instability and violence during 1999 in Indonesia. As the Commander-in-Chief of Falintil, I realise that we do not have the military capability to defeat and expel the occupying forces from our Homeland. But I know that we are capable of creating a greater and deeper instability throughout the territory, thus bringing about an even harder situation for Jakarta. And our motto would be *Pátria ou Morte*! Homeland or Death! And there would be no more compromise.

Maybe I am a coward for not choosing this path. Or maybe I am just waiting to run out of patience with the intransigent attitude of the Indonesian generals, given the stubbornness of Indonesian politicians and diplomats.

I wish to state that CNRT took the following considerations into account: first, its responsibility to preventing an increase in the number of victims among the East Timorese population. Second, CNRT believes that dialogue is the best way to reach a just and long-lasting solution, via international means. Third, CNRT does not wish that independence be the cause of conflict among the East Timorese themselves or between East Timor and Indonesia.

Some have been suggesting that we should prepare ourselves to proclaim independence if the situation in Indonesia gets out of control. I do not accept this idea, but not because I do not want independence. I do not accept it because I have my own notion of independence. I do not wish to be witness to a chaotic type of independence, one which would lead to violence between brothers. We all understand that independence is a means and not an end in itself. Independence must guarantee peace, tranquillity, harmony and safety to all, with no exception, so that everyone may be committed to national development and reconstruction. Independence must be forged in such a way as to ensure the best possible relationship of cooperation with our great neighbour, Indonesia.

Independence must not mean the closing of doors to the world. Independence is nothing more than the ability to be managers of our own destiny. For some politicians, to manage is to govern and to hold power. Rather, to manage is an act which all the people will carry out through full participation in the nation's future.

Our struggle for national liberation gave us more than enough time to study the history of liberation movements around the world. Many independent countries have yet to prove their understanding of the meaning of the 'right to manage the country's fate'; their leaders are now facing serious social and political problems and regrettable economic hardships. In those countries, independence did not bring peace and understanding to their citizens; it did not help improve the living conditions of the population.

Indonesia itself mirrors this Third World policy. Poverty and misery hide behind the beautiful buildings of metropolitan Jakarta. Fifty years after independence, social conflicts are almost intractable, external debt has reached four million rupiahs per person and over 90 million Indonesians are living below the poverty line.

Above all, we must avoid the independence euphoria which always emerges in the wake of a war of liberation. If it is not one party claiming to have led the whole struggle, it is individuals who paint themselves as heroes, claiming that because they have worked the most and suffered the longest they deserve to be rewarded.

Independence is yearned for as a means of placing heroes in the leading bodies of the government. Independence is a way of showing who fought and who did not; independence is a way for people to dream for themselves or for their group, or party. Independence gains a new meaning: conflict of opportunities! I am aware that the Peniche Convention brought bitter feelings to many East Timorese and that the composition of CNRT in East Timor was a disappointment to many politicians and heroes. We are not even independent yet and we are already thinking about who will be a minister and who will not. Even before becoming independent we are already trying to write our name in the Heroes' Book of Honour, the book of those who have done all, who have suffered the most. And we forget that the true heroes are our people and the guerrilla fighters in the bush!

Independence is already losing its character; independence is already concealing personal and group ambitions. It was common in Third World countries for heroes of the liberation movement to become heroes of independence. In most cases this was a huge mistake. And it is from this mistake that the East Timorese should learn.

We should all understand that the liberation of our Homeland is only the halfway mark on the road to achieving the goal of independence.

However, independence can only enable the development of our initiative and creativity if all East Timorese can reassure themselves and everybody else that East Timor is for all and that in East Timor we can all live in peace and harmony so that the just solution we will achieve may be a long-lasting one.

With this thought I wish to clarify that if the CNRT has accepted the idea of autonomy it is not because we do not yet have the infrastructure or human resources that will guarantee our ability to rebuild our nation.

During the first three years after the invasion, our people showed extraordinary courage in mobilising themselves to face the war that Suharto's generals waged against us. I believe that by living on cassava during the first five years we, the East Timorese, will be selling rice to the Indonesians a year later.

However, our problem is not as simple as it might seem. Today, feelings that separate, divide and lead to conflict between us still exist in East Timorese society, although at the National Conference, held in March 1981 we identified National Unity as a prime objective of our struggle; in 1986 we set up the Nationalist Convergence; in 1987, CNRM followed as a means of opening the way for new prospects of National Reconciliation, and CNRT's establishment represented a refinement of this process of uniting the East Timorese.

These are the wounds that must be healed. It is very easy for independence 'heroes' to think that tomorrow we will throw all integrationists into jail and that is it! Peace will prevail then! Will that really be peace? Is that what we yearn for? Those who killed ought to be killed? Those who arrested should be arrested? Those who tortured should be tortured? Those who stole should be stolen from? It is easy: they would be all thrown into jail. We will then crown ourselves with the glory of being the great heroes of National Liberation!

The history of the Third World is repeating itself: the leader of the resistance will end up as president, even if he is not up to the task; guerrilla commanders will be generals and politicians will strive to become ministers. All because we were the heroes; all because we worked hard, suffered more than others! If this were to happen, it would be an outrage to the whole meaning of our struggle, the whole meaning of the sacrifices made by our people. It would be a betrayal!

Then these 23 years of struggle would not put an end to bloodshed and violence. Our wish would be one for revenge and an appeal for justice to be done. These 23 years would not be enough for us to adopt a different political stance. After all, we fought for 23 years without trying to understand politics!

CNRT accepted the idea of autonomy for political reasons, because it wishes to implement genuine National Reconciliation and not an AIETD-type of reconciliation. We need a period of time to eradicate every feeling of hatred and revenge and to create a genuine harmony based on mutual respect and democracy.

This is hard to achieve. CNRT rejects the easy way towards a solution and accepts the challenge of having to face the hard way because CNRT believes that everyone, veteran politicians or beginners, should refuse to stain their hands with further violence in East Timor, where the victims will be the East Timorese themselves.

This is CNRT's commitment; this is my personal commitment!

If a majority votes for integration in a referendum, those who defend independence will be free to keep their opinions but will not have the right to provoke riots because of ideas. If the people choose independence in a referendum, the integrationists will continue being East Timorese and, as any other East Timorese, will rightfully live in East Timor if committed to not provoking instability in the reconstruction and development process of our Homeland.

CNRT does not dream about independence; CNRT can already see independence before its very eyes. Whether Habibie likes it or not, whether Wiranto may feel angry or not, whether Alatas feels furious or not, the independence of East Timor is an irreversible fact.

However, CNRT does not advocate an independence where the East Timorese will live in constant fear. When we proclaim independence, the East Timorese people will sing joyfully and feel genuine confidence in the future. No East Timorese will be cast aside; no East Timorese will feel alien to the process. We do not accept autonomy with Indonesian involvement because we 'love' Indonesia or because we expect some sort of compensation from Jakarta. Indonesia has a responsibility to contribute to the solution. Indonesia incited disagreement between the East Timorese; Indonesia must help the East Timorese to reconcile. Only by doing so will Indonesia save its face. Indonesia cannot leave the East Timorese to kill each other just because a majority wants independence. Otherwise, the crimes Indonesia perpetrated with the invasion and annexation of East Timor will multiply and be added to the shame of having created conflict and then having abandoned the East Timorese.

A just solution must be combined with something else: it must be long-lasting. During the autonomy period, as a transitional phase in preparation for a referendum, Indonesia will cooperate with the East Timorese in establishing a climate of total harmony guided by tolerance and mutual respect. If we can achieve this, Indonesia will have fulfilled its responsibility to finding a just and lasting solution for East Timor. A just and lasting solution will be of mutual benefit to both countries, ensuring a future relationship of cooperation and mutual assistance.

If Indonesia is willing to co-operate in establishing a political climate of genuine national reconciliation, I believe that our people will close the book on the chapter of the past 23 years. East Timor and Indonesia will then open a new chapter of history, with their eyes set on a future of peace in the region, as a contribution to world peace.

This is our people's commitment, because the East Timorese people want to live in genuine peace and prosperity for the sake of their children.

Companheiros da Luta! Let us concentrate on the problems we face and be concerned with future problems if we are serious about overcoming the current ones. Instead of discussing time frames, be they a month, six months, a year, two, three or ten years, let us concentrate on understanding the issues placed before us so that we may make decisions; the fate of our Homeland must be our prime concern.

An erroneous analysis of the situation has led the people of East Timor to take sides—either with those who defend autonomy or with those who defend a referendum. Those who defend the holding of a referendum forget that CNRT 'accepts' autonomy as a period of transition in the lead-up to a referendum.

What I can guarantee to all is that if Indonesia is to continue with its arrogance and inflexibility, insisting on autonomy as a final solution, there will be no autonomy in East Timor.

What I can guarantee is that before autonomy is established in East Timor, our people will be enlightened as to the true meaning of autonomy and its representatives will only sign an agreement if it is in the interests of the people. There will be no autonomy without the agreement of the East Timorese. And our motto would be, 'The struggle continues on all fronts! No truce!'

I have stated in a former message that it will all depend on the political stance adopted by the Habibie Government; a government which so far seems to be an extension of Suharto's colonial-expansionist regime. If the Habibie Government does not have the political courage to recognise Suharto's mistake, East Timor will remain a UN question; and when we lose our patience there will be no concern about saving Indonesia's face! Indonesia's face is stained with the blood of the Indonesian people and of over 200,000 East Timorese.

The Suharto regime used to say that the clock of history cannot be turned back; we say that the clock is running far too fast for Indonesia's rulers and their desperate bid to maintain the status quo.

Companheiros da Luta! My personal opinion is that Jakarta is not ready to move forward in a constructive way in the negotiation process during 1999. The Habibie colonialist government does not wish to find a solution for East Timor which will respect international law; right up to today, it has shown the arrogance which is typical of colonialists, stating that what they did was legal and therefore it is up to Portugal to recognise Indonesia's sovereignty over East Timor.

I am certain of one thing: 1999 will be yet another year of deadlock. We, the East Timorese, will have to wait for a new truly democratic government to be installed.

I will not call for an increase in tensions in our Homeland, nor for a greater level of confrontation with the occupying forces. One day we might have to make a decision on this if after the elections nothing changes in Indonesia and if the *Orde Baru* regime prolongs the current status quo. But not now. Let us concentrate on focusing our efforts on achieving:

— an end to military hostilities;

— a climate of greater political tolerance.

This stance aims at preventing further East Timorese casualties. The occupiers are arming the East Timorese and telling them to kill their own brothers and sisters. Instead of allowing ourselves to be consumed by anger, let us make an effort to think in a balanced political manner. Otherwise we will be playing the colonialists' game; we will be reinforcing the Indonesian argument that the East Timorese are threatened with a new civil war.

Politically we have not yet been able to neutralise these ancient tactics of the enemy: divide and rule. But the problem does not lie solely in the division; the problem is that they divide and distribute weapons to kill our own brothers and sisters. I wish to draw attention to the fact that all those who are instigating physical violence among Timorese are doing nothing more than helping the enemy to remain in East Timor. Whether they are aware of it or not, those who provoke conflict between the East Timorese do not wish for a speedy solution to the East Timorese problem.

Let us all accept the responsibility for creating a climate of political tolerance. Only such a climate will enable us to meet the challenge of initiating the process of conceiving ideas and plans and of starting to implement them.

Let us all try to be politically mature; let us avoid imitating the ways of the 'politicians' of 1974. Let us learn from our own mistakes before looking at those made in other countries. Let us try to be ourselves, mature in our political thinking, knowledgeable about our own process and capable of an objective analysis of reality. Let us not be bullies just because we carry some memories from the bush, nor let us be heroes just because we are holders of a 'long experience' diploma. Let us not be demanding just because the 'world' does not recognise our work or our sacrifices, nor act with pride because we can now lead or represent groups or parties.

Let us be humble in this struggle, because it does not belong to any single individual. The struggle has always been of the people! Let us not allow the meaning of our struggle to be sullied by personal ambition. The interests of the people must always stand above everything else. No matter how much or whom it may hurt, as the Falintil Commander, and in order to defend the supreme interests of our people, I will not hesitate to make the decisions that may better serve them.

Nineteen ninety-nine must be the year of a new political dynamic; 1999 must be the year for rethinking attitudes and for redoubling our commitment to achieving a positive future for our Homeland. Instead of just waiting for a referendum or autonomy, let us educate ourselves to realise that it is we, the East Timorese, who bear the enormous responsibility for solving our own problems; that it is up to us, the East Timorese, to formulate ideas, design plans and seek the means of bringing them to fruition.

Nineteen ninety-nine must be the year of joining forces in preparation for the challenges of the future!

Pátria ou Morte! A Luta continua em todas as frentes! Resistir é vencer!

Homeland or death! The struggle continues on all fronts! To resist is to win!

President of the CNRT
Kay Rala Xanana Gusmão
Falintil Commander-in-Chief
Cipinang, 31 December 1998

From the Dreams of the Mountains

Message to the Strategic Development Conference

This message, played on video, was Xanana's official opening of the April 1999 Melbourne Conference 'Strategic Development Planning for East Timor'. This working conference brought East Timorese together from around the world, many from East Timor, to produce a basic strategic development plan for a future independent East Timor in the areas of government, health, education, economy, agriculture and environment. The video was filmed in the Salemba prison house he had been moved to in February.

The presence here today of the indigenous members of Australia is of tremendous significance to my people and me. The Aboriginal people of Australia and the East Timorese people share a common historical anguish and yearning for full recognition of their inalienable rights.

Honoured Participants and Dear Friends of the People of East Timor.

In the name of the Martyred People of East Timor, I wish to thank:

the Victoria University of Technology, the Australian Government, Caritas Australia, Archbishop George Pell, the Overseas Service Bureau, the Marist Brothers, the Myer Foundation, the Fred Hollows Foundation, ACFOA, the Victoria Foundation for Survivors of Torture, the Timorese Association in Victoria, members of the East Timorese Community in Victoria, members of the Australian community, Oxfam and CAFOD of England, the Gulbenkian Foundation, CCODP of Canada, CCFD of France, the Australian Education Union, and the Norwegian Government,

who made it possible for this conference to take place and become a hope for our people.

We are touched by the enormous interest and concern that the international community is expressing for the future of East Timor. We are also touched by the incomparable dedication that NGOs have shown and continue to give to our people. We cannot proceed without acknowledging the presence of representatives of friendly governments and, on the last day, the presence of a representative from the World Bank who kindly wants to witness the efforts made by the Timorese to produce ideas and create a vision for the future. I also welcome representatives of NGOs who will provide stimulus, and, obviously, the presence of international experts who I am sure will give us a hand in areas where our experience has yet to be revealed or in areas where our lack of expertise will require advice, amendments and improvement. Your consideration is a great motivation and your support will make us more able and resolute in overcoming our difficulties.

To all of you, our many thanks.

Dear Compatriots, this is the first time in the history of East Timor that its children are gathered together for a real analysis and to plan a development strategy for the first years which will mark the beginning of a new future, towards the direction of independence, full of our yearnings and toil.

It is the first time in our history that the Timorese assume with great enthusiasm and confidence their responsibilities as the future builders of a small nation that wants to assert itself in the world after more than two decades of criminal repression.

The members of Falintil were given the sacred mission to liberate the nation from domination. Today you receive a mission no less sublime: to formulate its construction. Here you will debate how to develop our beloved East Timor.

These last 23 years of military annexation of East Timor were presented as years of 'development'. Beyond the criminal repression of the population, the said 'development' did not change the images of illiteracy, illness, disease, misery and malnutrition of our people. On the contrary, it created a psychological state of terror, uncertainty and moral dilemma. The said 'development' of these 23 years did not find a formula to improve the nutritional levels of our people; could not discover a formula to diversify the agricultural production of our people, not even a formula to explore the potential of our natural resources; nor was it able to discover methodical and harmonious regional planning, not even a formula to guarantee self-sufficiency of the territory.

All that has occurred is a continual dependency on annual budgets from outside East Timor in which, from the beginning, any initiatives were limited and any capacity minimised in a routine of doing the same thing, every year.

Honoured Participants, dear Compatriots, the economic development process in the nations of the south has been the object of permanent studies at the level of bilateral and multilateral relationships between governments and has also been a constant worry to NGOs and associations of humanitarian character.

The failure of the majority of developing countries, which were not able to support continuous economic growth without incurring heavy external debt, should serve as a lesson to us in how to direct, from the first hour, our strategic development.

Bad management and incorrect strategies of competitive, accelerated industrialisation were the principal causes of failure of developing nations. It is the global perspective of the continuous dependency of developing nations, less developed nations or underdeveloped nations which has led to us throwing ourselves into this task of preparing our own project of development.

We are practically starting from zero in all areas. It is necessary to identify each area, research it and program it, with relation to the global picture in which we will engage thereafter, in a synergy of adjustment, reflection and evaluation, so that we can obtain the necessary short, medium and long term sustainability. Let us not be captivated by the methodologies of solving social emergency problems with which we are lately preoccupied. Let us conceive of structured projects that guarantee sustainable development in East Timor.

We are conscious that for any development process to succeed well, it basically depends on factors such as human resources, natural resources, capital and technological formation. Nevertheless, a promising starting point in the effective continuity of any development plan requires making the correct use of human resources. This also implies the necessity for total transparency within the apparatuses and organisations of power and in the management and accountability of funds provided by international aid to civic and social organisations, so that from the first moment we can firmly combat corruption and all temptation to debase the objectives of sustainable development. Only with such political commitment can we improve the living conditions of the rural people who will be called on to play an integral role in the gradual and persistent elimination of the main causes of poverty.

We will stimulate a civil society by the conception and promotion of economic and social development in East Timor. We will need, without doubt, outside help in many areas, from the legislative and administrative restructure to infrastructure, from education to investment management, among others.

The challenge that is facing us is one of whether our natural potential can attract foreign investors to stimulate our economic development. Will we be able to produce something that truly represents a strategy for development and which has as the main objective the improvement of the living conditions of our people? Will we also be able to produce something here that guarantees to the international community that the Timorese are prepared to avoid the mistakes of other developing nations, and that shows the beginnings of the principles of cooperation that do not entail total or prolonged dependence on our partners?

Dear Compatriots, I am not the right person to give an expert opinion on the development program for East Timor. Nevertheless, if you allow me, I will try to draw the vision that our Falintil fighters have always carried with them to justify their sacrifices.

The cornerstone of the rapid and efficient development of any country is the cultural strength of its people. What we see now is that the Timorese people are unable to provide for their children's school expenses. Hence they are not motivated to attend school. It should be the policy of our new East Timor state that there is compulsory and free education for all.

Allied with this policy, the state must pay careful attention to realistic programs of professional development oriented to the needs of our human resources.

But the serious health problems of our population also deserve our concern. TB and malaria characterise the general state of health of our people. Leprosy, goitre, elephantiasis and infant mortality constitute areas where medical assistance is inadequate and are evidence of the absence of preventative measures. Our children are born and are growing up in poor health and nutritional conditions; hence we need to provide free health assistance to the whole population of East Timor. Let us not be tempted to build and develop modern hospitals that are costly and in which only half a dozen people benefit from good treatment. Let us concentrate above all on planning intensive campaigns of sanitation and prevention, and the treatment of epidemics and endemics for the whole population.

Vitamins will not be useful while malnutrition continues to grip the villages, whilst our people continue to be condemned to a subsistence production which offers very little quality and quantity, and which will continue to leave people hungry for most of the year. Let us try to understand the variety of conditions in our territory so as to enable us to implement an agricultural policy that promotes the harmonious growth of the districts, allowing self-sufficiency to each of them through a wealth of methods and organised traditional techniques. This diversification itself will be useful in promoting and enriching rural communities.

Parallel to this, we should provide incentives for agribusiness and the fishing industry as the two main sources of our people's diet. The potential resources in these two sectors are enormous and their gradual growth will bring much needed industrialisation in food preparation and distribution.

Speaking of industries, we will perhaps have to attend to three sectors:

— small industries concentrating on the manufacture of primary goods;
— medium-term industries for the production of goods and services necessary for the revitalisation of the nation;
— strategic industries specialising in the production of export items to generate revenue for the nation.

A beautiful country like East Timor, with its determined and heroic history, must not be promoted through a tourist industry which creates a small modern world of luxury hotels. Rather, we should accelerate the creation of conditions for ecotourism as a means to promote the unique identity, personality and character of our people, with a dimension of more humane relationships between people.

It is necessary that we be uncompromising in our defence of the environment, with all the consequences this may bring, because we should never lose sight of the small language of the land which is our nation, which has to be preserved as our birthplace, as the green lawn from where the future generations will grow, and as a grave full of flowers for all the generations that have gone before.

You have heard the Falintil fighter's dream, shrouded in the mist from the mountains.

Finally, I wish to appeal to all Timorese to be prudent in our actions and behaviour. We must learn to be tolerant and patient, given that there may be others who have not yet been called upon to contribute better ideas. Let us try to construct our nation collectively and, although I respect political parties, I appeal to everyone to consider this first effort as essentially a technical and professional task.

In this context, all Timorese professionals have an obligation in the present and in the future to contribute within a strong civil and wholesome democratic society, to the great undertaking that East Timor demands from its children.

I do not want to miss this opportunity to appeal to governments and NGOs to define together with us, the Timorese, a concerted aid package with which to create the best conditions to construct the new nation, where we will secure respect for human rights, promote equality of rights and opportunities for all components of the Timorese society and defend the Timorese culture and identity.

Peace is possible in East Timor.

Viva the martyred people of East Timor!

Xanana Gusmão
CNRT President
Falintil Commander

Message to Dare II

The Dare II Peace and Reconciliation Conference, which began 25 June in Jakarta, was to consist of three phases. Dare, the small town 20 km south of Dili, is the location of a seminary from which a number of East Timorese leaders graduated, including Xanana Gusmão and Nicolau Lobato. The first Dare meeting took place, in Baucau, at the initiative of Bishop Belo in 1998. This June conference was the second phase. The gatherings discussed a comprehensive and peaceful solution to the question of East Timor. The two sides, pro-independence and pro-integration, sent 30 representatives each. Delegates from pro-integration and pro-independence groups refined a statement of the basic ideas they could agree on but could find little common ground on a joint committee for the implementation of these ideas. Xanana was convinced the Indonesian Government and military unduly influenced the pro-autonomy delegates.

Distinguished Representative of the United Nations, Tamrat Samuel
Excellencies, Ambassadors of Friendly Governments
Distinguished Representatives of the Government of Indonesia
Honourable Representatives of the Church of Indonesia
Ladies and Gentlemen
Respected Bishops of East Timor, D. Carlos Filipe Ximenes and D. Basilio do Nascimento

The presence here today of so many distinguished figures is a great honour and testimony to the tremendous faith placed in this set of meetings of dialogue and reconciliation.

I wish to express our appreciation to the Indonesian Government which has contributed admirably to the realisation of Dare II through granting visas to our brothers and sisters from the diaspora.

This occasion constitutes, above all, a responsibility for the more than 60 Timorese gathered here who are conscious that peace is a universal value and the right of each and every human being.

This meeting, witnessed by the international community, is of particular relevance in view of the fact that the Timorese are fully committing themselves, through their presence here, to returning peace to the people of Timor Loro Sa'e.

The people of Timor *Loro Sa'e* have experienced periods of war throughout their history, most notably over the past 23 years. If we have inherited from our ancestors the spirit of rebellion, today the Timorese people wish to hand down something new to future generations—real and lasting peace!

Dear Timorese Brothers and Sisters, the New York agreement of 5 May has rendered this process, the process of reconciliation, irreversible. No son or daughter of Timor Loro Sa'e can or will be able to avoid feeling responsible for and committed to the process of dialogue and reconciliation.

The fundamental objective of reconciliation is peace. Reconciliation represents a deliberate break with an atmosphere of confrontation. The most difficult step has been taken—that of accepting the need for dialogue as the means of reaching a better understanding of one another's ideas, of putting an end to apprehensions and of rejecting violence.

The first two days of meetings, while perhaps falling short of our expectations, were of crucial importance in paving the way to improved communication and to a more conscious assumption of our responsibilities as sons and daughters of Timor *Loro Sa'e* to our beloved people and to the international community.

Our long-suffering people have placed all their hopes in Dare II. These final three days of meetings are vitally important to our people. It is their hope that their sons and daughters, with greater capabilities, may embrace the spirit of fraternity, of mutual respect, and may commit themselves to the ideal of peace.

On our part, I reaffirm our unqualified support to contributing in all aspects in order to ensure that the consultation process is free, just and democratic.

I invite all my Timorese brothers and sisters, once and for all, to break down the barriers constructed between us. May brotherhood be the new guiding force in our relations.

Peace is possible in Timor *Loro Sa'e*!

Kay Rala Xanana Gusmão
President of CNRT

Afterword

In early 1999 the new Indonesian President, B. J. Habibie, made a surprise announcement that if, in a 'process of consultation', the majority of East Timorese rejected autonomy in favor of independence Indonesia would grant independence. With the prospects for referendum imminent, Xanana began calling for a cease-fire, disarmament and real Indonesian troop reductions. In February he was moved to house arrest to facilitate his participation in further negotiations. CNRT began warning about possible violence and called for armed international peacekeepers, but nevertheless agreed to proceed with the referendum.

The ballot was carried out on 30 August 1999 with UN officials saying that up to half of the estimated 450,000 voters were waiting outside booths within the first few hours of them opening across the country. Some 78.5 per cent of East Timorese voted for independence by indicating the CNRT flag on the ballot paper. The pro-integration militias, with substantial Indonesian military backing, took their revenge. An unknown number of East Timorese were killed and over 200,000 forcibly displaced into West Timor and other parts of Indonesia.

In September the Indonesian Government released Xanana from prison amidst the extensive military slayings in East Timor. Initially taking refuge in the British Embassy in Jakarta, after receiving death threats Xanana fled to Australia to the northern city of Darwin. The terrifying violence in East Timor finally spurred the United States to pressure Indonesia into accepting a peacekeeping force and on 15 September the UN Security Council, authorised an Australian-led multinational force to restore peace and security in East Timor. Xanana returned home to a devastated East Timor and made emotional pleas for all Timorese to return home, to forgive and to rebuild.

Select Bibliography

Aubrey, Jim (1998), *Free East Timor: Australia's Culpability in East Timor's Genocide*, Random House, Sydney.

Borja da Costa, Francisco (1976), *Revolutionary Poems in the Struggle against Colonialism: Timorese national verse*, Jill Jolliffe (ed), Wild & Woolley, Glebe.

Budiardjo, Carmel and Liong, Liem Soei (1984), *War Against East Timor*, Zed Books, London.

Carey, Peter and Bentley, G. Carter (1995), *East Timor at the Crossroads: the forging of a nation*, Social Science Research Council, New York.

Domm, Robert (1990), *Report from the Mountains of East Timor: Interview with resistance guerrilla commander, Shanana Gusmão*, ABC transcript of Background Briefing broadcast on ABC radio 28, 29, 30 October 1990.

Dunn, James (1996), *Timor: A People Betrayed*, ABC Books, Sydney.

Frederico, Joao (1993), *The Fusion of Religion and Nationalism in East Timor: A Culture in the Making*, Boavida, Masters thesis, Oxford University.

Gusmão, Xanana (1994), *Timor Leste: Um Povo, Uma Patria* [East Timor: One People, One Homeland], Edicoes Colibri, Lisbon.

Gutteres, Justino (1997a), *The Makasae of East Timor: The Structure of Affinal Alliance Systems*, Masters thesis, University of Melbourne.

Hill, Helen (1978), *FRETILIN: The origins, ideologies and strategies of a nationalist movement in East Timor*, Masters thesis, Monash University.

Jannisa, Gudmund (1997), *The Crocodile's Tears: East Timor in the Making*, Lund Dissertations in Sociology 14, Lund University.

Jolliffe, Jill (1978), *East Timor: Nationalism and Colonialism*, University of Queensland Press, St Lucia.

Lawson, Yvette (1989), *East Timor: Roots Continue to Grow*, University of Amsterdam.

Pinto, Constancio, (1997), *East Timor's Unfinished Struggle: Inside the Timorese Resistance*, South End Press, Boston.

Ramos-Horta, José (1987), *Funu*, Red Sea Press, New York.

Scott, David (1994), *Ten Days in East Timor and the Case for Talks*, East Timor Talks Campaign, Melbourne.

Taylor, John (1991), *Indonesia's Forgotten War*, Pluto Press, London.

Thatcher, Patricia, (1988), *The Role of Women in Timorese Society*, Honours Year thesis, Monash University.

Thatcher, Patricia, (1993), *The Timor-Born in Exile in Australia*, Master of Arts thesis, Monash University.

Traube, Elizabeth (1986), *Cosmology and Social Life: Ritual Exchange among the Mambai of East Timor*, University of Chicago Press.

Turner, Michele (1992b), *Telling*, University of NSW Press, Sydney.

Glossary

(i) Indonesian word; (p) Portuguese word; (t) tetum word

ABRI: *Angkatan Bersenjata Republik Indonesia*, Armed Forces of the Republic of Indonesia

ACFOA: Australian Council for Overseas Aid

Ai bubur (t): eucalyptus trees

AIETD: All Inclusive East Timorese Dialogue

AMF: Armed Forces Movement (Portuguese)

ANP: *Associao National Popular*, the official government political party in Portuguese Timor

Apartismo (p): neutrality, nonpartisanship

APEC: Asian Pacific Economic Cooperation

Apodeti: Associao Popular Democratica Timorense, Timorese Popular Democratic Association (first called the Association for the Integration of Timor into Indonesia)

ASDT: *Associao Sosial Democratica Timorenses*, Timorese Association of Social Democrats

ASEAN: Association of South East Asian Nations

Aswains (t): warriors

BAIS: Indonesian Strategic Intelligence Agency

Bapak (i): deferential Indonesian term of address meaning father

Bupat (i): administrator

Cadre: member of left-wing resistance

Camat (i): administrator

Chefe do Posto (p): Chief administrator of a *Posto*, an administrative area in Portuguese Timor

CNRM: *Conselho Nacional da Resistencia Maubere*, National Council of Maubere Resistence

CNRT: *Conselho Nacional da Resistencia Timorenses*, National Council of Timorese Resistence

Comando da Luta (p): Command Headquarters

Companheiro (p): close comrade; companion or mate

Concelho (p): administrative council or division. There were 13 *concelhos* in Portuguese Timor

CP: *Commisao Politica*, Political Commission (Fretilin)

CRRN: *Conselho Nacional da Resistencia Revolutionario*, National Council for Revolutionary Resistance

Deportado (p): Portuguese political deportee

Desa (i): village

DFSE: Delegation of Fretilin in Overseas Service

DOPI: *Departmento de Orientacao Politica e Ideologica*, Department of Political and Ideological Orientation (Fretilin)

DRET: Democratic Republic of East Timor

EEC: European Economic Community

Escudo: Portuguese currency

Falintil: Armed Forces for the National Liberation of East Timor

Fataluku (t): people from the far east of Timor

Firaku (t): people from the eastern part of East Timor

Fretilin: Frente Revolucionaria de Timor Leste Independente, Revolutionary Front for an Independent East Timor

Garuda: Indonesia's national bird and national airline

Golkar: Indonesia's official government party under Suharto, now one of many in democratic Indonesia

Gubernor (i): Governor

Guerilheiros (p): guerrilla fighters

Hansips (i): official civilian guard

Intel (i): Indonesian Political Police Organisation

Jutas (i): one million or millionaire

Kaladi (t): people of the western part of East Timor

Katuas (t): term of respect for a veteran or elder

Kepala (i): Chief

Kodim (i): *Komando Daerah Militar*, district military command

Kooperasi (i): shops

Kopussus (i): Indonesian military elite troops
Koramil (i):Indonesian Military Command
Kore-metan (t): Parties that signal the end of the one year morning period, open to everyone who attended the funeral.
Leste (p): East
Liceu (p): secondary college
Liurai (t): indigenous king or part of that royal class
Loro S'ae (t): East; where the sun sets
Lulik (t): can be an adjective or noun, describes a sacred item or something pertaining to the indigenous belief system of Timor, eg, *lulik* house, *lulik* talisman
Luta (p): the struggle
Mambai (t): one of the largest of the 13 main ethno-liguistic groups in East Timor
Maubere (t): Son of Timor; originally My Brother (see footnote p.3 for political meaning)
MEAU: *Missao de Estudos Agronomicos do Ultramar*, Mission of Colonial Agricultural Studies
Mesticos (p): people of Portuguese and Timorese mixed race
NAM: Non-Aligned Movement
Nangala: knife-throwing terrorists
NATO: North Atlantic Treaty Organisation
NGO: Non Government Organisation, usually referring to aid or humanitarian agencies
Ninja: black-masked armed gangs trained by Indonesian military
Nureps: nucleos de resistencia popular, Popular Resistence centres
OPEC: Organisation of the Petroleum Exporting Countries
Orde Baru (i): New Order
Palapa (p/t): local palm leaf used as traditional building material and many other uses
Palmatoria: a device for physical punishment used by striking the palm of the hand
PALOP: *Países Africanos de Língua Oficial Portuguesa*, Organisation of Official Portuguese Speaking African Countries
Pancacila (i): official Indonesian government ideology
Pataca (p): Old Portuguese currency
Pegawai (i): public servant
Pembangunan (i): official Indonesian development program
Pemuda (i): youth
PIDE: *Policia Internactional de Defensa do Estada*, Portuguese Political Police
Polwil (i): Indonesian regional police command
Posto (p): an administrative district within a concelho. There were 58 *Postos* in Portuguese Timor.
Praca (p): the central town square that usually houses the market place
Quartel-General (p): army headquarters
RER: *Readjustamento Estrutural do Resistencia*, Reorganisation of the Structure of the Resistance that established CNRM (December 1988)
Rupiah (i): Indonesian currency
SAPT: *Sociedade Agricola Patria e Trabalho*, Agricultural Society of Fatherland and Work
Senhor (p): formal, Mr
Suco/Suku (p/t): a small administration area, many of which make up a *Posto*
Tentaras (i): Indonesian soldiers
Tetum/n: Lingua franca of East Timor
TNI: National Indonesian Army
Transmigrasi (t): Indonesian transmigrants to East Timor (and other parts of Indonesia)
UDT: *Uniao Democratica Timorense*, Timorese Democratic Union
Ukun rasik an (t): self-determination
UN: United Nations
UNAMET: United Nations Mission to East Timor
Uniao (p): 'the Union' or 'the League', the indigenous sporting club
Unimog: brand of military vehicle
UNITIM: East Timorese Student Union
UNTAET: United Nations Transitional Administration in East Timor
Viva (p): Long live!

Index

In the text, both Portuguese and indigenous spellings are used for the same place names. In the index, alternative versions are given in brackets.